Globalization and Belonging

NEW MILLENNIUM BOOKS
IN INTERNATIONAL STUDIES

Deborah J. Gerner, Series Editor

NEW MILLENNIUM BOOKS issue out of the unique position of the global system at the end of the Cold War, the end of the twentieth century, and the beginning of a new millennium in which our understandings about war, peace, identity, sovereignty, security, and sustainability— whether economic, environmental, or ethical—are likely to be challenged. In the new millennium of international relations, new theories, new actors, and new policies and processes are all bound to be engaged. Books in the series are of three types: compact core texts, supplementary texts, and readers.

Editorial Board

Titles in the Series

Globalization and Belonging: The Politics of Identity in a Changing World
Sheila L. Croucher

The Global New Deal: Economic and Social Human Rights in World Politics
William F. Felice

*The New Foreign Policy: U.S. and Comparative Foreign Policy
in the 21st Century*
Laura Neack

Global Backlash: Citizen Initiatives for a Just World Economy
Edited by Robin Broad

*Negotiating a Complex World: An Introduction to
International Negotiation*
Brigid Starkey, Mark A. Boyer, and Jonathan Wilkenfeld

Military–Civilian Interactions: Intervening in Humanitarian Crises
Thomas G. Weiss

Forthcoming in the Series

Introduction to Global Studies
Patricia J. Campbell and Aran S. MacKinnon

Liberals and Criminals: IPE in the New Millennium
H. Richard Friman

Law in International Politics: Key Issues and Incidents
B. Welling Hall

International Law in the 21st Century
Christopher C. Joyner

*Global Politics as If People Mattered: World Political Economy
from the Ground Up*
Ronnie D. Lipschutz and Mary Ann Tetreault

The Peace Puzzle: Ending Violent Conflict in the 21st Century
George A. Lopez

Elusive Security: State, International, and Human Security in the 21st Century
Laura Neack

Political Violence
Philip A. Schrodt

Globalization and Belonging

The Politics of Identity in a Changing World

Sheila L. Croucher

ROWMAN & LITTLEFIELD PUBLISHERS, INC.
Lanham • Boulder • New York • Toronto • Oxford

ROWMAN & LITTLEFIELD PUBLISHERS, INC.

Published in the United States of America
by Rowman & Littlefield Publishers, Inc.
A wholly owned subsidiary of The Rowman & Littlefield Publishing Group, Inc.
4501 Forbes Boulevard, Suite 200, Lanham, Maryland 20706
www.rowmanlittlefield.com

P.O. Box 317, Oxford, OX2 9RU, United Kingdom

British Library Cataloguing in Publication Information Available

Library of Congress Cataloging-in-Publication Data

Croucher, Sheila L.
    Globalization and belonging : the politics of identity in a changing world /
Sheila L. Croucher.
        p.   cm.—(New millennium books in international studies)
    Includes bibliographical references and index.
    ISBN 0-7425-1678-4 (alk. paper)—ISBN 0-7425-1679-2 (paper : alk. paper)
    1. Group identity.   2. Citizenship.   3. Globalization.   I. Title.   II. Series.
HM753 .C76   2004
302.4—dc21   2003008105

Printed in the United States of America

♾™ The paper used in this publication meets the minimum requirements of
American National Standard for Information Sciences—Permanence of Paper
for Printed Library Materials, ANSI/NISO Z39.48-1992.

Contents

Acknowledgments

I began work on this book just weeks before the hijackers flew the deadly planes into the World Trade Center. Like many in the United States and around the world, I reacted with deep sadness to the events of September 11, 2001, and those since. At a more selfish level, I was initially frustrated by the ways in which 9/11 and the unrelenting media coverage distracted me from work on the book. I realized quickly, however, that 9/11 spoke powerfully to the very themes I was exploring in this book, and I welcomed the excuse to channel emotional energy into more cerebral activity.

The ideas presented in this book are the culmination of several years of thinking, teaching, and writing about identity and are motivated by my own personal and political interest in questions of belonging. Along the way, various colleagues, students, friends, and family members lent valuable intellectual and emotional support. At Miami University, Will Hazleton, Mary McDonald, Laura Neack, and Susan Kay read drafts of chapters, exchanged information and ideas, and encouraged me when I needed it most. During my semester leave from the University of Florida in the spring of 2002, Jim Button, Barbara Rienzo, Amanda Wolfe, Marie McGhee, Philip Williams, Charles Wood, and Patricia Woods provided me with needed support, encouragement, and intellectual exchange. Alexander Motyl at Rutgers University was kind enough to provide helpful feedback on chapter 3. Throughout this process, Jennifer Knerr at Rowman & Littlefield was everything one hopes an editor will be—competent, efficient, and kind. Finally, I am particularly grateful to Carolyn Haynes whose emotional and intellectual generosity is unsurpassed.

Introduction

The year was 2001—the first year of a new millennium filled with the promise of progress and change. Automobile manufacturers were selling electric cars, private citizens were purchasing trips into outer space, and scientists were on the verge of solving the mysteries of the human genetic code. Russia was joining NATO; the pope was visiting Cuba, and Europe was counting down the days to a common currency. Global travel had reached an all-time high of 698.8 million international arrivals a year; and over 400 million people around the world had regular access to the Internet (*Foreign Policy* 2002). For many people, however, and certainly a majority of Americans, 2001 will be most remembered for the tragic day of September 11. At first glance, an unforeseen terrorist attack on the United States by Muslim fundamentalists seems not only impossible to predict, but strangely out of place in a high-tech, globally interconnected world. On second glance, what looks like a paradox reveals itself as a complex, contradictory, overlapping set of realities that entail both integration and disintegration, homogenization and fragmentation. This book focuses on the seeming contradiction and the interaction between globalization on one hand, and the power and passion of cultural and political belonging on the other.

The sequence of events that transpired the morning of September 11 is now well known. At 8:48 A.M. EST the first plane crashed into the north tower of the World Trade Center in New York City. At 9:03 A.M., a second plane crashed into the south tower of the World Trade Center. At 9:43 A.M. a third plane flew into the Pentagon, and at 10:10 A.M. a fourth plane, later reported to be headed for the White House, crashed in a field outside Pittsburgh, Pennsylvania. The horrific images of those events are also emblazoned in the minds of people around the world: concrete symbols of the United States' power and prestige crumbling into dust while terrified victims covered in molten ash ran screaming or jumped from fiery buildings. Interpretations or explanations of the attack—what its implica-

1

tions are and why it happened—are far from settled. Widespread, however, is a sense, or at least the proclamation, that "things will never be the same." This reflects the view of many analysts and observers that 9/11 marked a fundamental rupture in the patterns and flow of world events—a veritable paradigm shift in how people and states think about and exist in the world.

Other indicators suggest that 9/11 represents not a break with the past, but a return to the no-so-distant paranoia and hostility of the Cold War era. President George W. Bush's provocative invocation of an "axis of evil" is reminiscent of Ronald Reagan's reference to the USSR as the "Evil Empire." The frequent post-9/11 refrain of many in the United States that "You're either with us or against us" portrays a bipolar world order not unlike the one that divided East from West during the decades-long Cold War. And for many concerned citizens and lawmakers, the suspension and violation of civil liberties in the name of national security run the risk of replicating some of the most shameful chapters in American history, from the internment of Japanese Americans to the McCarthy-era witch hunts for suspected communists. Whether it represents a rupture with or resurrection of the past (and it is likely some combination of both), what is certain is that 9/11 has been and will continue to be a powerful and poignant touchstone for understanding and acting upon world affairs.

This book is not about terrorism, international security, or foreign policy—at least not directly. Instead, the focus is on identity and belonging, and, specifically, on how citizenship, nationhood, ethnicity, and gender are being affected by processes of globalization. September 11 is illustrative of certain trends, contradictions, and reconfigurations that comprise the themes and relationships explored in this book. For example, the events surrounding the terrorist attacks and the U.S. response bring into sharp relief the ambivalent role of states as actors in the world system. They also highlight the power and multidimensionality of identity and belonging.

Finally, and perhaps most vividly, the events of 9/11 encapsulate a commonly observed paradox of the contemporary world—a paradox that Benjamin Barber has labeled "Jihad vs. McWorld." "Jihad" refers to "a retribalization of large swaths of humankind by war and bloodshed . . . in which culture is pitted against culture, people against people, tribe against tribe." "McWorld" conveys the onrush of "forces that demand integration and

"the events surrounding the terrorist attacks and the U.S. response bring into sharp relief the ambivalent role of states as actors in the world system. They also highlight the power and multidimensionality of identity and belonging."

uniformity . . . pressing nations into one commercially homogenous global network" (1992, 53). In other words, globalization is bringing the world closer together while varied forms of sociocultural and political differentiation threaten to tear it apart.

September 11 is just one tragic example of how analysts of and participants in international affairs seem ill-prepared to understand or anticipate the ebb and flow of a world that commutes busily along the information super-highway while victims of various forms of hatred and hostility languish along the roadside amid disorder and despair. In the aftermath of the collapse of the Soviet Union, many world leaders and policymakers, former U.S. president George H. W. Bush prominent among them, triumphantly proclaimed the advent of a New World Order. Some academics such as political scientist Lucian Pye joined in declaring that a world culture of modernization had ushered in the twilight of authoritarianism (1990, 3). For Pye, this "great transformation" vindicated modernization theorists of the 1950s who had predicted that economic growth, the spread of science and technology, and the acceleration and spread of communications would bring about democratic transitions worldwide (p. 7). In other words, socioeconomic development, technological advancement, and democratization seemed finally to have triumphed over parochial attachments and ties such as ethnicity and nationalism. For some scholars this meant "the end of history," or in the words of Francis Fukuyama, "the endpoint of mankind's ideological evolution and the universalization of Western liberal democracy as the final form of human government" (1989, 4).

These enthusiastic visions did not anticipate and could not accommodate the turmoil that would soon follow: ethnic cleansing in the Balkans, genocide in Rwanda, and an indigenous revolution in Mexico, to name just a few. There was no place in this view of a New World Order for the surge and scourge of modern-day slavery, the sexual trafficking of women, and certainly not for the brand of Islamic fundamentalism that fueled the terror of September 11. Nor did post–Cold War pronouncements of an emergent global village acknowledge the individuals and groups throughout the developed and developing world that were already mobilized around issues of cultural recognition, autonomy, and in some cases separateness. This latter category includes indigenous peoples, women, and the ongoing struggles of groups like the Québécois in Canada, the Basques in northern Spain, or the Kurdish peoples spread across Turkey, Iraq, and Iran. Not only did these social and revolutionary movements fail to dissipate with the onset of the New World Order, many were invigorated. The persistence or eruption of identity-based conflicts not only contradicted many of the claims and celebratory assessments of globalization or a New World Order, but also reacted against it. In other words, the trends that Benjamin Barber describes as Jihad and McWorld not only coexist uncomfortably, but also closely interrelate, playing off each other with sometimes explosive consequences. This was certainly the case on September 11.

A majority of people throughout the world agree that there is no justification for the death and destruction that took place on that fateful day in September. However, there are many legitimate and well-reasoned responses to the desperate question posed by so many Americans in the wake of September 11: "Why do they hate us?" Answers to that question point invariably to aspects of globalization and to many of the same circumstances and trends celebrated by the proponents of a New World Order—namely the spread of global capitalism, Western liberal democracy, and American culture.

Interestingly, however, the terrorists not only reacted against certain aspects of globalization, but they also utilized, relied upon, perpetuated, and at the very least provided evidence of others. The events of 9/11 could not have been planned or executed without the existence of and widespread access to advanced technology. The individuals that flew the deadly planes were terrorists prepared to kill and die in the name of their god and in opposition to the political and cultural imperialism of the West. They were also well educated, traveled, and experienced participants in a global world. In fact, al Qaeda's very existence and the success of its mission in the United States relied heavily upon airplanes, cell phones, the Internet, ATMs, CNN, video recorders, satellite technology, and a sophisticated system of international financial exchange. Mohamed Atta made his plane reservations online via his laptop, and several fellow hijackers relied upon Travelocity.com. One hijacker spent the last night of his life in a bar in Florida playing video games; and months after the attacks in Pakistan, the kidnappers, and ultimately the killers, of U.S. journalist Daniel Pearl used e-mail to negotiate a ransom for his release. Moreover, although the hijackers may have intended to harm Americans, the realities of global interconnectedness guaranteed that citizens from at least seventy other countries around the world were also in the World Trade Center that day and perished alongside Americans. Five hundred Colombians were unaccounted for in the days following the attacks. At least one hundred Japanese nationals, including dozens of tourists, are unaccounted for. Fifty Bangladeshis were confirmed dead. Twenty-seven South Koreans are missing. Nine Australians were confirmed dead by September 14, with eighty-five still missing. And two Canadians were killed in the planes that crashed (*Associated Press* 2001a).

Another aspect and contradiction of global change that became evident amid the events of 9/11 was the ambivalent role of the nation-state in the contemporary world order. Accounts and analyses of globalization point repeatedly to the declining relevance of states in an increasingly interconnected world system dominated by transnational organizations and corporations. To some extent, 9/11 supported this thesis in that the enemy was not a state or an alliance of states. Instead, the enemy was a vast network of terrorists who came from more than twenty different countries and had spread their organization across as many as sixty different states. As Robert Jervis writes: "Were this a peaceful enterprise, we would celebrate it as showing the ability of people from different countries, social classes, and experiences to work together" (2002, 40). Allegations about the decline of the modern state are accompanied by the view that citizenship or formal membership in a state has also diminished in importance. Indeed, evidence that came forth in the aftermath of 9/11 suggests that throughout much of the world, individuals move (or at least did so prior to 9/11) freely and relatively unencumbered by the formality of passports and visas. Even in the states that are the most guarded or technologically sophisticated in terms of surveillance, borders appeared remarkably porous.

From another perspective, however, September 11 attests to the continuing centrality and significance of states in the international system and formal membership in them. Although the perpetrator of the violence was not a state, states were called upon to join the United States in an antiterrorism alliance, and states, primarily Afghanistan, were the targets of U.S.-led military action. Moreover, the stakes of membership in a state seemed to skyrocket. In the United States, for example, demonstrations of loyalty and attachment to the state have been pervasive and dramatic. Stores set unprecedented records for the sale of flags. Flag owners adorned their cars, clothes, houses, barns, and businesses with the red, white, and blue. Many people rushed to join the U.S. armed services, and a remarkable expression of sympathy, financial and otherwise, poured forth for "fellow Americans."

Meanwhile, as is discussed further in chapter 2, noncitizens living in the United States, even very long-term residents, experienced the increasing and sometimes frightening stakes of not having formal membership in the United States. Newspapers in cities throughout the United States reported hate crimes against Arab residents, and in the case of one Arizona town, a Sikh, mistaken as an Arab due to his long facial hair and turban, was murdered (Billeaud 2001). In the five months following the attacks, the Equal Employment Opportunity Commission received 260 claims of workplace discrimination from Muslims, an increase of 168 percent over the same period a year earlier. The Council on American-Islamic Relations received more than 1,700 reports of public harassment, ethnic slurs, hate mail, and other claims of discrimination (Lichtblau 2002). Mohamed Majad of the All Dulles Area Muslim Society in Washington, D.C., said in an interview with the *Financial Times*: "As a community, we feel hurt. Our kids are afraid to sleep at night" (quoted in Dunne 2002, 4).

In response to 9/11, the U.S. government sought and acquired expanded powers to arrest, search, and detain noncitizens suspected of terrorism. The

USA PATRIOT Act, an acronym for Uniting and Strengthening America by Providing Appropriate Tools Required to Intercept and Obstruct Terrorism, expands, among other things, the government's legal use of surveillance, including accessing e-mail and cell phone conversations, and the definition of terrorist to include those who "lend support" to terrorist organizations. Meanwhile, lawmakers as well as citizens called for tightened control over U.S. borders and stricter immigration policies. New York congressman Peter King proposed halting all further immigration from Arab states because, in his opinion, most of them support terrorism ("Rep. King" 2002); and a Zogby poll on immigration and terrorism found that 85 percent of voters in the United States believed that lax enforcement of border controls and immigration laws contributed to the terrorist attacks (Camarota 2001b).

At the turn of the millennium, globalization was in full swing, but belonging to a state still mattered, and after 9/11 mattered even more. In addition, the events surrounding 9/11 revealed the multiplicity and complexity of different forms of belonging and identity. For some Muslims in the United States, or individuals of Middle Eastern descent, formal citizenship in the United States was not a sufficient criterion for belonging. As hostility against Arab Americans by other American citizens and by the government increased, U.S. citizenship appeared to be as much about race and religion as it did about a belief in liberty or an allegiance to the U.S. Constitution. Alternatively, stories about newly arrived residents from diverse ethnic backgrounds joining together to sing the U.S. national anthem in broken English suggested that the category "American" remained a fluid and potentially inclusive one. Some of these immigrants, like the ones who approached a news photographer asking, in thick Spanish accents, for help with the words to the national anthem, felt like Americans on September 11 (Grier 2001a). Yet they may also have felt at that time, and certainly at many other times, like Latinos, and perhaps Catholics. Many presumably remain in close contact with their homelands and consider themselves members of a national community outside of or other than the United States. And all are no doubt aware in their daily lives of belonging or being assigned to a particular gender.

For the terrorists, and certainly for many individuals and groups around the globe who are not terrorists, religion was and is a more fundamental source of identity and belonging than is any government or state. Osama bin Laden, for example, had rejected his homeland of Saudi Arabia (and vice versa) because he perceived it as complicit in the American-led evil he so adamantly despised. And for some, attachment to New York City was more salient than attachment to the United States. Alexandr Manin, a recent immigrant from Kazakhstan and not a U.S. citizen, joined the U.S. military after the September 11 attacks explaining: "It doesn't matter that America is not my country. New York is my city" ("War on Terror" 2001b, 25). Gender also came into play as an administration that had in no way concerned itself with women's rights at home or abroad, and a First Lady who actively eschewed a political role, came out strongly in defense of the women suffering under the Taliban regime. Meanwhile, sexual orientation, an otherwise controversial dimension of belonging, likely did not become divisive when gay rugby player Mark Bingham joined fellow passengers in thwarting the fourth terrorist attack of the morning.

Everywhere there are individuals who on that day did and generally do feel the tug and pull of multiple attachments and identifications to family, country, ethnic group, neighborhood, and so forth. States were also confronted with the power and the fluidity of belonging. The September 12 newspaper headlines in France, a country that often prides itself on its differentiation from the United States, read "We're All Americans Now." Russia and China, both often at odds with the United States, pledged support for an antiterrorism alliance. Around the world, 9/11 brought to the fore for individuals, groups, and states the power and complexity of identity and belonging. That day and the surrounding events also brought into clear relief the extent to which the world had become interconnected, and simultaneously complicated assessments of that interconnectedness. In these ways, 9/11 is not merely a rupture nor a return to the past, but a lens or a spotlight on patterns and contradictions in the world system that have been intensifying for decades.

This book aims to improve understanding of these trends by examining how various forms of sociocultural and political identification and attachment are being affected by the increasing interconnectedness—economic, technological, political, and cultural—of the globe. Chapter 1 introduces the concepts of globalization and belonging and reviews the central questions and debates that characterize the growing literature on both of these themes. This chapter also discusses the role of the state as an entity that is critical to understanding the processes and politics of both globalization and belonging. Chapter 2 examines the implications of globalization for citizenship and how the centrality of citizenship as a form of belonging is being simultaneously diminished and heightened by processes of global

---

"Around the world, 9/11 brought to the fore for individuals, groups, and states the power and complexity of identity and belonging. That day and the surrounding events also brought into clear relief the extent to which the world had become interconnected, and simultaneously complicated assessments of that interconnectedness."

change. The topics of dual citizenship and European Union citizenship illustrate that globalization's impact on citizenship is best characterized in terms of reconfiguration.

Chapter 3 turns to the issue of nationhood as belonging and to competing views on the future of nations and nationalism in a global, postmodern world. Specifically, this chapter explains how and why nations are likely to persist even in the midst of profound social and political change.

Ethnicity is the focus of chapter 4. Using cases such as Rwanda, Cuban Americans, and the Zapatistas in southern Mexico, this chapter demonstrates both how ethnic identities and ethnic relations are constructed and how that construction is contingent upon global factors.

Chapter 5 turns to the topic of gender and specifically to the ways in which globalization has affected women's well-being and women's political mobilization worldwide. This chapter also highlights how forms of identity and belonging, treated separately throughout the book, are actually closely interrelated.

Chapter 6 sums up insights from the preceding chapters and highlights some normative and philosophical dimensions of the topics explored in the book. Is world citizenship as opposed to state citizenship possible, or even desirable? Is nationalism inherently exclusionary? Is ethnicity compatible with the liberal individualism, and how are women uniquely situated in relation to all these issues and trends?

When Benjamin Barber identified "Jihad and McWorld" as "two axial principles of our age," or "two possible political futures," his primary concern was that both were "bleak" and "neither democratic" (1992, 53). His essay focused, therefore, on the dangers associated with what he calls "tribalism" and a "threatened Lebonization of national states" on one hand, and a "commercialized, homogenized, depoliticized, bureaucratized" universal society on the other (p. 59). In spite of the valuable insights in Barber's analysis and the fact that the events of 9/11 can be interpreted in such a way as to make him appear remarkably prescient, much remains to be better understood about the origins and essence of belonging, about globalization, and about the interaction of the two. This book contributes to that understanding.

1

Globalization, Belonging, and the State

Few terms have been more widely and frequently used yet less clearly defined or understood than "globalization." Every year since the mid-1980s the number of books and articles with the term globalization central to their titles has grown exponentially (Scholte 2000, 14). It is also increasingly common for the authors of these works to begin their analyses bemoaning the lack of conceptual clarity surrounding their subject matter and promising to rectify it. Some progress has been made, but many of the aspirations for greater conceptual and analytical clarity remain unfulfilled. The challenge is a tall one, reflecting the genuine complexity of the topic at hand. Globalization is a reality that is so large, so multifaceted, so ongoing, and so defiant of conventional categories and methods of analysis that it frustrates social scientific precision even on the part of the most dedicated of scholars. On the other hand, some blame must also be attributed to sloppy scholarship and to the desire on the part of the media, politicians, and the general public for quick and easy explanations, or excuses, for complex, pervasive, and often unsettling economic, political, social, and cultural trends.

Because this book explores how globalization affects identity-based politics, it is imperative to begin with a general understanding of what globalization is. This chapter will review key statements and debates regarding the definition of globalization, its origins, and its consequences. Given the volume of published work on the topic of globalization, this overview will be relatively condensed, but bibliographic references point readers interested in various aspects of globalization to a wealth of resources that explore these topics in greater depth. The goal of this chapter is not necessarily to resolve ongoing debates or to defend a particular position regarding globalization, but instead to construct a working definition and framework that will inform the analysis in subsequent chapters. In each of the chapters that follow, aspects of globalization—its content, causes, and consequences—will be explored further in terms of their relationship to issues of citizenship, nationhood, ethnicity, and gender. Following the initial section on globalization, this chapter will also introduce the topic of identity politics and of the state as a mediator between globalization and various forms of belonging.

Globalization: What Is It?

Definitions of globalization range from the very general, such as Martin Albrow's claim that "Globalization refers to all those processes by which the peoples of the world are incorporated into a single world society, global society" (1990, 7) or Roland Robertson's definition of globalization as "the crystallization of the entire world as a single place" (1987, 38), to the very specific:

> [G]lobalization . . . include[s] the spatial reorganization of production, the interpenetration of industries across borders, the spread of financial markets, the diffusion of identical consumer goods to distant countries, massive transfers of population within the South as well as from the South and East to the West, resultant conflicts between immigrant and established communities in formerly tight-knit neighborhoods, and emerging world-wide preference for democracy. (Mittelman 1996, 2)

Definitions of globalization also vary in emphasis from the economic and technological to the sociocultural and political. While some scholars attempt to offer a purely descriptive, nonnormative definition, others convey within their definition an assessment, or in the case of Martin Khor's definition, an indictment: "Globalization is what we in the Third World have for several centuries called colonization" (1995, 16).

Complicating attempts to define globalization is the difficulty of sorting through which factors are causes and which are consequences, or untangling the complex web of interrelationships between different aspects and dimensions of global change. Many scholars point to economics as the engine of globalization, emphasizing, for example, the role of multinational corporations (MNCs) whose participation in global production and exchange is linking together far-flung regions of the world.

Yet, the dynamics of the marketplace do not occur in a political vacuum. States still act as regulators and/or resistors of globalization, as do a large and growing number of international governmental and non-governmental organizations (NGOs). Meanwhile, globalization as increased interpenetration and interdependence in the economic or political realm would not have been possible without significant technological innovations. Finally, culture comprises yet another dimension of globalization that is both affected by as well as an influence upon the other processes noted above. In this regard, Arie Kacowicz's definition of globalization as "a cluster of related changes" (1999, 528) is particularly useful, as is his analysis and that of other scholars who break down or "map" globalization in terms of its constituent parts.

David Held, for example, explains that:

Globalization is neither a singular condition nor a linear process. Rather, it is best thought of as a multidimensional phenomenon involving diverse domains of activity and interaction, including the economic, political, technological, military, legal, cultural and environmental. (1998, 13)

Anthony Giddens describes the current world system in terms of the world capitalist economy, the global information system, the world military order, and the nation-state system (1987, 276). Benjamin Barber characterizes globalization in terms of McWorld or one commercially homogenous global network, and identifies four imperatives that make up the dynamic of McWorld: a market imperative, technological imperative, resource imperative, and ecological imperative (1992, 1995). And, Arjun Appadurai (1990), who is primarily interested in the "global cultural economy," identifies five interrelated dimensions of globalization: ethnoscapes (flows of immigrants, refugees, exiles, guest workers, and tourists); technoscapes (rapid movement of technology, high and low, informational and mechanical, across previously impenetrable boundaries); finanscapes (rapid flows of money via currency markets and stock exchanges); mediascapes (flows of images and information via newspapers, magazines, television, and film); and ideoscapes (the spread of elements of the Western enlightenment worldview—namely, images of democracy, freedom, welfare, rights, and so forth).

In a more recent analysis, Jan Aart Scholte (2000) offers not so much a breakdown of what globalization entails, but rather a categorization of existing definitions of globalization and his own alternative conceptualization. Scholte's main argument is that most common definitions or uses of the term globalization reduce it to processes or interactions that are not necessarily new and that do not warrant or necessitate new terminology. Most treatments of globalization portray it as either internationalization (increased interaction and interdependence between countries and/or inhabitants of different countries); liberalization (the reduction in barriers to the cross-border movement of goods, services, money, and financial instruments); universalization (the spreading of objects and experiences to people worldwide); or, Westernization (modernization and processes of homogenization that lead the world to become more Western, or American). Although these various processes may be intensifying, Scholte argues, the terms already in use are sufficient, and the introduction of "globalization" is redundant at best and unnecessarily confusing at worse. More important, these existing definitions or operationalizations fail to capture what is new in the world system and what does warrant application of a term like globalization, namely, "far reaching transformations in the nature of social space" (p. 46). Globalization, then, for Scholte, entails the "spread of supraterritoriality," or "a reconfiguration of geography, so that social space is no longer wholly mapped in terms of territorial places, territorial distances, territorial borders" (p. 16).

> *"Whether the contemporary context is described as postmodern, late modern, postnational, or transnational, scholars from diverse disciplines are now emphasizing the disintegration of borders and a general unboundedness—economic, cultural, and political."*

Scholte is not alone in identifying deterritorialization as a central dimension of globalization. In fact, most scholars of the global condition now call attention to the declining centrality of geographic place and contrast this to the epoch of modernity—the central attribute of which was a "historically unique configuration of territorial space" (Ruggie 1993, 144). Whether the contemporary context is described as postmodern, late modern, postnational, or transnational, scholars from diverse disciplines are now emphasizing the disintegration of borders and a general unboundedness—economic, cultural, and political (Appadurai 1996; Bhabha 1990; Basch, Glick-Schiller, and Blanc 1994). In so doing, they draw a distinction between space and place, maintaining that we still witness and experience identifiable flows and social networks within emerging transnational spaces, but that these are not linked to geographic territory in the same way as is place. Although some scholars are willing to go far with the thesis of unboundedness (Appadurai 1996; Bhabha 1990), others stress the need to ground and contextualize global realities and flows (Guarnizo and Smith 1998). Scholte, for example, emphasizes *relative* deterritorialization: "while the spread of supraterritoriality means that some aspects of social space are no longer reducible to territorial geography, it by no means follows that territoriality has become irrelevant" (2000, 42–43).

Drawing from and building on this vast array of scholarship, this book will treat globalization as a cluster of related changes that are increasing the interconnectedness of the world. These changes are occurring in, but not limited to, economic, technological, cultural, and political realms. Furthermore, globalization is not restricted to merely enhancing the interdependence of already existing entities or the intensification of established networks or flows, but is also creating or facilitating the creation of new ones. What follows are examples or evidence of globalization in these four realms.

Economic Interconnectedness

Many analysts identify economics as the central dimension of globalization and focus the bulk of their attention on capitalism and the marketplace as the driving forces and primary indicators of global interconnectedness. For example, in 1997, the European Commission defined globalization as "the process by which markets and production in different countries are becoming increasingly interdependent due to the dynamics of trade in goods and services and flows of capital and technology" (cited in Held 2000, 92). More recently, a report by the Institute for National Strategic Studies defined globalization as follows: "Anchored in economic dynamics, it is a process of growing cross-border flows in many areas that are drawing countries and regions closer together, creating networks of expanded ties" (Flanagan, Frost, and Kugler 2001, 5).

Ample data are readily available to demonstrate that expanding and intensifying trade and investment networks are tying countries and regions closer together and are also, simultaneously, creating spaces and flows that extend beyond or exist outside of established boundaries of nation-states. World trade has expanded rapidly since World War II and has grown at twice the rate of world output since the early 1980s (Mittelman 2000, 21). Trade as a proportion of gross domestic product (GDP) has increased steadily since the 1970s, currently reaching ratios as high as 30 percent and higher in advanced industrialized countries (Held 2000, 97). Foreign direct investment has also climbed rapidly during the same period. In 1982, foreign direct investment inflows and outflows were $58 billion and $37 billion respectively (unless otherwise noted all dollar figures are in U.S. dollar amounts). By 1990 both figures had quadrupled to $209 billion and $245 billion, and by 2000, they had more than quadrupled once again to $1,271 billion and $1,150 respectively (UNCTAD 2001).

This increase and intensification of trade and exchange applies not only to goods and services, but also to money. World foreign exchange transactions have climbed from U.S.$15 billion a day in the 1970s to

U.S.$900 billion a day in the early 1990s. By the year 2001, financial markets were moving U.S.$1.5 trillion around the world every day. In the United States, cross-border flows of bonds and equities are fifty-four times higher today than they were in 1970, fifty-five times higher for Japan, and sixty times higher for Germany (*Foreign Policy* 2001, 58). Meanwhile, between 1975 and 1994, international bank lending grew from $265 billion to $4.2 trillion.

With regard to the supraterritorial or, specifically, suprastate dimensions of globalization, it is important to note the central role of MNCs in organizing the globalization of production and financial transactions. MNCs now account for more than one-third of world output, 70 percent of world trade, and 80 percent of direct international investment (Held 1998, 17). Facilitating the globalization of production are various forms of export processing zones (EPZs) or offshore manufacturing arrangements that allow companies to benefit from, among other things, tax exemptions and the suspension of certain labor regulations. According to data from the International Labour Organization, no such arrangement existed prior to 1954, and by 1998, these zones numbered 850. The largest number (320) are located in North America, but many (225) are located throughout Asia as well (ILO 1998). By 1990, Mexico alone was operating 1,938 individual maquiladora factories (Mittelman 2000, 42). Finally, the data indicate an expansion not only in trade flows, but also in integration. According to the recent study by the Institute for National Strategic Studies, "the *integration of capital and commodity markets* since the 1970s has surpassed all previous levels and is still spreading" (Flanagan, Frost, and Kugler 2001, 8, emphasis in the original). These data support the suggestion that economics is a, if not the primary, engine of globalization.

Technological Interconnectedness

Yet, the economic dynamics described above have been influenced profoundly by, and some argue would not have been possible without, the increased sophistication of technology, and specifically communication and information technologies. As early as 1976, Abdul Said and Luiz Simmons stated that "The dominant causal agent behind the emerging international political system is the technological revolution in communication" (1976, 14). Anthony Giddens recently identified the communications media as "the leading influence in the globalisation of society over the past 20 or 30 years" (1995, 10); and a 2001 report by the Institute for National Strategic Studies stated that "Globalization would not be occurring in its present form were it not for the business application of the knowledge revolution—for example, computers, e-mail, satellites, and other innovations" (cited in Flanagan, Frost, and Kugler 2001, 8). The introduction of satellites and fiber optics has led to a massive increase in transborder communications, as has the proliferation of cell phones, fax machines, and televisions. The number of television receivers in the world went from 192 million in 1965 to 1,361 million in 1996, and during that same period, the number of televisions per 1,000 people worldwide increased from 57 in 1965 to 240 in 1997 (Held 2000, 50; UNDP 2002, 77). In Latin America alone sales of television sets grew by over 500 percent (Vo 1998, 8). Radio ownership worldwide showed similar increases. In China, for example, radio receivers per 1,000 inhabitants grew from 16 in 1975 to 195 in 1996, and in Africa during the same period, the number of radios sold quadrupled (Held 2000, 52; Vo 1998, 8).

The best example of a newly emerged medium of communications is the Internet. In the year 2000, the online population was estimated at 349 million. Moreover, it was expected to reach a half-billion people worldwide by 2002 and to grow to nearly 1 billion by 2005 (UNDP 2002). Although it took radio broadcasting thirty-eight years from the time of its inception to reach fifty million people, and television thirteen years, the Internet did so in only four years (Simon 2001, 615). The number of computers in the world also soared over the past two decades, from 2 million, mostly mainframes, in 1980, to current estimates of over 150 million, 90 percent of which are personal computers (Mittelman 2000, 22). Owing to satellite technology, the price of a three-minute phone call from New York to London dropped from $244.65 in 1930, to $31.58 in 1970, to $3.32 in 1990, to 35 cents in 1999 (UNDP 1999, 28). And during the year 2000, traffic on international switchboards topped 100 billion minutes for the first time (*Foreign Policy* 2001, 58).

Cultural Interconnectedness

One obvious outcome or aspect of the revolutionary changes in technology described above is that information, ideas, and people are moving and interfacing worldwide more freely, rapidly, frequently, and at greater distances than ever before. These flows, in turn, have a significant, although somewhat less definitive, impact on the globalization of culture. As Hugh Mackay contends: "In recent decades, there has been a phenomenal growth in the global circulation—in terms of both distance and volume—of cultural goods" (2000, 49). Measured in terms of printed matter, music, visual arts, cinema and photographic, radio and television equipment, the value of cultural imports and exports almost tripled from an estimated $67 billion in 1980 to $200 billion in 1991 (UNDP 1999, 33). The proportion of world trade in cultural goods rose from 2.5 percent of all imports in 1980 to 2.8 percent in 1997. Music goods dominate this market, comprising one-quarter of all cultural imports and exports, followed by what has been a significant increase in the market share for games and sporting goods (UNESCO 1999, 4–8). For the United States, for example, entertainment, specifically films and television programs, has become the largest single export industry. In 1997 alone, Hollywood films grossed more than $30 billion worldwide, and in 1998, one film, *Titanic*, grossed more than $1.8 billion (UNDP 1999, 33). This is just one indication of how the contemporary flow of culture and cultural goods is rapid and expansive, but also heavily weighted in one direction—from rich countries to poor. As will be discussed below, it is this imbalance that renders culture one of the most contested arenas of globalization.

Advances in technology affected the spread and exchange of not only cultural ideas, practices, and artifacts, but also people. Air traffic between countries grew from 25 million passengers per year in 1950 to almost 600 million in 1996 (ICAO 1998). In 1980, out of a world population of 4.4 billion, 287 million people traveled abroad. By 1996, the world population was 5.7 billion, and the number of people traveling to another country more than doubled to 595 million. By the year 2020, it is estimated that out of a worldwide population of 7.8 billion, 1.6 billion will travel abroad (Mittelman 2000, 21).

Beyond travel and tourism, recent decades have also witnessed a profound increase in more permanent forms of human migration. Notable movements and resettlements of people from their homelands to other areas have taken place since the 1500s, yet the magnitude as well as direction of human flows—whether immigrants, refugees, exiles, or guest workers—have shifted significantly. By 1996, it is estimated that one in every twenty-one people on Earth was on the move as either a refugee or displaced person. In 1999, the UNDP estimated that 130 to 145 million people lived outside their countries of birth, up from 104 million in 1985 and 84 million in 1975 (UNDP 1999, 32). The United Nations Economic Commission for Africa estimates that one out of eighteen Africans resides outside her or his country of origin, and that more than 30 percent of Africa's skilled workforce is living in Europe. As of 1999, foreign-born residents made up 24 percent of the population in Australia, up from 10 percent in 1947 (Australian Bureau of Statistics 1999). Canada's 1996 census marked the population of foreign born at 17.4 percent, and Germany's foreign population increased by 63 percent between 1988 and 1998, comprising 9 percent of the total population in 1998 (OECD 2000). By the year 2000, the population of foreign born in the United States had reached 11 percent—tripling in size since the 1970s (U.S. Census Bureau 2000a).

Throughout the 1990s, many cities throughout North America and Europe saw their percentage of foreign born exceed one-third of the total population. Yet, as will be discussed in subsequent chapters, these immigrants did not completely sever ties with their homelands. One indication of persistent ties is the more than $66 billion per year in remittances that immigrants send to family members in their country of origin. In the case of Mexico, wire remittances in 2001 surpassed tourism as the country's third-largest source of foreign income after manufacturing and oil (S. Jacobs 2001).

Political Interconnectedness

Economic, technological, or cultural globalization does not occur in a political vacuum. The term political in this case can be interpreted broadly and somewhat loosely to encompass an array of circumstances that range from state relations to trans-state organizations and networks. Globalization or global interconnectedness is intimately related to the nation-state form, and because this political formation has been predominant since the eighteenth century, much of what constitutes global interaction and exchange is mediated through or in some way shaped by states and the state system. In this regard, political interconnectedness relates to what international relations (IR) scholars have termed interdependence.

By the 1970s, many IR theorists began to recognize that realism, a theory that posits an anarchic international system of zero-sum power relations among autonomous states, did not account for the many ways that states, even the most powerful ones, were dependent upon other states (Keohane and Nye 1977). Some of that interdependence relates to resource needs, such as oil; but there is also evidence of a degree of coordination and cooperation among states that is not reducible to the realist model of brute power relations. In fact, the international system comprises an array of regimes, sometimes deliberately codified in formal agreements or organizations and other times the result of less formal but still familiar and widely accepted practices that serve to manage activities and address policy problems that transcend the boundaries and capacities of states. These regimes range in focus from human rights and refugee issues to the control of natural resources and weapons systems.

More recently, this political interconnectedness is being addressed in terms of issues of governance, or what Scholte calls "post-sovereign governance" (2000). The various aspects of supraterritoriality discussed earlier promote a situation of multilayered governance where regulation not only is the purview or responsibility of the sovereign nation-state, but is dispersed across various international or suprastate agencies as well as substate agencies. International organizations or associations that are engaged in some sort of global governance are not new, but have expanded significantly in both number and charge in recent years. In 1909, there were only thirty-seven international governmental organizations (IGOs) and by 1989 there were three hundred. Similarly, in the middle of the nineteenth century there were two or three conferences or congresses per year sponsored by IGOs; today, there are more than 4,000 held each year (Held 1998, 20). The World Trade Organization (WTO), created in 1995, is a recent and marked example of the degree to which individual states are willing to commit themselves to comply with international law. Under WTO rules, a Trade Policy Review Body monitors member governments' commercial activities. Any alleged violations of WTO regulations are reviewed by a panel of experts, whose decisions are binding, and the consensus principle that prevailed under the General Agreement on Tariffs and Trade (GATT) has been replaced by one of majority rule. Nonetheless, there has been no shortage of states around the world lining up for membership in the WTO (Scholte 2000, 149; J. H. Jackson 1998).

Some of the growing political interconnectedness is regional in character, more so than worldwide, but represents the same tendency toward postsovereign governance. The European Union (EU) is the most widely known example of regional integration, and its member states (with the current exception of Britain) took a giant step toward transborder harmonization in January 2002 when they willingly traded in their national currencies for the euro. There have in the past and continue to be countless other examples of regional frameworks for governance in areas outside of Europe, including Central America, South America, North America, Southeast Asia, Southern Africa, and others. In fact, between 1948 and 1994, 109 regional agreements were reported to GATT, the bulk of which were formed in the 1970s and 1990s (Scholte 2000, 146). Although arguably a subset of more expansive worldwide integration, processes of regionalization are generally convergent with globalization in that both entail suprastate frameworks of governance and a commitment to harmonization and standardization in areas that range from finance and accounting, to communications and navigation, to labor and the environment.

Increasing interconnectedness of states in the world system is a powerful example of political globalization, but so, too, are the growing number and transborder activities of NGOs. Whether the International Red Cross, Amnesty International, Oxfam, or the International Planned Parenthood Federation, there has been a proliferation of organizations and associations whose mission and membership is not tied to a state. In 1909, international nongovernmental organizations (INGOs) numbered 176; by 1993, that number had soared to 28,900, and by the year 2000 to 37,000 (UNDP 2002, 10). Furthermore, many NGOs with a previously domestic focus or mission and the social movements that surround them have expanded their reach to incorporate issues and clientele not necessarily confined within the sovereign state. These organizations and associations recognize the transborder nature of the issues that concern them, and their transborder or extrastate responses further contribute to global political interconnectedness.

Beyond international IGOs and NGOs, another category of extra- or illegal organizations and networks also demonstrate a growing degree of worldwide interconnectedness. In fact, the same technological innovations that facilitate economic and cultural interaction also provide fertile ground for international organized crime and terrorism. Global criminal activity ranges from worldwide trade in arms and drugs, complex money-laundering schemes, international financial fraud, trade in biological and chemical technology and human organs, and the smuggling of illegal migrants and endangered species (Thachuk 2001, 746). In 1995, the illegal drug trade was estimated at $400 billion, representing about 8 percent of world trade and more than the share of iron and steel or of motor vehicles. The UNDP also estimated that a global network of organized crime syndicates grosses $1.5 trillion a year: "All have operations extending beyond national borders, and they are now developing strategic alliances linked in a global network, reaping the benefits of globalization" (UNDP 1999, 41–42).

In February 2001, during the trial of suspects in the 1998 bombings of the U.S. embassies in Tanzania and Kenya, many public officials and journalists issued eerily prescient portrayals of Osama bin Laden's vast global terrorist network, al Qaeda. Described as a "terrorist NATO," the *Christian Science Monitor* wrote: "bin Laden may have constructed something that is bigger than a guerrilla group and more complex than a multinational corporation. Call it a virtual country—the Republic of Jihadistan" (Grier 2001b, 1). Meanwhile, University of California political scientist and terrorism expert Richard Rosecrance stated: "It [al Qaeda] has state-like aspects, but without state borders," and the head of the U.S. National Security Agency publicly complained that al Qaeda's sophisticated use of the Internet defied Western eavesdropping attempts (Grier 2001b, 1).

Some scholars of globalization continue to emphasize a specific economic, technological, cultural, or political dimension; many others acknowledge its multidimensionality. Either way, there is an abundant supply of evidence to support the claims that the contemporary world is a tightly interconnected one.

Globalization: Old or New?

Closely related to and often implicit in definitions of what globalization is are questions of when it began. There is a widespread tendency to emphasize the novelty of globalization, but also indications that it dates much farther back in history. For example, if globalization is defined in terms of a focus on the world as a whole, or on existing or recognized relationships between the universal and the particular, then it is possible to go back to the second century B.C. when Polybius, in *Universal History*, wrote in reference to the Roman Empire: "Formerly the things which happened in the world had no connection among themselves. . . . But since then all events are united in a common bundle" (quoted in Robertson 1990, 21). There is also evidence of a global consciousness among various religious faiths—or "world religions"—dating as far back as the fifth and sixth centuries B.C.

(Scholte 2000, 64). If, on the other hand, globalization is intended to refer to increased interconnectedness among states, and particularly economic connections, some scholars mark the early emergence of a world system in the sixteenth century (Wallerstein 1974). Meanwhile, still others point to the rise and consolidation of transnational corporations in the 1970s as the beginning of globalization as we know it today (Marchand and Runyan 2000, 4).

Some analysts approach the origins of globalization by way of a map or model that presents a chronology of distinct phases in a long evolution of globalization. Roland Robertson offers one such model of globalization through five phases. For Robertson, the evolution and acceleration of globalization must be understood in relation to the simultaneous diffusion of the idea and reality of the nation-state. Hence, his five phases are differentiated, largely, by the changing role and nature of national societies. Phase 1, the *Germinal Phase*, takes place in Europe between the early fifteenth and mid-eighteenth centuries and entails, among other things, the emergence and growth of national communities and the accentuation of concepts of the individual and of ideas about humanity as a whole. Phase 2, the *Incipient Phase*, occurs between the mid-eighteenth century and the 1870s, also mainly in Europe, and entails a "sharp shift towards the idea of the homogenous, unitary state," and the "crystallization of conceptions of formalized international relations" (1990, 26).

Phase 3, the *Take-Off Phase*, takes place between the 1870s and the mid-1920s. This crucial time period witnesses increasingly global conceptions of what constitutes an "acceptable" national society, the inclusion of some non-European societies in "international society," a very pronounced increase in the number and speed of global forms of communications, and the founding of the League of Nations. Phase 4, the *Struggle for Hegemony Phase*, lasts from the early 1920s until the mid-1960s. Robertson characterizes this period as one primarily of "disputes and wars about the fragile terms of the globalization process established by the end of the take-off period" (1990, 27). He points also to the founding of the United Nations. The final phase, or *Uncertainty Phase*, begins in the 1960s with a heightening of global consciousness and carries into what Robertson describes as the crisis tendencies of the early 1990s. This period includes a dramatic increase in the number of global institutions and movements, a growing interest in world civil society, and the consolidation of a global media system. It also witnesses the end of the Cold War, the spread of nuclear weapons, and the increase in problems related to multiculturality in societies around the world.

Jan Scholte also maps the evolution of globalization by reference to distinct phases, in his case three. Scholte assigns no exact starting point to globalization, but identifies different factors that demonstrate a long gestation period up to the eighteenth century. He terms this first phase the "emergence of a global imagination" (2000, 63). Religious faiths dating back to the fifth and sixth centuries B.C., such as Buddhism, were premised on the notion of supraterritorial world community. Writers and thinkers from the fourteenth to the sixteenth centuries, ranging from Dante to Shakespeare, evinced secular global thinking, as did Herder, Condorcet, Hume, and other Enlightenment thinkers of the eighteenth century. Nonetheless, Scholte concludes that "prior to the nineteenth century, globality had little existence outside the mind" (p. 65).

Phase 2, incipient globalization, begins in the 1850s and lasts through the 1950s. This one-hundred-year period saw the emergence and consolidation of global communications technologies, global markets, and some degree of globality in finance and organization. The spread of telegraph lines began in the 1850s, transborder telephone and radio communications in the 1890s, and intercontinental air transport in 1919. Global distribution and sale of some commodities also began during this period. Within twenty years of its introduction in 1886, Coca-Cola was being marketed in Great Britain, Canada, Cuba, Mexico, and the United States. As a result of the gold standard, some national currencies—most notably the British pound—circulated globally, and several worldwide organizations and movements also emerged. The International Red Cross was started in 1863, the International Telecommunication Union was founded in 1865, the labor movement maintained its First International from 1864 to 1872, and two more before 1943. There is also evidence of frequent transborder activities on the part of other movements, such as that for women's suffrage (Scholte 2000, 71).

Because Scholte defines globalization as the growth of supraterritorial spaces, he marks its "full-scale" emergence, phase 3, in the 1960s, and its most significant, qualitative expansion in the decades since. "These years have seen far and away the greatest increase in the number, variety, intensity, institutionalization, awareness and impact of supraterritorial phenomena" (2000, 74). For example, in contrast to the period prior to the 1950s when some global products appeared in markets, today's stores are heavily, if not primarily, stocked with transborder items. The World Wide Web has contributed to a burgeoning growth in electronic commerce, estimated to expand from $2.6 billion in 1996 to over $300 billion in 2002 (UNDP 1999, 60). Meanwhile, money has become global as well. Scholte calls attention to the fact that the decades since the 1960s have witnessed unprecedented global circulation and exchange of national currencies, and the emergence of suprastate currencies such as the International Monetary Fund's (IMF) Special Drawing Rights (SDR), and, more recently, the euro. Furthermore, there are currently an estimated one-half million automatic teller machines (ATMs) worldwide that typically allow bank customers to extract money anywhere, anytime, and in countless different currencies (Scholte 2000, 79).

For the purposes of this analysis, it is not necessary to determine the novelty, or lack thereof, of globalization. Rather, it seems reasonable to conclude that whether or not the processes and patterns of contemporary worldwide interconnectedness are fundamentally and qualitatively new or different from those of the past, they are intensified. Time and space have, in David Harvey's (1990) words, become compressed. And chronologies like Robertson's and Scholte's are useful for tracing the intensification of interconnectedness.

> *"whether or not the processes and patterns of contemporary worldwide interconnectedness are fundamentally and qualitatively new or different from those of the past, they are intensified. Time and space have . . . become compressed."*

Globalization: Good or Bad?

More contentious and arguably more significant to the discussion of globalization than debates about when it began are the debates about its implications. No phenomenon this complex and multifaceted can be evaluated in simple terms of good versus bad, yet many of the debates, or positions within the debate, tend to lend themselves to just that sort of characterization. On one side are those who see and welcome the emergence of a global village, and on the other are those who see only global pillage and fear the worst is yet to come. A number of norms and values characterize the contours of this debate, but most frequently at issue are questions of equality, diversity, and democracy. This section will sort briefly through these debates, keeping in mind that the values or ideals listed above are themselves frequently contested concepts and closely interrelated as well. The purpose here is simply to introduce the normative dimensions of the globalization question. The final chapter will return to these issues as they relate to globalization's impact on belonging.

Equality

Debates about globalization's implications for equality typically focus on issues of economic and social justice. For example, are the costs and the benefits of globalization being fairly distributed between countries and between classes or groups within countries? Or, similarly, is globalization a force for greater social and economic equity, or is it an ever more sophisticated mechanism for exploitation and oppression? Proponents or defenders of globalization, like defenders of trade liberalization more generally, argue that the deregulation of trade, investment, and the movement of capital improves market efficiency and greatly benefits both producers and consumers (Wolf 2000). This argument is put forth by analysts, but also by policymakers and politicians. Former Mexican president Ernesto Zedillo recently delivered a speech titled "More, Not Less, Globalization Is the Answer." In that speech Zedillo acknowledged persistent worldwide poverty and extreme disparities in wealth and resources, but he emphasized that globalization should be viewed not as a cause of the disparity, but rather as "a vital part of the solution":

> More international trade, more investment flowing across countries, more knowledge diffused internationally among communities and individuals, by creating wealth, shared opportunities and common interests, will do much to defeat the evils of conflict and poverty during this new century. (2001, 515)

A recent report in *Foreign Policy* also claims positive benefits of globalization, or, more accurately, refutes claims that globalization increases inequality. *Foreign Policy* recently joined efforts with A.T. Kearney, Inc. to construct a globalization index that allows measurement and comparison of levels of global integration in fifty countries worldwide. The index also facilitates analyses of the relationship between globalization and other factors such as income disparity. In contradiction to the claims of some antiglobalization critics, the magazine reports that the more highly globalized a country the more egalitarian, not less, is the distribution of income. The report acknowledged persistent inequalities, but argued that income disparity in an economy likely has "more to do with history, economic growth, price and wage controls, welfare programs, and education policies than it does with globalization or trade liberalization" (*Foreign Policy* 2001, 64).

From an alternative perspective, critics or detractors of globalization point to growing gaps between rich and poor that have coincided with globalization. In recent years, income gaps have reportedly grown wider in almost every country, as well as between countries (Hurrell and Woods 1999). The United Nations, in 1999, issued a report on globalization decrying the growing gulf between rich and poor and reporting that the combined wealth of the world's three richest families was greater than the annual income of 600 million people in the least developed countries. Thirty years ago, the gap between the richest fifth of the world's people and the poorest was 30 to 1. By 1990, it had widened to 60 to 1, and today stands at 74 to 1 (Held 2000, 112). Several recent studies, some under the auspices of the World Bank, have also revealed a "startling" increase in inequality worldwide. One report noted that between 1988 and 1993 the share of world income going to the poorest 10 percent of the world's population fell by over a quarter; whereas the share of the richest 10 percent rose by 8 percent. Another study found a significant 6 percent increase in the Gini coefficient (a commonly used measure for inequality) for world income inequality. Economist Robert Wade from the London School of Economics claims that "the bulk of the evidence on trends in world income distribution runs against the claim that world income inequality has fallen sharply in the past half century" (2001, 73). Furthermore, the evidence of persistent worldwide inequality reveals that the implications of globalization are not neutral with regard to race, ethnicity, or gender (Richmond 1994; Peterson and Runyan 1999).

Those who are skeptical of globalization question not only the claims of supporters that globalization reduces inequalities, but also the very values that economic globalization promotes. Rigoberta Menchu, passionate spokesperson for Mayans in Guatemala and winner of the 1992 Nobel Peace Prize explains:

> None of the Western development programs or models understand the difference between the organizing principles of the market— banking, corporations and enterprises—and our organizing principle: community life. We want holistic integrated development that holds the community sacred. We see the community, not the market, as the building block of a model of self-reliant development based on cooperative village life. (1994, 59)

Diversity

Menchu's concern about the impact of the market on the Mayan way of life speaks to another hotly debated aspect of globalization—increasing cultural interconnectedness. Specifically, questions arise as to whether globalization is replacing cultural pluralism and local diversity with a mass, homogenized world culture. As Arjun Appadurai explains: "The central problem of today's global interactions is the tension between cultural homogenization and cultural heterogenization" (1990, 295). Few will deny the reality of the increased cultural flows outlined earlier, or, specifically, that advances in communications and transportation technology have led to a rapid and intensified exchange of ideas, information, cultural symbols, lifestyle preferences, and modes of behavior. The debate arises over whether the outcome of this interchange is the convergence and uniformity of a Western-imposed and commodity-driven world culture, or, a more dialectical, multilateral, reflexive process of negotiating the local meaning and significance of global cultural symbols. The contours of this debate are complex and it is a difficult debate to settle empirically. Nonetheless, it has captured a great deal of attention and spawned intriguing analyses of cultural politics.

Typically, the homogenization thesis is simultaneously an argument about and against Westernization or Americanization. The focus is on a global culture industry that has people worldwide, from Johannesburg, Rio de Janeiro, and Paris to Bangkok, Los Angeles, and Cairo, from townships, favelas, and barrios to upscale apartments, office complexes, shopping malls, and villas wearing Levi's, watching MTV, drinking Coca-Cola, smoking Marlboro cigarettes, and visiting, or dreaming of visiting, a Disney theme park. This is a reality that analysts have come to describe as McDonaldization, or what Benjamin Barber terms "McWorld" (1992). From this perspective, cultural globalization represents nothing more than a form of cultural imperialism. Cultural flows are profoundly imbalanced, and what is sometimes described as global culture is really Western, or American, culture. Furthermore, the far-reaching distribution and dominance of commodified Western culture is said to work to the advantage of the United States and other Western nations while threatening more vulnerable cultures (Schiller 1991). As John Tomlinson writes:

> The globalised culture that is currently emerging is not a global culture in any utopian sense. It is not a culture that has arisen out of the mutual experiences and needs of all of humanity. It does not draw equally on the world's diverse cultural traditions. It is neither inclusive, balanced, nor, in the best sense, synthesising. Rather, globalised culture is the installation, world-wide, of one particular culture born out of one particular, privileged historical experience. It is, in short, simply the global expression of Western culture. (1999, 23)

It is not difficult to find evidence to support the cultural imperialism thesis. To take television, for example, fully 40 percent of worldwide exports of programming hours come from the United States. In Latin America, for example, 77 percent of imports are from the United States, and in Canada, the percentage is 70. The United States, on the other hand, imports only 1 percent of its commercial programming and 2 percent of public service programming (MacKay quoted in Held 2000, 63). Similar patterns are evident in the film industry. In 1995, Barber published a list of the top-ten grossing films in 1991 in countries ranging from Argentina and Hungary to Malaysia and Switzerland. Only in the rarest of cases did Hollywood films not dominate all of the top-ten slots. In Europe, by the late 1990s, 60 to 90 percent of box office receipts came from foreign films (Held 1998, 18).

Language, and in this case, English, also figures prominently into the pattern of cultural dominance. English is spoken by an estimated quarter of the human race, and not only by large numbers of people, but also by the most affluent. English is the main language for communication within and between global organizations and for the codification of a majority of the world's scientific knowledge (MacKay 2000, 63). Experts estimate that there are currently six thousand different tongues existing in the world, and 90 to 95 percent of these will be extinct in the coming century (Cowen 1995, 1).

The predominance of U.S. culture has not gone unnoticed around the world. Many countries, France and Canada foremost among them, have mounted campaigns against *Americanization*. In France in 1999, French farmer José Bové achieved hero-like status after he was arrested for vandalizing a local McDonald's in an act of protest. These and other governments have taken specific steps to protect their national culture—including their magazine, film, and music industries as well as the use of English on the Internet in the case of France. In 1998, Canada sponsored a two-day International Meeting on Cultural Policy. Twenty-two countries attended the conference, which focused on protecting indigenous cultures, but as Canadian cultural heritage minister Sheila Copps acknowledged, "Americanization of cultures is a major concern" (quoted in Stewart 1998, A10).

Despite the amount of attention focused on globalization as cultural homogenization, many analysts question whether this portrays accurately what is indeed occurring in the world. Jan Pieterse, for example, argues that globalization, rather than being viewed in terms of standardization and uniformity, should be recognized as a process of "hybridization" that gives rise to "translocal mélange cultures." To view globalization as a one-dimensional process of homogenization obscures, according to Pieterse, its fluid, indeterminant, open-ended, and multidimensional nature (1994, 161–62). Appadurai agrees with Pieterse, and in arguing against the "globalization as Westernization" thesis writes:

> What these arguments fail to consider is that at least as rapidly as forces from various metropolises are brought into new societies they tend to become indigenized in one or other way: this is true of music and housing styles as much as it is true of science and terrorism, spectacles and constitutions. (1990, 295)

Roland Robertson (1995) proposes that instead of focusing on the global and the local as opposing forces, we employ the term "glocalization" to capture the dialectical and contingent interchange between local cultures and global trends.

In other words, in addition to downplaying the multidimensionality of global forces, the homogenization argument also tends to overlook the fluidity and dynamism of local cultures around the world. Cultures are not static, uniform, organic entities highly vulnerable to poisoning or imposed alteration by outside forces. Instead, what is meant by hybridization or creolization is that when different cultures interact over an extended time period, even if on unequal terms, what typically emerges are new cultural forms that are not merely derived from one or the other culture (Hannerz 1990). McDonald's may have penetrated the far corners of the globe, but when Indian residents, for example, enter the local McDonald's in New Delhi or Bombay, they choose between 100 percent beefless Maharaja Mac or Vegetable McNuggets with McMasala or McImli (tamarind) sauces (Zubrzycki 1996, 6).

> *"in addition to downplaying the multidimensionality of global forces, the homogenization argument also tends to overlook the fluidity and dynamism of local cultures around the world. Cultures are not static, uniform, organic entities highly vulnerable to poisoning or imposed alteration by outside forces."*

Scholars of popular culture have also pointed out that what might look like Americanization is actually a far more complex fusion, incorporation, and reinterpretation of cultural symbols. American bands with messages of rebellion resonated in a particular way in communist Czechoslovakia, as did Spike Lee's *Malcom X* in Haiti. And rather than drowning out local, indigenous cultures, Orlando Patterson (1994) argues that the diffusion of Western popular culture often generates hypercreativity in cultures around the world. Not to recognize this smacks of cultural chauvinism on the part of the West. Furthermore, as Patterson and others have pointed out, arguments and actions on the part of some leaders around the world against Westernization are often no more than thinly veiled attempts at maintaining the power and prestige of an entrenched political elite.

Latin American novelist and intellectual Mario Vargas Llosa makes this point when he argues that globalization does not suffocate local cultures, but rather, liberates them from the ideological conformity of nationalism. Vargas Llosa uses the example of Spanish.

Half a century ago, Spanish speakers were an inward-looking community. . . . Today, Spanish is dynamic and thriving, gaining beachheads or even vast landholdings on all five continents. The fact that there are some 25 to 30 million Spanish speakers in the US today explains why the two recent US presidential candidates, Texas Governor George W. Bush and Vice President Al Gore, campaigned not only in English but also in Spanish. (2001, 70)

Finally, Appadurai makes a similar claim when he cautions that "for the people of Irian Jaya, Indonesianization may be more worrisome than Americanization, as Japanization may be for Koreans, Indianization for Sri Lankans, Vietnamization for the Cambodians" (1990, 295).

As was the case with the issue of equity, assessing globalization's impact on or relationship with culture is often a matter of perspective. Furthermore, there is perhaps no more complex concept in social analysis than "culture"—making it even less amenable to definitive analysis than equity or, as will be discussed below, democracy.

Democracy

Closely intertwined with the previous normative implications and aspects of globalization is the question of democracy, or the principle that members of a polity should have an equal capacity to shape the decisions that affect their lives. This question is also multifaceted and complicated by the fact that democracy itself is a contested concept. Typically defined as "rule by the people," heated debates about democracy emerge around questions such as: Who constitutes the people, and What precisely does it mean to rule? Some participants in the debate utilize a formal conceptualization of democracy as a political system characterized by free and fair multiparty elections. Others invoke broader and more substantive definitions of democracy that incorporate issues of social and economic justice.

Relying on more procedural definitions of democracy, some scholars credit globalization with facilitating the worldwide spread of liberal democratic principles and practices and the demise of dictatorial regimes (Pye 1990). Francis Fukuyama's confidence in the appeal of liberal democracy is so strong that he has proclaimed the "end of history" (1989, 4). For scholars like these, globalization tends to be synonymous with Westernization; but even scholars who have a more expansive conceptualization of globalization as the increased interaction and interdependence among countries and peoples of the world maintain that the opening up which it entails has positive implications for democracy. This is the case both in terms of increased levels of governance above the state and movements that exist below or transcend the level of states. From this perspective, the proliferation of regional and international agreements and organizations has opened up new and multiple levels of access and opportunity through which individuals can pursue rights and participate in politics outside of simply an assigned state. Whether through the additional levels of protection guaranteed by EU institutions and EU citizenship, North American Free Trade Agreement's (NAFTA) regulations relating to fair wages and environmental standards, or the multitude of UN and related international covenants that increase human rights protections, globalization can be seen as fueling or facilitating democratization.

The same argument can be and is made with regard to growing pressures and demands made upon states from below in the form of increasingly sophisticated and well-organized social movements, which are often transnational in membership and scope. Operating on and advocating more substantive conceptualizations of democracy, these groups, whether labor, women, indigenous peoples, or gays and lesbians, are demanding democratization in realms that range from fair wages, to civil rights, to environmental protection and make up what many have come to describe as a global civil society (Lipschutz 1992). Furthermore, many have argued that this transnational civil society or the "third sector" is fueled by the increasing availability of sophisticated communications and transportation technologies (Waterman 1998). One notable example involved the remarkably effective use of the Internet by the Zapatista rebels in Mexico during the early 1990s. Daily e-mail updates of their struggle were transmitted worldwide from the remote jungle areas of the southern state of Chiapas. Similar tactics were used by the Chinese student dissidents during the Tiananmen Square massacre in 1989.

Many other analysts and observers of globalization have a much less optimistic view of its democratic outcomes. First, it is important to question whether what many celebrate as a wave of democratization sweeping the globe is indeed democratization or, as often seems to be the case, economic liberalization and capitalist integration. The two, capitalism and democracy, do not necessarily go hand-in-hand. Furthermore, it is not clear that celebrating state regimes, even democratic ones, makes much sense when, as will be discussed briefly below, one central characteristic of contemporary globalization is the declining significance of the modern state. In other words, whatever their shortcomings as mechanisms of democratic governance, states may have offered individuals better political access and been held to higher standards of accountability than the various suprastate organizations, such as the WTO, that have gained power and prominence in recent decades. This is certainly a primary concern of the growing antiglobalization movement that has made itself heard from Seattle, to Prague, to Quebec City, to the fatal demonstrations in Genoa that ended in the loss of one protestor's life. Transnational corporations, this movement argues, are not beholden to the rules of democratic practice that govern most states, nor are international intergovernmental organizations like the WTO accountable to a constituency or polity in the same way that are the states that comprise its membership (Broad 2002).

Furthermore, and regarding the democratic potential of technological innovation, it is important to keep in mind that access to the Internet and fax machines is not equally distributed around the world. Moreover, the same technology that assists social movements in their pursuit of democracy also assists states and suprastate organizations in their subversion and surveillance of these movements. Even in the United States, one of the wealthiest countries in the world, a disproportionate share of poor Americans do not have access to home computers or the Internet. Whereas 80 percent of households with annual incomes over $100,000 own personal computers, among households with incomes under $30,000 only 25 percent own a personal computer. Meanwhile, although the national ratio of students per classroom computer in the United States is 10 to 1, in schools with 90 percent or more low-income minority students, the ratio is 30 to 1 (Holtzman 1998, 11).

This pattern of inequality is similar between rich and poor states around the world. In fact, in 1999, the United Nations reported that 88 percent of all Internet users in the world live in the West (Held 2000, 112). In many countries where the Internet has become increasingly popular, governments have sought, and often gained, control over its use and content. China has been remarkably effective at controlling information and access to it—often resorting to the massive shutdown of Internet cafés. And software companies, most of them American, have found a lucrative market in helping countries throughout the Middle East, particularly Saudi Arabia, block access to web sites the government deems inappropriate. In the Saudi case, the government is largely concerned with pornographic sites, but has also blacklisted, as has China, various foreign media and human rights web sites. Among the sites banned by the Saudi government were the Committee for the Defense of Human Rights in the Arabian Peninsula and the Movement for Islamic Reform in Arabia (Lee 2001, C1).

None of these debates about the normative implications of globalization have been settled, nor are they likely to be any time soon. This is due in part to the fact that the debates involve value judgments around which consensus rarely exists. Part of the challenge also has to do with the relative newness and the complexity of the topics at hand. In this regard, further research on globalization in all its dimensions will, if not provide material for a more definitive stance, at least bring into sharper focus what is at stake with regard to globalization, along with questions of why and how. At this point, and before turning to the second theme of "belonging," it is important to clarify an undercurrent that runs throughout much of the preceding discussion of globalization, one that is essential to understanding globalization's relationship to belonging—namely, the role and relevance of the modern state.

The State

Few discussions of globalization proceed without reference to the state. Whether interest lies in the meaning of globalization, its evolution, or its consequences, the state surfaces as playing a significant role. In some cases that role entails actively facilitating or participating centrally in processes of global integration. In other cases, the state is resisting some aspect of globalization or is conceptualized as an obstacle that the forces of globalization seek to overcome. In many portrayals or analyses of globalization, the state is significant in its absence. In other words, a declining role or relevance of the state is considered an indicator, or part and parcel, of the globalization process itself. This last point, dealing specifically with the issue of state sovereignty, is one around which much of the current debate on globalization and its relationship to the state revolves (Lapidoth 1992). Some observers maintain that the ushering in of the era of globalization marks the retreat of the sovereign state (Strange 1996). Others argue, however, that it is much too soon to write the obituary of the state—a still privileged form of polity (Tölölyan 1991, 5).

"Whether interest lies in the meaning of globalization, its evolution, or its consequences, the state surfaces as playing a significant role. In some cases that role entails actively facilitating or participating centrally in processes of global integration. In other cases, the state is resisting some aspect of globalization or is conceptualized as an obstacle that the forces of globalization seek to overcome."

Challenges to State Sovereignty

What is clear from the preceding discussion of globalization is that its very parameters, whether in the realm of economics, technology, culture, or politics, are defined in large part by their relationship to the state. And that relationship is typically one of transcendence. Economic interconnectedness, for example, is driven by the rise of transnational corporations that have the capacity to make decisions and engage in business practices that are outside of and largely detached from the arena of state politics and policies. States, then, have seen their power wane in the face of highly mobile transnational corporations and global capital and are loath to use the regulatory mechanisms that do remain at their disposal for fear of losing out in a highly competitive global marketplace. Within the realm of technology, what is often considered remarkable and transformative is that, in Barber's words: "Satellite footprints do not respect national borders; telephone wires penetrate the most closed societies" (1992, 58). The borders referred to by Barber and others, borders that are being erased by globalization, are typically those of states.

With regard to cultural interconnectedness, the very fact that countries like Canada, France, and others aim to protect their "national" culture from global penetration implies that there is or should be something "national" about culture. In other words the assumption is that culture is somehow, has been, or should be the purview of states, and that globalization threatens that purview. Similarly, so many examples of what constitutes interconnectedness in the political realm are examples of governance that take place beyond, beneath, outside, or somehow other than, the modern state. In fact, regimes of international governance, which both comprise and are designed to manage globalization, limit, by definition, the autonomy and sovereignty of individual states. Finally, in the literature on globalization's repeated references to deterritorialization, or in Scholte's words "supraterritoriality," the territory being transcended is most often the territory of the modern, sovereign state.

The claim is more explicit in some analyses than others, but the decline or demise of the state is a central theme running throughout the contemporary literature and discourse on globalization. In his 1995 book *The End of the Nation State*, Kenichi Ohmae contends that today's nation-state has lost its capacity to control exchange rates and protect its currencies. The nation-state no longer generates real economic activity, and as a result has forfeited its role as a critical participant in the global economy. In her book, *The Retreat of the State*, Susan Strange argues that "Today it is much more doubtful that the state—or at least the great majority of states—can still claim a degree of loyalty from the citizen greater than the loyalty given to family, to the firm, to the political party or even in some cases to the local football team" (1996, 72). Meanwhile, there is a growing body of work characterized as "postnational" that emphasizes the complex, ad hoc, nonterritorial social formations and allegiances that exist outside of and largely disconnected from the nation-state (Appadurai 1996; Bhabha 1990). In these analyses and others, scholars are pointing to the many ways in which the state is being challenged from above—via transnational organizations, agreements, and flows—and from below—via transnational social movements and the enhanced competencies on the part of individuals and groups to resist the hegemony of the state (J. Rosenau 1990; Scholte 2000, 132–58). Their portrayals are compelling, but there is also an opposing viewpoint that insists that this case is overdrawn.

Persistence of the State

Just as some observers question whether current processes of globalization indeed represent new, profound, fundamental alterations in the world system, many also question the extent to which the state is actually fading from the world scene. It is not difficult to find evidence of the state as a key actor in globalization, whether economic, technological, cultural, or political. In each of these realms, the state plays a role in facilitating, even stimulating, globalization, as well as mediating or regulating it. In fact, much of what constitutes globalization happens in and through international institutions created by states. States join organizations ranging from the WTO and the IMF to the International Telecommunication Union and the International Organization for Standardization (ISO), and states sign onto treaties, protocols, and conventions, all of which set standards and establish procedures for global trade and commerce and technological, financial, and cultural exchange. Much of this activity is designed to encourage global interconnectedness, yet states also enact legislation and implement policies that regulate and monitor the impact of this interconnectedness. The increase in global flows has motivated many states to pass laws focused on protecting the environment, consumers, data, and so forth (Scholte 2000, 134).

The discourse on MNCs typically focuses on cross-border transactions and the mobility of capital, but as Robert Holton writes, most MNCs have headquarters within a single nation, hold annual shareholders' meetings within that nation, and cultivate close relations with the government of the country in which they are domiciled. In a number of sectors, such as banking, telecommunications, and the media, they are often subject to national controls limiting foreign ownership (1998, 82–83). Migration is another arena in which states act to resist the impact of globalization, and their continued power and prominence is evinced in the increasingly strict attitudes, policy proposals, and surveillance activity designed to restrict the free movement of people across state borders. Meanwhile, and as noted above, technology, in whatever ways it has increased suprastate flows and interactions, has also strengthened and empowered states in their surveillance and military capacities, both at home and abroad.

Political scientist Stephen Krasner (1999, 2001) has been one of the most persistent and persuasive voices arguing against the view of a declining state. According to Krasner, an inherent weakness in the "retreating state" thesis is the fact that the sovereignty of states was never as robust as is often believed. States, particularly weaker ones but also strong ones, have always been forced to contend with challenges to their sovereignty from outside and from within. For centuries, states have struggled to maintain international peace and promote universal human rights and have sacrificed autonomy to international agreements and organization in order to do so. Technology has also been, for at least two hundred years, posing challenges to state sovereignty. Krasner maintains, for example, that the current impact of the global media on political authority pales in comparison to the havoc unleashed by the invention of the printing press (2001, 24). Similarly, the nineteenth century was characterized by booms and busts in the world economy that revealed a remarkably high degree of economic interdependence among states. Not only is what is happening now not necessarily new, Krasner argues, but there is also evidence that states are now better prepared to respond to and manage global processes. The fallout of the Asian financial crisis of the late 1990s was more easily maintained than previous economic crises, most governments have developed social welfare strategies to cushion the effect of such crises, and overall government activity as reflected in taxation and expenditures has, according to Krasner, increased as a percentage of national income since the 1950s (2001, 26).

Although Krasner rejects the "end of the nation-state" thesis, he shares the opinion of many other scholars who acknowledge the multiple changes now taking place in the world to which the state must, and is, adapting. Jessica Mathews, for example, writes:

> National governments are not simply losing autonomy in a globalizing economy. They are sharing powers—political, social, and security roles at the core of sovereignty—with businesses, with international organizations, and with a multitude of citizen groups, known as nongovernmental organizations (NGOs). (1997, 50)

Ronnie Lipschutz states: "In spite of forecasts of the 'end of the state,' there is little question that the 'state' will remain a central actor in world politics for some time to come. It will retain its capabilities, its material and discursive powers, and its domination of the political imaginary" (1999, 217).

States, then, continue to be prominent players on the global scene, but their role has not gone unchanged. Even the staunchest defenders of state sovereignty acknowledge that globalization, in all its guises, has challenged the centrality and primacy of the state. Nor are academics the only group aware of the ambivalent role of the state. In 1994, as Nelson Mandela began his term as the first president of a post-Apartheid South Africa, he noted the challenges his country's fragile democracy would face—challenges that relate to the simultaneous waning and resilience of the state. "Faced with the enormity of events, states appear too puny, too clumsy, to deal with diverse issues—from trade wars to public health—which now touch the lives of ordinary people. Sovereignty, once one of the central organizing principles of our world, has been profoundly disturbed" (1994, 58). Yet, at the close of his speech, Mandela invoked South Africa's sovereignty and vowed to use the power of the state to protect "the needs of the country's people," noting that "Any effort to force the reintegration of our country's trade regime into the global system will be resisted" (p. 60).

This is only a brief sampling of a burgeoning literature on the contemporary and future role of the state. Subsequent chapters will return to this topic in the context of exploring how the fate of the state interrelates with the form and content of different types of belonging.

Belonging

Belonging as an analytical concept or term does not have the same currency in the social sciences as does globalization, yet so much of the subject matter that currently consumes scholars and politicians can be characterized in relation to questions of belonging or identity. Conflicts in the former Yugoslavia, the Middle East, Northern Ireland, and Rwanda, while profoundly complicated in their origins and contemporary manifestations, are poignant examples of the power and passion that surround belonging. Movements toward greater regionalization in Europe, in North America, in Southern Africa, and elsewhere, although largely motivated by economic concerns, are also related to issues and aspects of belonging. The European Union, the most advanced example of regional integration, has established a new form of collectivity among its inhabitants. It has created additional or alternative levels of membership, heightened the salience of some previously existing forms of belonging and lessened others, and altered people's perceptions and actions with regard to how they identify themselves and attach themselves, or not, to those around them.

Meanwhile, the growing number and sophistication of various transnational movements and organizations, described above as part of an emerging global civil society, attests to the desire and the capacity of individuals and groups to negotiate new forms of belonging—many of which are disconnected from more familiar attachments to territory, geography, or polity. The literature on globalization points to a world in flux, and the politics of belonging is a central part of that flux. The remainder of this book is devoted to investigating how globalization and belonging interrelate. Before turning to that question, this section introduces the concept of belonging and some of the theoretical discussion and debate on related issues of identity and culture.

The terminology of belonging is only beginning to emerge (Bell 1999; Geddes and Favell 1999; Migdal forthcoming), and much of what is being described here as the politics of belonging is addressed most thoroughly by a burgeoning literature on identity, and to a lesser extent, culture. In recent years, there has been, as Stuart Hall notes, "a veritable discursive explosion" around the concept of identity (1996, 1). Identity now forms a central focus across a range of disciplines in both the social sciences and the humanities; and culture, although somewhat out of academic fashion in previous decades, has also staged a powerful comeback (Lapid and Kratochwill 1996). Josef Lapid, for example, notes "a cross-paradigmatic surge of interest in culture and identity" (1996, 3); and this interest is reflected in an array of books, journals, university courses, academic conferences, and associations devoted to the study of identity generally, and to ethnicity, nationalism, citizenship, and gender specifically.

As was the case with globalization, various debates characterize this literature—the most prominent of which revolves around whether identity is best conceptualized as static, essential, and unidimensional, or fluid, constructed, and multidimensional. The former view, known as *primordialism* or *essentialism*, treats identity as fixed and organic—something pregiven, predetermined, or "natural." From this perspective, identity is conceptualized as an independent variable. It is used to explain other phenomena—conflict, war, aggression, cooperation, coalition, and passivity. From a primordialist perspective, for example, it is natural for an American citizen to feel more compassion for a fellow American who died in the attacks on the World Trade Center than for an innocent Afghan citizen who died in the U.S. attacks on Kandahar. This is because the loyalty and attachment to one's own nation is presumed to be a natural, deeply felt, even spiritual bond. Relatedly, if ethnically diverse regions or locales are prone to conflict, many assume that this is because when different cultures come into close contact they are naturally prone to clash. Moreover, the explanation for the clash may also be assumed to inhere in the ethnic group's very nature: "Latins are hotheaded," or "the Irish are quick-tempered." Finally, when men engage in violence more frequently than women, primordialists or essentialists locate the explanation in natural or biological differences between the sexes. In each of these cases, identity is invoked as an explanation, but little effort is made to explain or understand identity itself—whether nationhood, ethnicity, or gender. The origins or essence of identity is taken for granted or rendered irrelevant.

Primordialism has fallen somewhat out of favor among academics; but, as will be shown in the chapters that follow, some scholars, politicians, media personalities, and other observers continue to describe identity—ethnic, national, gender, or otherwise—as primordial or organic, and invoke static or essentialist interpretations of identity and culture to explain a range of phenomena. Particularly notable is Samuel Huntington's treatise on the "Clash of Civilizations." Writing in 1993, Huntington sounded a somber warning about a new phase of world politics that he perceived as potentially more ominous than the Cold War era that preceded it. According to Huntington, ideology and economics will no longer predominate as the fundamental sources of conflict in the world. Rather, "the great divisions among humankind and the dominating source of conflict will be cultural" (p. 22). Huntington's thesis is based on the supposition that the world is comprised of distinct civilizations or cultural groupings, distinguished by different languages, history, religion, customs, and institutions. Civilizations will clash because the differences between them are "real and basic" (p. 25). They are also less mutable than economic or political differences. It is quite difficult, Huntington muses, "to be half-Catholic and half-Muslim" (p. 27). Moreover, as the world becomes smaller, the interactions between these cultural groupings increase, and, hence, so too the conflicts.

> *"some scholars, politicians, media personalities, and other observers continue to describe identity—ethnic, national, gender, or otherwise—as primordial or organic, and invoke static or essentialist interpretations of identity and culture to explain a range of phenomena."*

It is not difficult to find evidence to support Huntington's claims. The Balkans, for example, is a region through which the fault lines of several "civilizations" run, and indeed, since the end of the Cold War, has been the site of horrific conflicts. The events of 9/11 might also appear to validate Huntington's position with regard to civilizational differences between Islam and the West. Yet, it is also not difficult to identify evidence that undermines Huntington's belief in the distinctiveness of civilizations and the inevitably of conflict between them. In fact, a great deal of world conflict during the past decade has been within, not between, civilizations, and several opposing civilizations have found themselves in close cooperation. Africa, which Huntington tentatively labels a civilization, has been racked by intracivilizational conflict within and across the borders of Rwanda, Uganda, Kenya, Ethiopia, Somalia, and the Sudan. Meanwhile, Russia (part of what Huntington labels the "Slavic-Orthodox" civilization) and the United States (a member of Western civilization) have formed alliances around issues ranging from arms control to the economy to terrorism. Huntington's analysis also ignores the unprecedented movement of people across international borders—leading to the dilution of bounded civilizations and the deterritorialization of identity and belonging.

The weaknesses and inconsistencies of the primordial view of culture and identity are challenged by an alternative view, known as *constructivist* or *social constructionist*. This approach has gained recent popularity among scholars, and, as a result, many of the most central concepts and categories of social and political analysis have and continue to come under increased scrutiny. Few analyses of nationalism now proceed without deference to Benedict Anderson's (1991) notion of nations as "imagined communities," and nations themselves are most commonly conceptualized in terms of "becoming," "formation," or "narration" (Eley and Suny 1996). Discussions of ethnicity, too, have moved away from metaphors of blood and stone to those of clay and putty, and ethnic identities, however ancient or intractable they may seem, are frequently characterized as inventions (Sollors 1989). Race, as a valid or legitimate means for classifying the human species, has been discredited, and any attempts to use the term as such have been and are being thoroughly interrogated by analyses of "racial formation" (Omi and Winant 1986), or "race-making" (Marx 1998). Even the seemingly most primordial notions of sex and gender have also been recognized as constructions or performances (Butler 1990).

Critical of the primordialist approach, constructivists argue that treating any one identity, ethnicity, for example, as a basic group identity fails to appreciate that individuals have any number of identities. Some of those identities intersect or collide with others, and all vary in salience across time and across contexts. For example, any one individual might simultaneously be an adherent of a particular religious group, a member of a political party, a grandparent, parent, spouse, and child, a self-identified and/or other-identified member of one, or more (Tiger Woods), ethnic or racial categories, and, as will be discussed in chapter 2, a citizen of one or more states. As described in the introduction, at some points in an individual's life, ethnicity may be central, and at other times, citizenship will seem more important or meaningful.

In addition to multiplicity, constructivists also emphasize the malleability of identity. The content and meaning of identities shift across time and place, for individuals, groups, and whole societies. An individual's ethnic or racial identity can change, for example, when she or he moves, marries, or makes more money. (A common phrase in Latin America, "money whitens," attests to the fluidity of racial classifications and their link to financial status.) In some societies at some times, nationhood is critically relevant. In others it is a nonissue. And as chapter 5 points out, gender means different things in different places and times. In spite of the emphasis on multiplicity and malleability, constructivists do not, however, portray identity as arbitrary. Rather, they seek to explain the emergence, variation in, and reconfiguration of different identity/belonging formations by reference to political, economic, and sociocultural conditions. The origins of ethnic identity and ethnic conflict might be explained, for example, by reference to elites who manipulate ethnic symbols in pursuit of political gain (Bowen 1996). Nationalist movements can be attributed to uneven regional development (Hechter 1975); and gender can be traced to the interplay of power and politics (J. Scott 1986). In this way, constructivists, unlike primordialists, remain cognizant that nations, ethnic groups, gender, and culture more generally are dependent as well as independent variables. These identities and attachments warrant, in other words, as much explanation as they provide.

"constructivists, unlike primordialists, remain cognizant that nations, ethnic groups, gender, and culture more generally are dependent as well as independent variables. These identities and attachments warrant, in other words, as much explanation as they provide."

Yet, despite valuable insights, the constructivist approach must still contend with the powerful and seemingly irrational passion and sense of embeddedness that often surround identity. Constructivists also confront a troubling paradox of emphasizing the invented, constructed, imagined, and performed nature of identity while individuals and groups around the world continue to fall prey to and commit unspeakable violence and hatreds all in the name of these "inventions." This dilemma has led some analysts to combine insights from both approaches, or to speak of "constructed primordiality." When groups and circumstances construct identity, as Stephen Cornell and Douglas Hartmann explain:

> what they construct is an identity that typically claims for itself primordial moorings—an anchor in blood ties or common origins. . . .
> An essential aspect of these identities is the fact that, whatever their actual origins, they are experienced by many people as touching something deeper and more profound than labels or interests or contingency. (1998, 89)

In other words, a careful constructivist approach can preserve an appre-
ciation for the emotional appeal of belonging, while shifting needed attention to the dynamic processes and politics of identity formation and
reconfiguration. This book adopts such an approach, and the use of the
term belonging is intended to capture the affective dimensions of attachment and identity while preserving an awareness of their fluidity and
constructedness. Doing so, however, is complicated by the fact that
belonging is a frustratingly complex concept. It operates at the level of
individuals and groups, ranging from very small to very large, and can
connote juridical as well as emotional dimensions of status or attachment.
The term belong might be used to describe membership in the American
Automobile Association (AAA), as well as to convey a deep sense of security derived from membership in a family unit. Individuals have both an
emotional and a material need to belong, and an array of sociocultural,
political, and administrative groups, including families, churches,
schools, ethnic groups, nations, and states, fulfill that need.

Constructed primordiality also recognizes that identities are never
formed in isolation. An individual's or group's identity always emerges
in relation to others and in the context of specific opportunities and constraints. Kevin Yelvington emphasizes the role of opportunities and constraints in his paraphrase of Karl Marx: "People invent their ethnicity, as
they invent their history, but, not exactly in ways which they please"
(1992, 3). Cornell and Hartmann also capture the contextuality and rela-
tionality of identity through a focus on the interplay of assignment and
assertion. Identity and belonging can be and are assigned by organizations, states, census bureaus, politicians, and social groups. Individuals
and groups, however, are not merely passive recipients in the process.
Identity and belonging are something "that people accept, resist, choose,
specify, invent, redefine, reject, actively defend, and so forth" (Cornell and
Hartmann 1998, 77).

Also inherent in the concept and practice of belonging is the related
reality or fear of not belonging. Individuals, groups, nations, and so on
understand and define who they are by specifying who they are not. Identity, in other words, always relies upon an "Other," and belonging to an
"Us" necessitates the existence and recognition of a "Them." Belonging,
as such, necessitates and implies boundaries. The boundaries may be
social, cultural, political, or economic in nature, and, depending on the

> *"Identity . . . always relies upon an 'Other,' and belonging to
> an 'Us' necessitates the existence and recognition of a 'Them.'
> Belonging, as such, necessitates and implies boundaries."*

individual, the group, and the context, will range in importance or centrality from very low to very high. Schools, for example, or fraternities and sororities can constitute sites and sources of bounded belonging. So, too, can language, or religion. Most individuals in the world also belong to multiple levels of government—local, national, provincial, federal, regional, and international—and are thus subject to and/or protected by a range of different laws and legal distinctions. Socioeconomic status, or class, is yet another dimension of belonging.

This book focuses on the belongings of citizenship, nationhood, ethnicity, and gender. It takes to heart Vikki Bell's claim that "One does not simply or ontologically 'belong' to the world or to any group within it. Belonging is an achievement at several levels of abstraction"(1990, 3). Yet, also central to the analysis that follows is the realization that although constructed, identity and belonging are not arbitrary and not inconsequential. Words like "invention" are not intended to infer falsity or to juxtapose a true identity against a fake or artificial one. Nor is a term like "imagining" meant to signify something ethereal or unimportant. Belonging is very real and is also quintessentially political. The politics of belonging refer to the processes of individuals, groups, societies, and polities defining, negotiating, promoting, rejecting, violating, and transcending the boundaries of identities and belonging. These politics and processes are highly contextual, and although belonging and its fluid nature are as old as history, the contexts in which belonging is negotiated change. This book focuses on globalization as a contemporary and changing context and its implications for belonging. Specifically, each chapter illustrates how globalization affects the conditions and contours of belonging—namely, the perceived material and psychological need to belong, mechanisms for negotiating belonging, and available options for belonging. Some theorists have extended their analyses of globalization to include issues of identity, but tend to do so in ways that obscure the fluidity and multiplicity of belonging. Meanwhile, many scholars interested in belonging and its construction often fail to recognize the influence of globalization and the global context on the process of identity construction. This book seeks to fill some of those gaps.

As is the case with globalization, understanding belonging requires a focus on the role of the state. Each form of belonging examined in subsequent chapters—citizenship, nationhood, ethnicity, and gender—has a close relationship with the state. In some cases, the connection is relatively straightforward, as with citizenship, which is typically defined as membership in a state. In other cases, such as gender, how the state influences the form and content of belonging is less obviously apparent, but no less relevant to the study at hand. As noted above, belonging is heavily influenced by contexts and circumstances—political, economic, social, and cultural. Because the state plays a significant role in shaping these contexts and is shaped by them, it simultaneously influences the configuration of various forms of belonging (Migdal, forthcoming). States determine who can or cannot become a citizen. States also use the census and other mechanisms to designate official categories of ethnicity and race (Marx 1998). Economic interests and circumstances, shaped by states, also affect belonging. Meanwhile, states make countless policies or engage in regulatory practices in the social and cultural realms that impact belonging. Bilingual education and immigration policies, marriage laws and laws to regulate sexual behavior, and hate crimes legislation are only a few examples. These are not determinant or definitive aspects of belonging, but are relevant ones.

This book is primarily interested in the relationship between belonging and globalization. Yet, what will be evident in the subsequent analysis is that states are relevant, and often significant, factors in that relationship. Some aspects of the interaction between globalization and belonging, such as transnationalism discussed in chapter 3, exist outside of, and may even challenge, the state. Others are shaped by or manifest through the state. The result is a multifaceted and dynamic set of processes and relationships. Each subsequent chapter sorts through the contours of this interaction between globalization and belonging by focusing on specific formations of identity and belonging. Isolating citizenship, nationhood, ethnicity, and gender as distinct configurations is useful analytically in that it allows for a more focused analysis of how globalization is influencing belonging. The downside of this strategy is that it risks obscuring the ways in which these and other forms of identity are closely interrelated. Feminist theorists in particular have been at the forefront of theorizing the intersectionality of identity (Bhavnani 2001; Ifekwunigwe 1999), and chapters 5 and 6 draw upon those insights to highlight relationships between identity formations that are discussed separately in preceding chapters. The focus turns first to citizenship.

2

Reconfiguring Citizenship

In 1994 California citizens lobbied to place on the ballot an initiative that would deny public benefits and services to illegal immigrants. Proposition 187, or the "Save Our State" (SOS) initiative as it was known by its supporters, barred illegal immigrants from the state's public education system, from receiving nonemergency health care, and from receiving cash assistance or other welfare benefits. It also required all service providers to report suspected illegal immigrants to the Immigration and Naturalization Services (INS). The proposition passed with 58.8 percent of voters in favor and 41.2 percent opposed. Within months mobilization began around a second initiative to deny citizenship to the children born in the United States to undocumented migrants (Lennon 1998, 81).

Two years earlier and across the globe, Estonia held its first national election as a newly independent state of the former Soviet Union. Only citizens were permitted to vote in this founding election, a policy that in and of itself differs little from that of other states. Months prior, however, and because of its status as a newly independent state, Estonia confronted the question of who would or would not comprise its initial base of citizens. The response was an exclusionary policy that granted citizenship only to those who were citizens prior to the Soviet period and to their descendents. Those not deemed citizens could naturalize over time, but only after meeting stringent language requirements. The new Estonian constitution also prohibited noncitizens from holding national or local office or joining political parties. This policy disenfranchised, among other minority ethnic groups, a large population of ethnic Russians, which had grown from

23,000 to 475,000 between 1945 and 1992. When the founding election was complete, ethnic Estonians held all 101 seats of the new parliament (Barrington 2000).

Passage of Proposition 187 signaled a mood of intolerance and perhaps fear on the part of Californians with regard to who was entitled to the benefits of membership in their state and who belonged. They chose to clarify those boundaries, as did Estonia, with reference to citizenship. Both of these examples, and there are many others like them, are indicative of the power invested in citizenship, its utility as a mechanism for delineating an "Us" and a "Them," and its persistence as a predominant form of belonging. They also provide evidence of various contemporary realities and contexts—whether mass migration or the changing boundaries of states—that are complicating the practice and meaning of citizenship. Citizenship as an ideal dates back to ancient times. Although it made its debut in Athens in the fifth century B.C., citizenship as practiced and articulated by the Greeks took a back seat throughout the Middle Ages to other forms of human association. It returned, however, with the emergence and consolidation of the modern state in the sixteenth and seventeenth centuries and was given renewed significance with the advent of Western liberal philosophy and democracy in the eighteenth century.

Scholarly interest in the concept and practice of citizenship has also waxed and waned, but has been particularly energized in recent years. In a 1995 article titled "Return of the Citizen," Will Kymlicka and Wayne Norman note an explosion of interest in a concept that twenty years prior could accurately be characterized as "out of fashion." Today, however, "citizenship has become the 'buzzword' among thinkers on all points of the political spectrum" (p. 283). This renewed interest in citizenship reflects a variety of circumstances around the world—circumstances that comprise or are closely affiliated with globalization. This chapter explores the meaning of citizenship, the challenges to it, and the implications of these challenges for the form, content, and probable future of citizenship as a type of belonging. The bulk of the examples will be drawn from North America and Western Europe. Because these are societies that receive large numbers of newcomers and are founded on principles of political liberalism, the challenges to and changes in citizenship play out in particularly heightened ways.

Meanings and Variations

Nearly every pronouncement of the resurgent focus on citizenship is followed by an acknowledgment that there is currently no clear or widely agreed upon definition of what citizenship means. Charles Tilly helps elucidate the confusion when he explains that citizenship can refer to a category, tie, role, or identity (1995, 7). For the sake of theoretical and historical clarity, Tilly advocates defining citizenship as a tie and offers the following definition of citizenship:

> [A] continuing series of transactions between persons and agents of a given state in which each has enforceable rights and obligations uniquely by virtue of (1) the person's membership in an exclusive category, the native-born plus the naturalized and (2) the agent's relation to the state rather than any other authority the agent may enjoy. (p. 8)

Indeed, most scholarly definitions are consistent with Tilly's emphasis on citizenship as a tie or special sort of contract. Bryan Turner, for example, defines citizenship as "a collection of rights and obligations which give individuals a formal legal identity" within a state or society (1997, 5); and Thomas Faist writes, "Citizenship forms a continuing series of reciprocal transactions between a citizen and a state" (2000, 202).

This clarification regarding the definition of citizenship leaves open questions concerning the nature and strength of the tie. For example, what types of rights are emphasized, and what is the relative importance attached to rights versus responsibilities? Is the tie or set of ties that constitutes citizenship thick or thin? Are citizens expected to and do they play an active role in the polity, or is membership of a more passive quality? Beyond the difficulties associated with conceptualizing citizenship, even the briefest empirical examination of citizenship in practice reveals a staggering array of different policies and arrangements that further complicate any understanding of what precisely citizenship means. This section offers a brief historical and conceptual background on the meaning of and variations in citizenship.

As noted above, scholars typically trace the origins of the ideal of citizenship to ancient Greece, specifically the city-state of Athens in the fifth and fourth centuries B.C. and Rome in the third century B.C. It was a form of human association believed to be unique to these societies during this time. The *polis* about which Aristotle wrote was a small society that stood in contrast to the great orders of the time—Mesopotamia, Egypt, and China. Citizenship referred to membership in the *polis* and replaced other

---

"even the briefest empirical examination of citizenship in practice reveals a staggering array of different policies and arrangements that further complicate any understanding of what precisely citizenship means."

forms of blood-related belonging such as clan, kinship, or tribe. The citizen, according to Aristotle, was one who both rules and is ruled. Politics, the act of ruling and being ruled, was a public good of the highest order, and citizenship was not a means to some end, but an end in itself—a way of being fully human. A century or so later in ancient Rome, citizenship (referring, in this context, to membership in the *republic*) was also a primary form of human association, but one that became more closely affiliated with jurisprudence. As J. G. A. Pocock explains: "A 'citizen' came to mean someone free to act by law, free to ask and expect the law's protection, a citizen of such and such a legal community of such and such a legal standing in that community" (1995, 36). Citizen as political being shifted to citizen as legal being. The distinction at this time was subtle, but it foreshadowed several variations in and dichotomous conceptualizations of citizenship that would come to characterize discussion and debate centuries later.

After the celebrated experiences of citizenship in Greece and Rome, almost two thousand years passed before this form of human association—the ideal and the practice—reemerged. Throughout the Middle Ages, ruling and being ruled took place, to be sure, but belonging was rooted in blood or religion, and authority was invested in the hands of an elite few whose status was ascribed. Not only did participatory citizenship disappear, but this era was also characterized by a notable disconnect between political power and association on the one hand and territory or clearly demarcated political units on the other. Instead, authority was both "personalized and parcelized within and across territorial formations," and there was no "notion of firm boundary lines between the major territorial formations" (Ruggie 1993, 150). Perry Anderson offers a similar portrayal of the medieval period as one in which political space was characterized by "patchworks of overlapping and incomplete rights of government," which were "inextricably superimposed and tangled," and in which "different juridical instances were geographically interwoven and stratified, and plural allegiances, asymmetrical suzerainties and anomalous enclaves abounded" (1974, 37–38). The reason for calling attention to this lack of congruence between political authority and delimited territory is that it stands in stark contrast to the historical context in which citizenship reemerges—a context in which territorially defined political units, namely, states, come to constitute the major subdivisions of the globe.

It is impossible to identify a precise date or time when the modern state was born, but in Europe in the late sixteenth and seventeenth centuries not only had frontiers become more like boundaries, but rulership came to be constituted in a more impersonal domain distinct from family, business, and religion. States became entities unto themselves, not tied to any dynasty, independent of other states, and supreme in relation to other domains of human life (Ruggie 1993). The Treaty of Westphalia, signed in

1648 to end religious wars in Europe, is considered a key moment in the birth of the principle of state sovereignty and the inter-state system as we know it today.

It is also difficult to mark the precise date when citizenship reemerges as a focus or practice of political association. In its classical sense, particularly as practiced in the Roman republic, citizenship reenters political discourse during the Italian Renaissance and through writers such as Niccolò Machiavelli. It is also present in the philosophy of eighteenth-century liberal theorists like John Locke whose contention that sovereignty lies with the people was later influential in the American Revolution, and with Jean-Jacques Rousseau's *The Social Contract* (1762), which provided theoretical inspiration for the French Revolution and the *Declaration of the Rights of Man and Citizen*. Rousseau made the case for "popular sovereignty" and characterized the modern citizen as a free and autonomous individual who is entitled to take part in making decisions that all are required to obey.

These modern conceptualizations of citizenship drew heavily on the classical variant. Some, such as Rousseau, adopted a more active and engaged Aristotelian view; whereas others conveyed a more juridical notion of citizenship as based in rights. What is most clear by this point in the historical evolution of citizenship is the close, symbiotic relationship between citizenship and the state. Some scholars debate which actually emerged first, citizenship or the state, but most accept that the two were mutually constitutive (Behnke 1997). Each contributed, in other words, to the other's existence and form. States, defined in terms of sovereignty, territoriality, and bureaucratic-administrative apparati, comprise the containers in and mechanisms through which citizens rule and are ruled. Meanwhile, the authority and legitimacy states possess come from the citizens, the populations they represent, serve, protect, or defend—their members. Furthermore, the principle that each person must have a state has, over many years, been firmly codified in international law (Aleinikoff and Klusmeyer 2001, 72–73).

This syncretic relationship between citizenship and state has persisted throughout the modern era in both theory and practice. As noted above, most current definitions of citizenship refer to this relationship and emphasize it as one of mutual rights and responsibilities. Yet, the specifics of this relationship, "the institutional arrangements, rules, and understandings that guide and shape concurrent policy decisions and expenditures of states, problem definitions by states and citizens, and claims making by citizens"—what Jane Jenson (1997, 631) terms "citizenship regimes"—have and continue to vary. They vary across countries, within individual countries, and across time. One well-known and widely cited classification of citizenship rights is T. H. Marshall's 1950 classic *Citizenship and Social Class*. Using England as his case study, Marshall identified three distinct categories of citizenship rights that emerged over three successive centuries. The eighteenth century saw the emergence of *civil* rights, which entailed protection from illegal infringement on an individual's freedom and property. *Political* rights arose in the nineteenth century. These were rights of political participation or rights that enable citizens to take part in the democratic process and have an active voice in the formation of a collective will. The twentieth century witnessed the establishment of *social* rights or the rights of citizens to a minimum level of social security. These are rights associated with the emergence of the welfare state and entail, for example, public education, health care, unemployment insurance, and pensions for seniors. Citizenship, for Marshall, involves securing fair and equal treatment for all members of society, and the method for doing so is to increase not only the number of people accorded rights, but also the types of citizenship rights.

Marshall's typology has been widely applied and provides the foundation for much contemporary theorizing about citizenship. Some scholars have critiqued the assumption that the acquisition of citizenship rights is a linear, cumulative, or irreversible process. Jürgen Habermas (1995), for example, is concerned that civil rights and social rights can and do exist without substantive political rights and autonomy, which form the real foundation, in his view, of democracy. Others have also questioned the utility of Marshall's theory since it relies so heavily on the particular case of England. Nevertheless, Marshall's framework and Habermas's caution are both useful in accounting for variations in the meaning and practice of citizenship around the world. In the United States, for example, citizenship is most often discussed and defined in terms of civil rights, and great emphasis is placed on protections such as freedom of speech or religion. Yet, in many European countries, citizenship tends to be conceptualized more in terms of social rights, such as health care or public education.

A second important dimension of citizenship involves not just the type of rights, but the question of who is entitled to those rights, or who can be or become a citizen, why, and how. Despite the rhetoric of access and equality that surrounds citizenship discourse, its practice since antiquity has involved not just inclusion, but exclusion. Citizenship in ancient Greece was restricted to male Athenian property owners. The American Revolution, steeped in the language of rights and equality, set up a republic exclusionary in ways similar to Athens; full citizenship was a privilege reserved for white, male property owners. Although this changed gradually with the Fourteenth and Fifteenth Amendments that extended citizenship to blacks in the United States and the Nineteenth Amendment that gave women political voice, it was not until the civil rights movement in the 1960s, and in some cases more recently, that full membership rights were extended to many minority groups.

The history of U.S. immigration and naturalization policies is also full of similar exclusions. Not until the 1960s were various race-based exclusions fully eliminated, exclusions that barred many groups' entry into the United States based on their national origin; and as recently as 1990, for example, homosexuality was considered "bad moral character" and hence a justification for denial of citizenship. The United States is certainly not alone in this respect. In fact, most contemporary democracies around the world have a history, and in some cases a present, tainted with undemocratic exclusions. In South Africa, for example, blacks were not given full membership rights in the republic until 1994 when Nelson Mandela cast the first vote of his lifetime in the election that named him the country's first democratically elected president. Today, however, both South Africa and the United States are examples of countries that guarantee citizenship to anyone born in the country, who has resided in the country for a certain period of time, demonstrates some degree of understanding of the country's language and history, and is of good character (Weil 2001).

This emphasis on citizenship, as rooted in residency, points to another variation in citizenship practice and policy—that between the principles of *jus soli* and *jus sanguinis*. The former refers to membership rooted in soil and the latter to membership rooted in blood. In addition to the United States and South Africa, other well-known examples of the former model include France, Canada, New Zealand, and India. In these cases, citizenship is something to be achieved or earned, and the achievement is open, at least in theory, to anyone regardless of color, class, or creed. Among these countries that base their membership on the principle of *jus soli*, there are variations in their specific immigration and naturalization policies. Canada, for example, has been known to be particularly generous with receiving refugees; and France has the reputation of maintaining high expectations for assimilation to French culture (Esman 1994). Nevertheless, the principles of citizenship that prevail in these cases stand in contrast to membership that is determined by blood, or ancestry.

Germany is perhaps the best-known example of this latter category, but it also includes Israel, Greece, and Italy (Faist 2000, 205). Traditionally, one has not become a German citizen by being born in Germany, but rather by being born with German blood, German ethnicity, or Germany ancestry. The result is described by journalist Craig Whitney:

> In Germany, it can be easier for a child whose family lived in Russia for 200 years to become a German citizen than it is for an American or for the German-born child of a Turkish "guest worker," even if that child speaks no Turkish and has been educated in German schools. . . . Russian descendants of the ethnic Germans whom Catherine the Great brought over to farm the Volga River Valley can come back to Germany

as citizens under the country's law of return. But most others wanting to acquire German citizenship might find it easier to pass through the eye of a needle. (1996, 6)

Israel offers yet another example of a citizenship regime—one that emphasizes ethnicity, but also protects the rights of some who are members based only on residency. Similar to Germany's "law of return," Israel grants its state membership based on Jewish identity or ancestry, but it also provides citizenship to Palestinian Arabs living in Israel who comprise an estimated 15 percent of the population. As such, Israel has been described as practicing two types of citizenship simultaneously. Jews in Israel participate in a citizenship model that allows and expects them to contribute to the common good. Israeli Arabs, on the other hand, are excluded from the common good although they are formally entitled to equal rights under the law. One avenue of exclusion relates to the fact that military service is obligatory for Jews, is seen as a fundamental contribution to the common good, and entitles those who perform it to a range of social benefits. Arab citizens of Israel are barred from military service, from the social, cultural, political, and economic benefits that accompany it, and hence from what T. H. Marshall characterizes as full membership in the society (Peled 1992).

These variations in citizenship are closely linked to the related concepts of nationality and ethnicity and will be further developed in the chapters that follow. At this point, it is important to understand that none of these citizenship regimes is static. As Ronnie Lipschutz explains: "Constitutionally and legally, of course, states and governments do establish standard requirements for citizenship and naturalization, but even these change over time in response to the exigencies of everyday life" (1999, 206). In the mid-1990s, for example, France began tightening its citizenship rules while Germany, in the midst of fierce debates about immigration and asylum policy, began to lessen its restrictions on citizenship. In the United States and Canada, immigration and citizenship reform is consistently on the political agenda. In the United States, the INS recently initiated a review of the civics examination that prospective citizens must pass. That review opened up for discussion the type of questions on the exam and whether, for instance, it is imperative that a prospective citizen knows who wrote "The Star Spangled Banner," or an alternative knowledge that might be more useful (J. Jacobs 2000).

Not only are the questions "Who is entitled to citizenship and how?" up for debate in countries around the world, but so, too, are questions related to what citizenship entails: What specific rights are or should citizens be guaranteed? What specific responsibilities do states have toward their citizens and vice versa? Furthermore, how, if at all, do these rights and responsibilities differ between citizens and noncitizens? None of these questions is entirely new, but all have taken on heightened significance in the face of profound changes in the world—changes described here as globalization. The following sections explore these contemporary challenges—many of which are simultaneously challenges to the modern state—and their impact on citizenship.

Challenges to Citizenship: Erosion or Invigoration?

The last decade of the twentieth century was rife, and unexpectedly so, with the breakup and attempted breakup of various states. Widespread political fragmentation and the related tensions, ethnic and otherwise, contradicted proclamations regarding a New World Order and the "end of history" (Fukuyama 1989). The collapse of the Soviet Union, for example, unleashed countless movements for regional autonomy within the newly independent states. The former Yugoslavia, and the Balkans more generally, offer what are arguably the most tragic examples of reconfiguration in terms of bloodshed and human atrocities. Meanwhile, there are countless other examples that range from the peaceful separation of Czechoslovakia to the persistent and potent appeals of Québécois separatists for independence from the Canadian state. Given that citizenship refers, in part, to "what draws a body of citizens together into a coherent and stably organized political community, and keeps that allegiance durable" (Beiner 1995, 1), these examples of fragmenting political communities and fluid political allegiances bring into focus questions of citizenship—both the theory and the practice. Yet, the breakup of states is just one example of the challenges to citizenship in recent decades. Globalization, in its economic, technological, cultural, and political dimensions, has and continues to have a significant impact on citizenship as a form of belonging. In some cases, there is evidence that citizenship is eroding, or is experiencing a "crisis" (Lipschutz 1999). Meanwhile, there is also evidence that citizenship persists as a salient attachment and in some instances is experiencing a form of invigoration. This section examines the varied implications of globalization for citizenship, looking first at citizenship's apparent decline and then at evidence of its persistent appeal.

The Erosion of Citizenship

Over a decade ago, political scientist James Rosenau began to call attention to fundamental changes in the world system—what he described as "Turbulence" (1990). In that and later works, he focused on breakdowns in three basic parameters of the world system. At the "macro level," according to Rosenau, the overall structure of the global system is undergoing a transformation from a state-centric system to a multicentric system of diverse, sovereignty-free collectivities. In the process, the authority of states is being relocated outward to transnational collectivities and inward to subnational actors. At the micro level, factors including innovations in communications and transportation technology and education have left individuals better prepared for and with access to greater opportunities for collective action that significantly affects the macro level. Finally, and as both consequence and cause of the former two alterations, a third parameter, that which separates the micro and macro levels, is also under strain. This parameter encompasses the authority relationships whereby macro collectivities, typically states, achieve compliance of the micro actors who comprise their membership. Rosenau likens the turbulence of this shifting parameter to a global authority crisis:

> [A]s the sources of governance within and between societies become increasingly obscure, as crowds gather in city squares, as majorities give way to coalitions, as stalemates persist or cabinets fall, as transnational organizations tap the energies of individuals, and as long-standing social movements with homogenous memberships and clear-cut organizational structures give way to new movements that are less hierarchical and more local, disorganized, and fragmented . . . authority today has become problematic where it once was given in world politics. (1992, 282–83)

What Rosenau characterizes as turbulence is closely related to, and in some sense synonymous with, globalization. The alteration or breakdown in the three parameters is fueled and/or facilitated by growing economic, technological, cultural, and political interconnectedness in the world, and it facilitates that interconnectedness as well. This turbulence is also associated with the diminishing importance of territory. Specifically, what we are witnessing is a decline in the territorial integrity of the sovereign state and in the centrality of a territorially bounded state to the social and political identification or attachments of a populous. All of this has profound implications for citizenship as a form of belonging. As noted above, most definitions of citizenship point to a set of mutual obligations between states and their members. Globalization affects the capacity and willingness of both parties to meet those obligations. Not only does globalization weaken the ability of states to fulfill various responsibilities toward their citizens, but it also provides citizens with new avenues or outlets for protection of rights typically guaranteed by states and facilitates forms of mobilization

"Not only does globalization weaken the ability of states to fulfill various responsibilities toward their citizens, but it also provides citizens with new avenues or outlets for protection of rights typically guaranteed by states."

and attachment, often in pursuit of or in connection to those rights, that transcend the sovereign, territorial state.

One arena of state responsibility toward citizens involves the guarantee of some degree of economic well-being. This obligation evolved over time and varies by country, but has come to be accepted in both theory and practice as a central aspect of citizenship. Late in the nineteenth century and again early in the twentieth, many countries around the world suffered major economic depression. States responded with policies designed to ease the impact of some the worst features of industrial capitalism. Over time, states came to play an increasingly active role in protecting citizens from the vagaries of the marketplace, a reality known as the welfare state. The protection included not just fiscal and monetary policies designed to shelter a "national" economy, but also social welfare policies—unemployment compensation, social security, public education—designed to guarantee citizens a minimum degree of security and well-being. Referring again to T. H. Marshall's theory of expanding citizenship rights, this bundle of "social rights" constituted the final and necessary step of full membership in the political community. Without some degree of socioeconomic stability, individuals were not free to be or capable of being active participants in their political communities.

Unfortunately, many of the same factors that make the need for a welfare state so urgent today are the same factors that limit the ability of states to meet those obligations. Economic globalization has been driven, in part, by the growing power and presence of transnational corporations. Although many of these corporations are headquartered in a particular state, most have offices spread around the world and have the capacity to locate and relocate production and distribution in and to multiple sites in order to take advantage of inexpensive labor and avoid costly regulations and requirements issued by home governments. Increasingly, the neoliberal economic principles that underlie this type of world economy have been codified in trade pacts, regimes, and international governmental institutions. The result is a highly competitive marketplace, held in place by international economic agreements in which states have a limited capacity to exercise regulatory powers or protect a "domestic" economy. The revenues that states need to fund social welfare policies come, in part, from taxing corporations. States also hope to provide employment opportunities and decent wages to their citizens, and corporations contribute to this. Yet, the highly mobile nature of capital means that corporations have the upper hand in negotiating with states, and high taxes, for example, may provoke relocation. All of this, in turn, limits any state's capacity to meet its obligations toward its citizens.

Not only does economic globalization and the neoliberal tenets that underpin it limit the capacity of states to guarantee the welfare of their citizens, but threats to citizen well-being extend beyond the strictly economic realm as well. Increased interconnectedness has both created and exposed additional realities that challenge the capacity of states to protect their members. These include threats to physical security in the form of terrorism or nuclear weapons, environmental crises (ozone depletion, water and air pollution, destruction of natural resources), and large-scale movements of people across state borders whether as refugees or migrants, documented or not. National security, or protecting citizens from foreign invasion, has long been considered a key function of states, but technology, and specifically nuclear weaponry, has made threats to security more ominous and the role of states in managing them more limited. The nuclear threat is not a new one, but, ironically, the post–Cold War context has intensified the spread of these weapons, the use of terrorism, and the ambiguity of exactly who or what is the enemy (J. Rosenau 1990, 397). The 9/11 attacks on the United States offer a particularly powerful illustration of this new context.

Governments, meanwhile, may have the capacity to manage environmental crises, but not if they act alone or in isolation. International conventions ranging from the Rio Earth Summit in 1992 to the Kyoto Accord on reducing greenhouse gases in 1997 have emphasized the need for international cooperation on issues related to the environment. But these discussions and treaties also reveal that in order to protect their citizens, states must sacrifice a degree of autonomy to international organizations, treaties, or conventions, and doing so may be perceived as a threat to citizen well-being in another arena. This dilemma, often perceived as the environment versus the economy, is what motivated U.S. President George W. Bush's eventual refusal to sign the Kyoto Accord in 2001. Bush's decision was widely criticized, however, by other world leaders. The United States was seen as having a major leadership role to play, not only as the sole superpower, but as an industrial giant that comprises only 4 percent of the world's population yet produces 25 percent of the greenhouse gases that enter the Earth's atmosphere. Criticism was particularly harsh among leaders in Europe—all of whom had agreed to the mandatory reductions in the Kyoto Accord. France's minister for the environment called Bush's actions "completely provocative and irresponsible." German Chancellor Gerhard Schroeder remarked: "Nobody should be relieved from his responsibility for climate control"; and the president of the European Commission, Romano Prodi, stated that "If one wants to be a world leader, one must know how to look after the entire earth and not only American industry" (quote in D. Jackson 2001, A25).

For some citizens and from the perspective of some states, what is more frightening than the threat of terrorism or environmental devastation, and as difficult to manage, is the perceived threat of human migration. (Although in the wake of the 9/11 attacks on the United States many have come to view migration and terrorism as closely interrelated.) As noted in chapter 1, migration, while not new, has intensified in recent decades and been characterized by profound shifts in the patterns of who moves where, why, and for how long. The controversies surrounding immigration in advanced industrialized economies of the West are well publicized, but less well-developed countries from Costa Rica and the Dominican Republic to Uganda and South Africa are also experiencing large-scale movement of people across borders. For the resident populations and governments of these regions, the perceived threats of migration range from a loss of jobs to the spread of disease. Yet there is also a less clearly articulated, but still pervasive, concern regarding the implications of migration not just for the availability of material resources but for the meaning and practice of citizenship itself. For one thing, because much of the movement of peoples across states is unregulated or illegal, it calls into question the capacity of states to control their borders. In the United States, for example, the census estimated that in 2000 approximately eight million illegal immigrants were residing in the United States (U.S. Census 2000b). Furthermore, because citizenship is closely tied to the notion of membership within a territorial entity, porous territorial boundaries simultaneously call into question the meaning and integrity of membership in a state.

The largest portion of migration in the world today, however, is not illegal or clandestine, but is regulated, or at least supervised, by states. Yet, this, too, poses numerous challenges to the meaning and practice of citizenship. According to T. H. Marshall's model, expanding categories of rights should be bestowed equally on expanding categories of persons irrespective of their inherent characteristics. Not only does the prospect of doing so with regard to migrants prompt concerns among established residents over limited resources, but it also weakens the notion of citizenship as a privileged form of membership in a political community and downplays the obligations, responsibilities, and commitments that citizenship is presumed to entail. In other words, what, if anything, is the value of citizenship if it is widely and indiscriminately available to all and demands little of the recipient in return? Peter Schuck (1989) examines this challenge to citizenship in the U.S. case in an essay titled "The Devaluation of American Citizenship." Schuck argues that two deeply ingrained principles of the American polity, equality and due process, have been so expansively interpreted and applied in recent years as to reduce to almost nothing the value of citizenship as compared to resident alien status.

> *"what, if anything, is the value of citizenship if it is widely and indiscriminately available to all and demands little of the recipient in return?"*

Similar claims have been made in and about other countries as well. In 1986, French nationalist Jacques Toybon proclaimed that "On the pretext of humanism . . . France has received and conferred its nationality on families whose sole bond of attachment to the national community consists in pecuniary advantages. What is more, the persons concerned preserve their original allegiance and often take French nationality as one takes the Carte Orange [the subway and bus pass used by Parisian commuters]" (quoted in Brubaker 1992, 147). Furthermore, a 1989 study of immigration and citizenship in North America (the United States and Canada) and Western Europe (specifically France, Germany, Sweden, and Britain) concluded that these states confer few exclusive rights on their citizens. Instead, most political, economic, and social privileges that citizens value and expect from their states are simultaneously guaranteed or available to residents—specifically permanent residents (Brubaker 1989).

The right to vote, the right to serve on a jury, the right to run for or be appointed to high governmental offices, and immunity from deportation are among the benefits typically reserved for citizens. None of these rights is meaningless, but, as some argue, nor are they indispensable. Jury duty is something that most citizens perceive as just that—a "duty," and, according to Schuck (1989), the principle and practice of due process limits, at least in the U.S. case, the actual risk to permanent residents of deportation. Furthermore, some of the restrictions historically applied to noncitizens are being lessened. Voting, for example, is a valuable mechanism of political influence and voice, and individuals or groups to whom it is denied are at a distinct disadvantage. Yet, many states and/or locales have, in recent decades, extended voting privileges to noncitizens. Beginning in the mid-1970s, several Western European countries, including Sweden, Switzerland, Denmark, Norway, and the Netherlands, extended municipal voting rights to noncitizens. Britain grants voting privileges to immigrants who are citizens of Commonwealth countries, and several Canadian provinces give voting rights to British subjects in nonfederal elections (M. Miller 1989). In the United States, citizenship status remains crucial for voting in federal elections, but various cities and states have passed legislation allowing noncitizens who are permanent residents to vote in local elections. Tacoma Park, Maryland, and Amherst, Massachusetts, for example, both allow noncitizens to vote in municipal elections, and several other cities including New York, Chicago, and Cambridge, Massachusetts, allow noncitizen participation in school board elections (McLaughlin 1998, 3).

Meanwhile, there are various avenues beyond voting by which individuals and groups make demands, access rights, and influence politics—few of which are restricted on the basis of citizenship status. In many countries, the United States, Canada, France, Germany, and Sweden among them, citizenship is not a prerequisite for union membership; and in some cases, neither is legal or permanent resident status. In fact, in some parts of the world, organized labor has begun to champion the rights of foreign-born and even undocumented workers in an effort to incorporate them into the organized and politically mobilized workforce. In February 2000, the American Federation of Labor–Congress of Industrial Organizations (AFL-CIO) announced a dramatic shift in its historic position on immigrants and immigration to the United States. Officials announced that the organization would now support expanded immigration, lenient enforcement of immigration laws, and the broader legislative agenda of immigrants (Briggs 2001). In most cases, noncitizens not only have access to union membership, but also the right to vote in union elections and to serve in elected posts on factory councils or as shop stewards (Brubaker 1989; M. Miller 1989).

Beyond labor unions, there are a variety of other civic, religious, and political organizations that provide their members with influence and access, but that do not restrict membership or benefits on the basis of citizenship. Mark Miller offers the example of the American Civil Liberties Union (ACLU), a U.S. organization focused on protecting individual rights, that frequently acts on behalf of noncitizens (1989, 139). Nor are political rights the only category of privileges associated with state membership but widely extended to nonmembers as well. A whole array of social and economic benefits, ranging from health care and child care to education and unemployment insurance, are available, in many states, to noncitizens. In his comparative study of immigration and citizenship in North America and Europe, Rogers Brubaker concludes that "citizenship status is in fact relatively insignificant as a basis of access to social services" (1989, 155). A similar study on immigrants' eligibility for social benefits found that in the area of economic and social rights, citizenship matters little (p. 159).

One purported outcome of these circumstances is that immigrants have little incentive to naturalize, and according to some studies, fewer and fewer do. Schuck (1989) uses 1980 census data to demonstrate declining naturalization rates in the U.S. case, and a more recent study suggests a continuation of that trend. A 2001 report by Steven Camarota for the Center for Immigration Studies (CIS) found that naturalization rates among immigrants to the United States have dropped steadily and significantly since the 1970s. In 1970, 63.6 percent of immigrants in the United States had become citizens. By 2000, that proportion had dropped by 26 percentage points to 37.4 percent—a smaller proportion than at any other time in the past century. Because immigrants must reside in the United States five years before they are eligible for citizenship, it is important to distinguish between the naturalization rates of recent immigrants (those who have been in the country ten years or less and have had less opportunity to naturalize) and established immigrants (those in the country between eleven and twenty years). The CIS report identifies a decline in citizenship among both groups, but finds a "very substantial decline" among established immigrants. Sixty-three percent of immigrants arriving in the United States in the 1950s had become citizens by 1970; but only 38.9 percent of immigrants arriving in the 1980s had nationalized by the year 2000. In other words, the percentage of established immigrants in the United States who are citizens fell by more than one-third from 1970 to 2000 (Camarota 2001a). Brubaker finds similar trends, pointing out that in Europe as in North America "settlement without citizenship has become increasingly prevalent" (1989, 145).

In addition to the fact that states appear less capable of meeting their citizens' needs, and many noncitizens see only marginal value in seeking formal membership in a state, citizenship is also challenged by the growing opportunities for individuals and groups to access rights and secure benefits outside of the sovereign, territorial state. Several scholars have pointed to an emerging array of international or regional organizations, conventions, and regimes that in Yasemin Soysal's words "have complicated the national order of citizenship and introduced new dynamics for membership and participation in the public sphere" (2000, 4). Specifically, Soysal (1994) argues that since World War II, the world has witnessed a recasting of citizenship rights as human (or personhood) rights. Using the example of guest worker rights in postwar Europe, she maintains that guest workers have achieved safe membership status without becoming citizens. Their ability to do so relies on the role of international organizations such as the United Nations, UNESCO, and the Council of Europe. In a similar study of *Rights across Borders*, David Jacobson (1996) points to a shift in the international system away from principles of state sovereignty to those of international human rights. He maintains that human rights, although originating in the very documents, practices, and institutions that gave rights to states, have now come to transcend and transform states and, in the process, lessened the centrality of states and state membership as the means by which to guarantee human rights or seek redress for their violation. Soysal describes this reality as the "increasing decoupling of rights and identity" (2000, 5).

Operating on the premise of universal personhood, the human rights instruments and codes associated with the United Nations and other international organizations are dedicated to protecting the human rights and dignity of all individuals regardless of their citizenship status. At the same time, however, they also contribute to increasing and/or maintaining the legitimacy of an individual's right to her or his "own culture"— whether ethnic, gendered, sexual, religious, regional, or otherwise. This array of attachments and identifications and their proliferation as sources of solidarity and mobilization are typically discussed under the rubric of multiculturalism. While many of the globalization-related challenges to the state and to citizenship outlined above are considered challenges "from above," multiculturalism and the various related forms of identity-based social movements are examples of challenges to the state and to citizenship that come "from below" (Smith and Guarnizo 1998). Nor is cultural identity the only basis for challenges from below. A growing number of movements and organizations emphasize the "local" in reaction or response to the "global"—a phenomenon sometimes described as "the new localism" (Goetz and Clarke 1993) and frequently analyzed in a burgeoning literature on the global/local nexus (Robertson 1995). The focus of these efforts is typically on returning power and control to the local level, and the individuals and communities involved are reacting to the more egregious implications of unrestrained globalism as well as challenging the hegemony of the nation-state. J. Rosenau describes this range of attachments and mobilizations as subgroupism: "a generic term which encompasses the drive for autonomy that is not necessarily associated with the aspiration for statehood" (1992, 282).

> *"While many of the globalization-related challenges to the state and to citizenship outlined above are considered challenges 'from above,' multiculturalism and the various related forms of identity-based social movements are examples of challenges to the state and to citizenship that come 'from below.'"*

The real and potential challenges of subgroupism to citizenship are multifold and affect not only its practice, but also our theoretical understandings of what it means. Localism entails demands for the devolution and decentralization of state power and control. In this regard, the state loses its privileged position as a primary site, referent, or coordinator of belonging. The popular bumper sticker "Think Globally, Act Locally" captures some of this sentiment and reveals how both trends—globalization and localization—minimize the relevance of the state and, by connection, the centrality of citizenship when understood as membership in the state. Meanwhile, multiculturalism poses additional but different challenges to citizenship. As Christian Joppke notes:

Even if immigrants have acquired the citizenship of (or, at least safe membership status in the receiving state), they are often not content with enjoying equal rights. As carriers of ethnic difference, immigrants notice that even liberal states, which are philosophically indifferent to the cultural preferences of their members, are couched in distinct cultural colours—its official language, holidays, or church relations cannot but privilege the ethnic majority population over the immigrant minorities. (1999, 630)

Often members of different "cultural" groups make demands on the state that go beyond the practice of individual rights, particularly as these have been conceived in Western liberal democracies, to the protection of cultural or group rights. Examples of the tension that may ensue range from the French state's attempt to prevent Muslim schoolgirls from wearing headscarves (Gorjanicyn 2000), to controversy surrounding Sikhs wearing turbans in the main hall of the Royal Canadian Legion (Bissoondath 1994), to a U.S. Supreme Court case protecting the rights of Cuban immigrants in South Florida to practice *Santería*—an Afro-Cuban religion that involves the sacrifice of animals (Greenhouse 1993).

These circumstances challenge citizenship in various ways. Many of the individuals and groups engaging in these practices are citizens (although some are not), and all, in any event, are entitled to equal protection under the law. Yet, their demands are often not made in the name of universal personhood or individual rights. The state, then, must grapple with how to accommodate the distinctive needs of different cultural groups—needs that in some cases clash with the cultural preferences and practices of the majority population and may also come into conflict with or violate the protection and promotion of the individual rights of members of a given group. In other words, the presence of culturally diverse groups within one state—often, but not always, the product of migration—also challenges citizenship in that it exposes the myth that citizenship's meaning and content are blind with regard to ethnicity, sex, color, or creed. The rights some groups request are deemed "special" or particular not simply in that they differ from a neutral or universal model, but from one that reflects and is rooted in the interests and experiences of a dominant group within a state.

This realization has led to calls for and efforts to theorize the contours of a more democratic form of citizenship. In addition to demands for more multicultural forms of citizenship, activists and academics are simultaneously emphasizing the need for more substantive citizenship practice that goes beyond formal membership in the state. As noted above, formal membership in a state is no longer a necessary condition for access to many rights and privileges associated with citizenship, but, as John Holston and Arjun Appadurai explain, nor is it a sufficient one: "That it is not sufficient is obvious for many poor citizens who have formal membership in the state but who are excluded in fact or law from enjoying the rights of citizenship and participating effectively in its organization" (1996, 190). That gay and lesbian citizens in most parts of the world do not have the right to marry, to adopt children, or to secure immigrant visas for their domestic partners is another example of granting individuals formal membership in a state but denying them substantive citizenship rights.

Formally, then, citizenship refers to membership in a state, but in substance it involves a broad array of civil, political, socioeconomic, and cultural rights people possess and exercise. In various ways, globalization has affected the availability, access, and awareness regarding these substantive rights and demands for their fuller and fairer extension. The sacred bond between states and citizens has weakened as the former find their power and autonomy shrinking and the latter find their options for and capacity to pursue rights elsewhere enhanced. Returning to the example of immigrants and guest workers in Western Europe, Yasemin Soysal offers the following illustration:

> Regardless of their historical or cultural ties to the German nation, and even without a formal German nationality, Turkish immigrants in Berlin make claims on Berlin's authority structures and participate in Berlin's public institutions. When they make demands for the teaching of Islam in state schools, the Pakistani immigrants in Britain mobilize around a Muslim identity, but they appeal to a universalistic language of "human rights" to justify their claims. And, they not only mobilize to affect the local school authorities, but also pressure the national government, and take their case to the European Court of Human Rights. (2000, 4)

Soysal's example is a poignant, but not an isolated one. Nevertheless, just as it has been deemed premature to write the obituary of the state, so too, as the next section will argue, is the case with citizenship.

The Persistent Appeal of Citizenship

Globalization, according to the examples outlined above, has contributed to a context in which citizens have less faith in and need for states, and immigrants have less need to pursue citizenship status in the states where they reside. Yet, despite the very real challenges of globalization, there is also ample evidence of citizenship's persistent power and appeal. This is evident with regard to the people who possess citizenship in a given state and want to exclude others from it, on the part of those excluded from its rights and privileges who desire access to them, and on the part of states whose very raison d'être is defined by and through citizenship. In other words, citizenship's apparent demise as a central or salient form of belonging exists alongside equally persuasive examples of its invigoration or reinvigoration. And, ironically, citizenship's invigoration is often a reaction or response to many of the same aspects of globalization that are deemed responsible for its demise.

One indication of citizenship's persistent appeal lies in the energy and passion that those who possess it devote to keeping it to themselves and excluding others from it. Over the past two decades, many countries around the world have experienced xenophobic outbursts among their citizens, the rise of political parties that seize upon and fuel this antiforeign sentiment, and the passage of legislation designed to restrict the influx of migrants and/or limit the benefits to which they are entitled. In the United States, California's Proposition 187 is one notable example, but throughout the 1990s immigration and related questions of citizenship also consumed a great deal of energy at the federal government level. In 1994, the Commission on Immigration Reform (CIR), a nonpartisan advisory body that grew out of the 1990 Immigration Act, published a set of recommendations that included tighter border control, steps toward a national system for worker verification, and an overall reduction in the annual intake of legal immigrants (CIR 1994). By the 1996 presidential election, immigration and citizenship practice had become the focus of heated debate, and among other measures, the republican platform included a call for a constitutional amendment denying automatic citizenship to the U.S.-born children of illegal immigrants. In 1996 and again in 2000, Reform Party candidate Patrick Buchanan called for the construction of a wall along the border between the United States and Mexico.

> *"One indication of citizenship's persistent appeal lies in the energy and passion that those who possess it devote to keeping it to themselves and excluding others from it."*

In addition to public officials and campaigns, anti-immigrant rhetoric also found an outlet in the academic and popular press. Richard Lamm's (former governor of Colorado) book *Immigration Time Bomb: The Fragmenting of America* (1985) and Peter Brimelow's *Alien Nation: Common Sense about America's Immigration Disaster* (1995) are just two of many works published in the 1980s and 1990s expressing great concern over America's capacity to absorb the large influx of immigrants arriving on her shores and issuing apocalyptic warnings about what might happen if borders are not tightened. Brimelow, for example, warned that if immigration was not brought under control, during the next century, "American patriots will be fighting to salvage as much as possible from the shipwreck of their great republic" (1995, 23).

During 1996, the U.S. Congress also passed two critical pieces of legislation, both of which served to widen the gulf between citizens and legal immigrants. The 1996 Illegal Immigration Reform and Immigrant Responsibility Act (IIRIRA) brought new and retroactive definitions of criminality that rendered legal immigrants and permanent noncitizen residents subject to deportation for felony and many misdemeanor offenses committed anytime in the past. IIRIRA also granted immigrant officials the authority to order summary exclusion and eliminated avenues for the appeal of deportation orders to an immigration judge. During the same year, Congress also passed a welfare reform law—the Personal Responsibility and Work Opportunity Reconciliation Act of 1996. This legislation declared legal immigrants ineligible for many kinds of cash and nutritional aid benefits. Specifically, most future immigrants were barred from applying for benefits under federal means-tested programs for their first five years in the United States. Although legal immigrants, like citizens, are required to pay taxes into social safety-net programs, based on this law, they were no longer able to receive the benefits of many of those programs (Fragomen 1997). Interestingly, in 2002, President George W. Bush and several Republican lawmakers who strongly supported the welfare reform bill did an about-face and proposed restoring food stamp eligibility to many legal immigrants. Bush cited hardship for immigrants resulting from the economic downturn as the reason for his proposal. More cynical interpretations of the policy reversal acknowledge that the majority of the legal immigrants who will benefit from Bush's proposal are Hispanics—an ethnic group in the United States whose support he needs to win the next election (Pear 2002).

U.S. government policies and rhetoric with regard to fortifying the boundaries between citizens and noncitizens both reflected and fueled negative public opinion toward immigration and immigrants. Between 1977 and 1999, when asked whether immigration should be kept at its present level, increased, or decreased, a steady plurality of Americans favored decreasing the number of immigrants entering the country. During the mid-1990s, a full two-thirds of Americans surveyed (65 percent in 1993 and 1995) advocated a decrease in immigration. When polled about the impact of immigration, similarly high numbers (64 percent in 1993) believed that immigrants hurt the U.S. economy. By the start of the new millennium, there was some indication that Americans' views toward immigration were softening. A Gallup poll conducted in September 2000 showed that for the first time in over thirty years, a plurality of Americans (41 percent) believed that immigration should be kept at its present level, 38 percent favored a decrease, and 13 percent supported an increase (Jones 2000).

The thaw in attitude, however, was short lived. One year later, after the September 11, 2001, terrorist attacks on the United States, immigration and immigrants became targets of blame. Energy was immediately focused on fortifying U.S. borders, tightening visa requirements, and monitoring and restricting the rights of immigrants in response to the security and surveillance needs of the United States. Attorney General John Ashcroft resurrected a long-ignored, fifty-year-old requirement that noncitizens notify the U.S. government of any address changes within ten days of a move. An estimated 11.5 million legal residents are affected by the requirement; and one individual, a thirty-year-old Palestinian immigrant, has already faced deportation charges for failing to report an address change (Malone 2002). As further evidence of the appeal that access to citizenship may hold, in November 2001, the U.S. Justice Department offered the prospect of American citizenship, including a promise to ignore visa problems, for any foreigner willing to come forward with information about the 9/11 terrorist attacks. Ashcroft stated: "The people who have the courage to make the right choice deserve to be welcome as guests into our country and perhaps to one day become fellow citizens" (Gullo 2001, A3). Citizenship became a rallying point after 9/11, and the stakes of not possessing it have been high.

The United States has not been the only country to experience antiforeigner sentiment or widespread support for tightening the territorial and political boundaries between citizens and noncitizens. In the 1980s and 1990s countries throughout Western Europe were wracked by xenophobic tension and by the rising popularity of extremist right-wing political parties. Neonazism in Germany typically receives a great deal of media attention due to that country's troubling past; but many other countries such as Britain, France, Austria, and more recently, Italy and Spain have experienced similar sociocultural and political phenomena. As with the United States, these governments both responded and often contributed to the perceived threat of foreigners with legislation designed to restrict the influx of immigrants, tighten access to citizenship, and make more exclusive the benefits associated with it. France offers an interesting example in that its relatively liberal citizenship regime, rooted in the principle of *jus soli*, is frequently contrasted with Germany's more restrictive model based on *jus sanguinis* (Brubaker 1992). Yet, a close analysis of France's immigration and citizenship politics since the 1980s supports Katrina Gorjanicyn's (2000) claim that the French Revolutionary tradition of universal citizenship has shifted more closely to the conservative tradition of rootedness and *jus sanguinis*.

Throughout the 1960s and 1970s, large numbers of immigrants arrived in France, coming mainly from North and West Africa, and specifically from former French colonies of Algeria, Morocco, and Tunisia. Many were recruited, even imported, by French businesses, and many entered without documentation; but the French government was willing to accept and even regularize their presence as they contributed to labor market needs of the time. By the mid-1970s, however, the welcome wore thin. In 1974, amid fears of a severe economic downturn, the center-right presidency of Valéry Giscard d' Estaing officially froze further inward migration. Since that time, different parties and political figures in France have advocated similar positions. The emergence in the late 1980s of Jean-Marie Le Pen's right-wing National Front and the party's growing dynamism during the 1990s served to ratchet antiforeigner sentiment and keep restrictionist immigration and citizenship policies on France's public agenda. Among the various proposals Le Pen has advocated are denying social benefits to immigrants, targeting immigrants first when cutting jobs, and granting citizenship at birth only to the children of "blood" French (Hargreaves 1995). Over time, proposals that had once seemed extreme entered the mainstream. In 1993, a center-right government came to power in France declaring as one of its primary objectives "zero immigration." That same year, the French government succeeded at tightening its citizenship laws through a reform of the French Nationality Code. Children born on French soil to foreign parents would now be required to apply for French citizenship, where it had previously been granted automatically (Whitney 1996).

At the turn of the new millennium, not only did countries like France, Germany, and Austria continue to struggle with issues of immigration and belonging, new countries in Europe also emerged as key sites of conflict. Spain, for example, which has not historically been a predominant destination of migrants, is now confronted with a large and continual influx of immigrants from Africa. Reminiscent of the Cubans and Haitians arriving in the United States, these migrants board rickety rafts to risk a perilous journey across the Strait of Gibraltar, and like Cuban and Haitian refugees, many do not survive the trip. As with their counterparts in the United States and other European countries, many Spanish citizens have reacted negatively to the influx of foreigners, and the country is experiencing what has become an all too familiar pattern around the world of growing xenophobia and racism (Cohen 2000). Meanwhile, the onward march of European integration is complicating questions of migration and citizenship around the region. Countries throughout Europe are struggling individually and as members of the European Union with questions of immigration and asylum policy, the need for closer coordination of policies among member states, and the issue of a common European border guard.

The intensity with which all of these topics are debated intensified in the aftermath of the 9/11 terrorist attacks on the United States. As in the United States, European governments came under pressure to respond to the threat of terrorism, and immigrants and migration became the surrogate targets. Governments proposed more restrictive membership laws and ceased efforts to liberalize existing ones. The European Union, for example, backed off plans to liberalize the region's refugee policy and notified Eastern European countries anxious to join the EU that they will now be required to meet stricter border and internal security requirements before entry into the EU (Lyons 2001). Meanwhile, far right political parties across the continent seized the opportunity to strengthen their campaigns against foreigners. In April 2002, National Front leader Jean-Marie Le Pen shocked many in France and across Europe when he captured 17 percent of the vote in the first round of France's presidential elections, second only to then-President Jacques Chirac's 19.6 percent (Riding 2002). Le Pen's platform included an end to legal immigration, deportation of illegal immigrants, elimination of dual nationality, priority for French citizens for all jobs and public housing, permitting only French citizens to teach in French schools, and outlawing yarmulkes and headscarves in schools. He eventually lost to Chirac in the final run-off election.

Europe and North America are not the only regions currently engaged in efforts to fortify borders, restrict the influx of immigrants, and differentiate clearly between citizens who belong and noncitizens who do not. Costa Rica, for example, announced in July 2001 that it was beefing up migration controls in response to an increase in the arrival of undocumented migrants from Nicaragua. This included the building of a seven-and-a-half-foot high and one-half-mile-long wall along its northern border (Elton 2001). Recent border tensions in other parts of Latin America have included the Dominican Republic's attempts to restrict the influx of undocumented Haitians and Mexico's efforts to control immigration from Guatemala.

Similar situations exist throughout Africa as well. South Africa, in particular, has adopted an almost fortress-like mentality in relation to its neighboring countries. However profound the democratic transition to a post-Apartheid state, many of the policies being pursued with regard to border control are strangely reminiscent of Apartheid—including South Africa's Minister of Home Affairs Mangosuthu Buthelezi's calls to turn the electric fence running along the border between South Africa and Mozambique to lethal mode. In fact, the stakes for a new South African state to clearly delineate membership and to restrict the benefits therein seem to have intensified in the fragile post-Apartheid context (Croucher 1998). In October 2001 and partially in response to the 9/11 attacks, South Africa's Ministry of Home Affairs put forth a proposal to make fraudulent acquisition of South African citizenship a crime of treason. In his support for the proposal, Home Affairs Director-General Billy Masethla repeatedly invoked the sanctity of South African citizenship and the state's sovereignty over it: "The department views activities that seek to undermine the credibility of this country's identification document system as an offense that should amount to highest punishment." He went on to say that "The issue of foreigners forging citizenship whether by false marriages or other means is posing a serious threat to this country's reputation to the outside world" (South African Press Agency 2001).

A variety of factors are typically invoked to explain exclusionary attitudes toward immigrants on the part of citizens (ranging from competition for scarce economic resources to a perceived threat of cultural anni-hilation). But the appeal of citizenship and its perpetuation as a sought-after membership rests not only with citizens. It rests also with states whose very existence is legitimated in large part by the role they play as purveyors of citizenship, or as the regulators of borders and the benefits that accrue to those who manage to find themselves within as opposed to outside of them. Roxanne Doty (1996a) describes this as "statecraft," and she and others have demonstrated the role that immigration and cit-izenship policies play in the construction and maintenance of the notion and practice of state sovereignty. Specifically, Doty examines various mechanisms—immigration policymaking and related rhetoric prominent among them—through which states are able "to impose fixed and stable meanings about who belongs and who does not belong," and "thereby to distinguish a specific political community—the inside—from all others—the outside" (1996b, 122). States act, in other words, to maintain their sovereignty, and they do so by reproducing boundaries—spatial, social, cultural, economic, and political. Immigration, particularly illegal immi-gration, challenges a fundamental element of sovereignty—the right to regulate entry—and states' responses to it simultaneously shore up key boundaries and their command over them (Doty 1996b). In a recent volume, *On Borders*, analyzing migration in Southern Africa, Belinda Dodson makes a related point when she writes that "Immigration policy is one of the last bastions of sovereign state power in an increasingly globalised world" (2000, 119). And contrary to some recent claims that states' capacity to control unwanted migration is declining, Christian Joppke (1997) finds, in a study of the United States, Germany, and Britain, an increased willingness and capacity of states to control mass asylum-seeking.

"the appeal of citizenship and its perpetuation as a sought-after membership rests not only with citizens. It rests also with states whose very existence is legitimated in large part by the role they play as purveyors of citizenship."

In addition to immigration policy there are countless other examples of states acting to protect and perpetuate their sovereignty by invoking citi-zenship, or their commitment to upholding the rights of their citizens. When U.S. president George W. Bush refused to sign the 1997 Kyoto Accord on global warming, he repeatedly emphasized the need to protect U.S. workers and the U.S. economy. In a widely quoted statement, Bush declared: "In terms of the CO_2 issue . . . we will not do anything that harms our economy. Because, first things first, are the people who live in America" (quoted in D. Jackson 2001, A25). Months later, in London, he reiterated his opposition to the agreement and stated: "Our strategy must make sure working people in America aren't thrown out of work" (quoted in Deans 2001, 1E). Nor is the United States alone in this regard. Despite declining sovereignty, states continue to be significant actors in the world system. The dynamics of that system challenge the autonomy of states, but it is also through their actions and interactions in the world system that states assert and fortify their existence. Citizenship has and continues to be a potent legitimating factor for doing so.

The examples discussed above indicate that attachments to citizenship remain strong in regions throughout the world, and in some cases have intensified. In addition to and often because of the desire on the part of those who possess citizenship to guard its benefits cautiously, there is evidence that citizenship still affords certain privileges that lead those excluded from it to seek access to it. In contradistinction to the examples presented in the previous section, which suggest that citizenship is no longer a necessary condition for the exercise of civil, political, or social rights, are alternative examples of its persistent value. For example, in his analysis of membership without citizenship, Rogers Brubaker acknowledges that "citizenship still confers certain significant privileges" (1989, 147). One obvious privilege within the political sphere is the right to vote, and despite the exceptions noted above, it is a privilege still largely reserved for citizens. Although the citizens of many countries, the United States prominent among them, take that privilege for granted, there is no denying that the right to vote affords a degree of access, voice, and power that is not available to noncitizens. There are also valuable benefits beyond the political realm that are still largely reserved for citizens—not the least of which is unconditional access to the labor market.

Nor is protection from deportation a right that should be taken lightly. For example, Schuck's (1989) claim that the expansive interpretation of due process in the United States renders the deportation of noncitizens highly unlikely is probably of little comfort to the hundreds of longtime legal residents with minor offenses who, on the basis of the 1996 IIRIRA, have been abruptly removed from their homes and sent back to their countries of origin. In fact, the INS reported that between 1996 and 2000 deportations from the United States increased by 164 percent. Many of those were legal residents who had been in the United States for decades and had committed only minor offenses, sometimes years prior. But, because IIRIRA made deportation for criminal offenses retroactive and failed to distinguish between serious felonies and lesser crimes, many otherwise law-abiding citizens, who had paid their debt to society, found themselves threatened with deportation (Casimir 2001, 4). Ironically, the

INS became aware of some of these individuals, and their offenses, when they applied for U.S. citizenship.

Examples of permanent residents and the crimes for which they were being deported ranged from a Korean immigrant and father, who had lived in the United States for twenty years and had been arrested for public drunkenness, to an immigrant in Atlanta who had been caught shoplifting a box of doughnuts and a $15 baby outfit (Bixler 2000). In 2000, a German woman who had lived in the United States since 1967 and had recently applied for U.S. citizenship was notified of her pending deportation due to an assault charge filed in 1989. She was twenty-three years old at the time of the crime, which consisted of pulling the hair of a woman whom she discovered on a date with her then boyfriend (NBC News 2000). As noted above, pressure on noncitizens intensified after 9/11, and in 2002, a twenty-two-year-old Afghan man who came to the United States as a small child of refugee parents faced deportation to Afghanistan (a country whose language and customs he did not know) because of a misdemeanor drug charge (Yates 2002).

In most cases, whether the privileges reserved for citizens are deemed significant or not is a matter of interpretation and context. In other words, "it depends." But the discussion above of growing xenophobia and support for measures to further restrict state benefits to formal members indicates that the demise of citizenship is far from complete; and in many countries around the world, noncitizens are well aware of and mobilized in response to that reality. Despite an overall decline in naturalization rates in the United States, for example, there was a notable surge in citizenship applications during the mid- to late 1990s. In fact, between 1993 and 1999, 6.4 million immigrants applied for citizenship—more than in the previous thirty-seven years combined. Analysts attributed this rush to citizenship to the anti-immigrant backlash evident among voters and Congress during the mid-1990s—whether because of Proposition 187 or 1996 legislative acts that took welfare benefits and due process rights away from noncitizens (Pan 2000).

Numerous reports of a "turn to citizenship for safety" were also reported in the United States in the aftermath of 9/11. In fact, applications for naturalization in October and November 2001 were up 61 percent over the same period of the previous year (Axtman 2002). Similarly, when Germany began to liberalize its citizenship policies in the early 1990s, the country experienced a dramatic increase in naturalization rates. In fact, the naturalization rates of Turkish immigrants in Germany, a group frequently the target of xenophobia and restrictionist policy proposals, almost tripled between 1993 and 1995 (Joppke 1999, 639). The same scenario has played out in the Baltic states as well. When the initially exclusionary citizenship policies of Estonia and Latvia, for example, were relaxed, or where opportunities for naturalization did exist, noncitizens typically rushed to seek the shelter of formal membership in a state (Barrington 2000).

The Reconfiguration of Citizenship

The discussion above supports contradictory conclusions with regard to the contemporary status of citizenship. On the one hand, citizenship as formal membership in a state seems to be declining as a central or salient form of belonging. On the other hand, there is ample evidence from around the world of individuals clinging to citizenship as a predominant method for separating "Us" from "Them," of states unwilling to give up their role as the regulators of membership and the benefits it entails, and of those excluded from citizenship—whether formal or substantive— actively seeking access to it. Yet, even the analysts and observers who emphasize citizenship's persistent power and appeal acknowledge the challenges, and as a consequence of those challenges, the current alterations in the form and content of citizenship. These alterations are closely linked to globalization, and, in fact, the very same elements of globalization often shape, simultaneously, both the demise and the invigoration of citizenship. In this regard, an emphasis on *reconfiguration* offers the greatest insight into the contemporary status or "crisis" of citizenship. Globalization is reconfiguring citizenship, but the shape of that reconfiguration varies widely and is closely related to competing visions and realities of the role and centrality of the state. This section reviews alternative forms and conceptions of citizenship in a globalizing world, namely, dual citizenship and EU citizenship.

Dual Citizenship

As noted above, current variations in the practice and conceptualization of citizenship can be distinguished in part by the continuing significance, or not, of the state. In some cases, the form and content of citizenship is shifting, yet the state continues to be the primary site and coordinator of belonging. From other perspectives, however, rights are being accessed and exercised, and belonging or attachment is being experienced and negotiated in ways that transcend the state entirely. Many contemporary configurations fall somewhere in between. One illustrative example of an emerging form of belonging that challenges conventional models of citizenship is the practice of dual citizenship. Dual citizenship, or what Schuck (1998) refers to as "plural citizenships," is becoming increasingly common and increasingly controversial as well (Renshon 2001). A variety of factors contribute to the current prevalence of dual citizenship—factors that range from the large-scale movement and resettlement of people across and outside of the borders of their home state to an emerging body of laws and regulations that reflect and respond to that contemporary reality.

Variations in specific citizenship policies are as numerous as states in the international system, and when people move and/or give birth outside of their home states, these distinct citizenship regimes interact in complex ways. For example, in the United States, citizenship is based on the principle of *jus soli*; but it also contains an element of *jus sanguinis* in that a child born outside of the United States to parents who are U.S. citizens is automatically entitled to U.S. citizenship. If that child is born in a country that also practices *jus soli* citizenship, Canada, for example, then the child is entitled to membership in two states. Naturalization results in similar outcomes. Naturalization refers to the process by which an individual not born into a particular state can gain membership in that state, whether by virtue of where the child was born or to whom. Again, the variation in naturalization regimes is immense, but in a situation where the new state does not require the naturalizing citizen to relinquish his or her former citizenship, or the original, home state does not revoke a citizen's membership when that person secures another, the result is dual citizenship.

The likelihood or prevalence of a situation like the one described above has increased significantly in recent decades not only because of an increase in international migration. Increased sophistication in communications and transportation technology facilitates the practice of multiple memberships, and global economic interconnectedness enhances the potential benefits. Because of the Internet, satellites, fax machines, and affordable high-speed travel, individuals can more easily remain connected to, physically and otherwise, and participate in more than one state. Because dual citizenship often affords enhanced opportunities in the way of investment, property holding, tax benefits, and travel, it can prove advantageous in an increasingly competitive global marketplace. Recognizing these benefits, individuals have increasingly lobbied for and attempted to secure access to multiple state memberships; and states, themselves, also recognizing potential benefits, have altered in both letter and spirit their laws pertaining to citizenship.

One recent and notable example involves Mexico's 1998 constitutional amendment that allows Mexicans who naturalize elsewhere to retain their Mexican nationality and those who have already lost it due to acquiring

"Increased sophistication in communications and transportation technology facilitates the practice of multiple memberships, and global economic interconnectedness enhances the potential benefits."

citizenship in another state to reacquire Mexican nationality. The law is directed primarily toward the very large number of Mexicans who migrate to the United States. Historically, emigrants from Mexico were disdained within their home country as traitors, referred to derogatorily as *pochos*, and harassed by Mexican border officials during temporary return visits (Shain 1999). This attitude began to change by the early 1990s and a number of factors may help explain the shift. The economic, social, and political trajectories of Mexico and the United States had always been closely intertwined, and amid negotiations for a free trade agreement were becoming more so. As noted above, technological advancements meant that a border and homeland that were always relatively close for most Mexicans and Mexican Americans in the United States seemed even more so. The Mexican government recognized its reliance upon the remittances of Mexicans working in the United States and became aware, particularly during negotiations for NAFTA, that its expatriates and fellow nationals could be valuable allies in the United States. This measure also reflected a desire on the part of the Mexican state to protect Mexicans in the United States from the harsh anti-immigrant sentiment expressed through measures such as California's Proposition 187 (Shain 1999).

The 1998 constitutional amendment's reference to Mexican "nationality" is intentionally distinct from citizenship. While granting broad property, investment, and inheritance rights, as well as the right to attend public schools and universities in Mexico, it stops short of granting voting rights, office-holding rights, and the right to serve in the Mexican armed forces, and, hence, full membership in the Mexican state. Technically, then, this is not an example of dual citizenship, but for people of Mexican origin living in the United States, the boundaries of membership in either Mexico or the United States continue to blur (Jones-Correa 2000; Renshon 2001). During Mexico's 2000 elections, three candidates for Mexican congress were residents of the United States, and one, Los Angeles businessman Eddie Varón Levy, won a seat. Candidates for Mexico's presidential spot, including the winner Vicente Fox, also campaigned in the United States, and the National Action Party (PAN) proposed adding another congressional district to give Mexicans living in the United States ten representatives in Mexico's five-hundred-member congress (LaFranchi 2000b).

Mexico is not the only country to extend membership and a sense of belonging to nationals living abroad even when they have also secured membership and a sense of belonging in their new state of residence. At least ninety-three countries now allow dual citizenship. A list of countries that have recently changed their laws to allow dual citizenship includes Argentina, Brazil, Canada, Colombia, Costa Rica, the Dominican Republic, Ecuador, El Salvador, France, Ireland, Israel, Italy, Panama, Switzerland, and the United Kingdom. Nor is the United States the only country in which migrants and refugees wish to resettle. However, many of the countries on the dual citizenship list are among the largest senders of migrants to the United States, and this, coupled with a relatively open immigration and naturalization policy, results in the prevalent practice and politics of dual citizenship in the United States. It is difficult if not impossible to know the precise number of people with dual citizenship living in the United States, but estimates suggest that over twenty million U.S. citizens also qualify as citizens of other countries (Renshon 2001). A half-million children are born in the United States each year with dual citizenship—meaning, for example, that their parents are immigrants from a country that grants *jus sanguinis* citizenship to the child and does not require emigrants to renounce their citizenship once they acquire citizenship in the United States. This estimate addresses only one of several ways dual citizenship may be attained (Aleinikoff 2000, 138–40).

Because the practice of dual citizenship has two sides, or, more specifically, involves the policies and politics of at least two states, it is critical to understand not just the sending country's position with regard to their citizens who emigrate, but also how the country of destination reacts to or receives the newcomers—as members or not. In the United States, for example, acquiring citizenship requires renouncing citizenship elsewhere. Specifically, the oath for U.S. citizenship requires that the applicant "renounce and abjure absolutely and entirely all allegiance and fidelity to any foreign prince, potentate, state, or sovereignty of whom or which the applicant was before a subject or citizen." In practice, identifying guidelines for the application of this requirement is complex and its enforcement highly impractical. While applicants must renounce their former citizenship, the United States requires no proof of its relinquishment. And if, like the many cases listed above, the home country does not consider naturalization elsewhere as expatriation and does not revoke the original citizenship, then the United States has little capacity to limit or regulate plural membership. Furthermore, although citizens naturalizing in the United States are required to renounce former memberships, a series of U.S. Supreme Court rulings and amendments to existing legislation has created a situation in which U.S. citizens who naturalize elsewhere do not automatically lose their U.S. citizenship. In fact, short of explicitly declaring an intention to give up U.S. citizenship, it has become virtually impossible to lose it (Aleinikoff 2000, 137).

The current status of both U.S. and international law with regard to dual citizenship is best characterized as moving in the direction of increased ambiguity or outright tolerance. In fact, one analyst likens the current U.S. policy to one of "don't ask, don't tell" (Jones-Correa 2000, 18). But this is not to suggest that the practices and policies surrounding dual citizenship are without controversy. In fact, the increased prevalence and visibility of plural state memberships has, particularly in the United States, ignited heated debates among policymakers and within the public at large. Those opposed to dual citizenship express some concern over what might be described as logistical problems. For example, on a practical level, dual citizenship may pose legal uncertainties with regard to the military, diplomatic, political, and commercial relationships among states (Schuck 1998, 157). Peter Spiro (1997), for example, analyzes how in the case of dual citizenship, one state's almost unfettered right to treat its own citizens as it chooses may clash with another state's right and obligation to diplomatic protection of its citizens while they are abroad.

Much more widespread, however, are concerns that focus on how dual citizenship violates the fundamental principle of citizenship as membership in one and only one state and the relationship of mutually exclusive rights and responsibilities between a state and its citizens and citizens and their state. In fact, opponents of dual citizenship frequently draw analogies to the institution of marriage. Some invoke the words of historian and diplomat George Bancroft who maintained that a state should "as soon tolerate a man with two wives as a man with two countries" (quoted in Gribbin 1999, 3). Others argue, as summarized by Noah Pickus, that "Citizenship, like marriage and religion, requires a strong sense of commitment. . . . Dual citizenship, in which individuals belong to two 'peoples,' is inconsistent with the moral and philosophical foundation of American constitutional democracy" (1998, 25). From this perspective, it is also not surprising that many agree with columnist Georgie Anne Geyer's contention that dual citizenship is "akin to bigamy" (quoted in Jones-Correa 2000, 19).

European Union Citizenship

The practice of dual citizenship indicates both the persistent significance of the state as a site and referent for belonging and the changing nature of this form of belonging. In other words, we see growing evidence of multiple, competing, and overlapping political allegiances, but states, even if more than one, are still the ultimate target or goal. The European Union offers a second and related example of a contemporary reconfiguration of citizenship. The process of European integration has been a lengthy one, formally dating back to the Treaty of Rome in 1957. During the early decades, the focus was exclusively on economic union, but more recently, efforts have been made toward social and political integration and the harmonization of a wide range of governance policies. A milestone in European integration was reached in 1993 when the Maastricht Treaty on European Union officially established a citizenship of the European Union. Article 8 of the treaty, entered into force on November 1, 1993, reads: "Citizenship of the Union is hereby established. Every person holding the nationality of a Member State shall be a citizen of the Union." Some analysts and observers interpret this as a profound shift in the nature of political belonging—a shift from citizenship defined by membership in a particular nation-state to multilayered memberships in a deterritorialized, postmodern form of political space (Behnke 1997). Others are more cautious in their interpretations of the events taking place in Europe. Marco Martiniello argues, for example, that European Union citizenship is, at most, a form of semicitizenship that emulates national models but does not actually create a new juridical and political subject (2000). These debates themselves reflect the complexity of a project that is still very much in the making, but regardless of whether EU citizenship is ultimately described as postnational or supranational or merely a sophisticated set of intergovernmental agreements that mimic federal arrangements such as that of the United States, it clearly entails a set of governance relationships and institutional arrangements not easily accounted for by the model of "citizenship as membership in a single state."

> *"whether EU citizenship is ultimately described as postnational or supranational or merely a sophisticated set of intergovernmental agreements that mimic federal arrangements such as that of the United States, it clearly entails a set of governance relationships and institutional arrangements not easily accounted for by the model of 'citizenship as membership in a single state.'"*

In T. H. Marshall's citizenship framework, the guarantee of social rights is said to follow civil and political rights and represents the ultimate extension of full membership in a polity. In the case of the European Union, the establishment of certain social rights actually predates the more recent guarantee of political rights. This has to do with what has historically been an emphasis in Europe on economic rather than political union and the related need for the coordination of policies with regard to the movement of workers and provisions for their social and material well-being. From the 1970s onward, common social policies began to emerge, including agreements related to sex equality, workers rights, and directives on workplace health and safety. In December 1989, all member states, except Britain, signed the Community Charter of Fundamental Rights for Workers. This charter set out a program for Community policy that focused on areas ranging from the entitlement to decent living and working conditions to the entitlement of workers to pensions, and provided citizens as workers with new rights vis-à-vis the Community (Wiener 1998, 176–78). As Elizabeth Meehan argues, even if not self-consciously intended by member state governments as a step toward a common citizenship, these social measures and many that preceded them cannot be discounted as a key dimension of European citizenship (1996, 207).

Prior to the 1970s, specific references to a common European citizenship were limited. During that decade, however, a paradigm shift began to take place in thinking about European integration, and European citizenship emerged as a central aspect of that shift. Europe was being affected by profound changes in the international political economy and the economic crisis reverberating across the globe. Meanwhile, the process of European integration was coming under increased criticism as one dominated exclusively by and for a small bureaucratic elite. Agents and supporters of European integration recognized that individuals had little or no attachment to the European Community, and that member states, in times of crisis, would, and indeed were, opting for more independent courses of action.

This set of circumstances motivated what one analyst called a shift in emphasis from a "Europe of materials to a Europe for citizens" (G. Van Den Berghe 1982, 22). Over the next decade, discourse on European unification came to include a focus on issues of identity and belonging. Various European Union dignitaries and foreign ministers of member states called for Europe to become more "personalized" and "more human" (Wiener 1998, 68). In other words, if Europe was to continue down the path of state or quasi-state building, it needs a *demos*, or a people. With this in mind, negotiations began over the establishment of a passport union based on the following objective: "the creation of a uniform passport to be issued by each member state to its nationals in place of the passports of varying appearance currently issued, and which would symbolize a definite connection with the community" (CEC 1975, 7). In the years following, efforts were also made to strengthen the European Community's image and identity through symbols such as a flag, emblem, and anthem. It would be years before many of these measures became formally instituted, but Europe was obviously experiencing a paradigm shift in that references to the "citizens of Europe" and "European citizenship" had taken center stage. European officials believed that citizenship was a necessary tool of institution building, but in the process, the focus on citizenship brought with it an emphasis on civil rights as well as the establishment of previously nonexistent political rights.

Particularly notable with regard to civil and/or legal rights is the way in which rulings by the European Court of Justice (ECJ) and the European Court of Human Rights (ECHR) have established a legal status for individuals within the European Union and a direct relationship between citizens and common European institutions. In this way, the emerging case law has not only acted as a powerful incentive for member states to comply with EU obligations, but has also contributed to the building of a meaningful notion of European citizenship (Vranken 1999, 28). The role and impact of these common juridical bodies have been further enhanced by various commitments on behalf of EU members and institutions to the protection of fundamental human rights and against various forms of discrimination. In 1950, a European Convention on Human Rights, signed in Rome under the aegis of the Council of Europe, established an unprecedented system of international protection for human rights. The convention, since ratified by all member states of the EU, created a number of supervisory bodies which, in 1989, were consolidated under a single European Court of Human Rights. The Treaty of Amsterdam, adopted in 1997, reinforced the principle of human rights, emphasizing the EU's commitment to the fundamental rights guaranteed by the convention and the responsibility of member states to respect those guarantees as well. The Amsterdam Treaty also included the adoption of an Anti-Discrimination Clause, which empowers the Council of Europe to institute measures to combat discrimination on the basis of gender, race, ethnicity, religion, age, sexual preference, and handicap, and provides additional legal ground on which EU citizens can base a claim against discrimination (Martiniello 2000, 350).

Meanwhile, in 1999, the European Council began work on drafting a charter of fundamental rights. The council was motivated by a belief that fundamental rights applicable at the EU level should be consolidated in a charter and by the desire to raise awareness of those rights. The Charter of Fundamental Rights of the European Union was completed on December 7, 2000, in Nice, and its Preamble reads:

> The peoples of Europe, in creating an ever closer union among them, are resolved to share a peaceful future based on common values. Conscious of its spiritual and moral heritage, the Union is founded on the indivisible, universal values of human dignity, freedom, equality and solidarity; it is based on the principles of democracy and the rule of law. It places the individual at the heart of its activities, by establishing the citizenship of the Union and by creating an area of freedom, security and justice. (Charter of Fundamental Rights 2000)

The Preamble goes on to locate the origins, related support, and mechanisms for protecting these rights with member states as well as with an array of preexisting treaties, conventions, charters, and EU institutions. The cumulative effect of all of this is a common European legal and political status that transcends the authority of member states and contributes to the concept and practice of EU citizenship. As Meehan explains, this common legal status gives "private individuals a role in defending the Community's 'public interest' by contributing, through their cases, to the supervision of the actions of member states and Community institutions" (1996, 210). Recent examples of how that role has been exercised include a 1998 ruling by the ECHR that Britain's law banning campaign expenditures by ordinary citizens was illegal and a breach of the European Convention on Human Rights (Meade 1998). The following year, the ECHR issued two landmark rulings overturning British laws pertaining to gays and lesbians. The Court declared that both Britain's ban on gays serving in the military and a law against consensual adult gay sex were discriminatory and a breach of human rights (Purnell 1999).

In some cases, the references to the social and civil rights of EU citizens in both the Treaty of Maastricht and Amsterdam simply reinforced or confirmed already existing guarantees, but explicit inclusion of political rights in Maastricht marked an important shift in the policies and practice of EU citizenship. The specific rights guaranteed to EU citizens by the Maastricht Treaty include the right to move and reside freely within the territory of the member states; the right to vote and to stand as a candidate in elections to the European Parliament and in municipal elections in the member state in which they reside; the right to diplomatic protection in the territory of a non-EU state by any EU member state; the right to petition the European Parliament and apply to the ombudsman concerning instances of maladministration in the activities of the community institutions or bodies. Particularly significant are the provisions for transnational voting rights. To reiterate, all EU citizens, regardless of their member state nationality, have the right to vote in local elections and stand for local office in their current member state of residence. The same holds true for voting and candidacy in European elections. Nor is national citizenship in a particular member state a prerequisite for diplomatic protection from or by that member state. EU citizenship guarantees EU citizens who are in a non-European state diplomatic protection from any member state no matter their specific nationality or residency. Each of these provisions represents a significant breech of the long-established link between citizenship and a territorially bounded nation-state.

All of this seems to suggest the emergence of new forms of political membership and belonging. Yet skeptics are quick to caution against declaring EU citizenship the marker of a transition to a postnational era. States still retain control over their own nationality policies, and this determines access or lack thereof to EU citizenship. Article 8 of Maastricht grants EU citizenship to "Every person holding the nationality of a Member State," and five years later the Amsterdam Treaty clarified and rein-

> *"skeptics are quick to caution against declaring EU citizenship the marker of a transition to a postnational era. States still retain control over their own nationality policies, and this determines access or lack thereof to EU citizenship."*

forced this with the statement "Citizenship of the Union shall comple-
ment and not replace national citizenship" (Europa 2002). Furthermore, a
close look at the actual implementation and practice of EU citizenship
reveals a continued preeminence of the nation-state. Martiniello (2000)
notes, for example, that the free movement of EU citizens within the EU
has been impeded by member states reluctant to give up control over
their internal borders. And the provisions related to voting rights also
leave wide discretion to member states. For example, a member state in
which the proportion of nonnational European citizens of voting age
exceeds 20 percent of the total electorate can restrict the right to vote and
the right to stand for office based on a minimum period of residency in
that state (Martiniello 2000, 364).

It is the fact that EU citizenship is confined exclusively to nationals of a
member state that leads critics to question its revolutionary status. Proclamations such as Andreas Behnke's that the EU represents "the first postmodern form of political space" (1997, 262) may be exaggerated, but this is
still something more and different with regard to belonging. The bundle of
rights—social, civil, and political—that are guaranteed by Article 8 and
other parts of the Treaty on European Union clearly qualify as a form of citizenship, and one that transcends the nature of the relationship of rights
and responsibilities typically associated with membership in a nation-
state. Moreover, these rights are associated with and guaranteed by a political arena that is not fixed but is in a continuous state of construction
(Wiener 1998, 5). As Elizabeth Meehan explains, it represents a new form
of citizenship that is multiple in that "identities, rights and obligations . . .
are expressed through an increasingly complex configuration of common
European Community institutions, states, national and transnational voluntary associations, regions and alliances of regions" (1996, 201–2).

Conclusion

Globalization has thrust citizenship squarely into the spotlight. Citizenship now figures prominently on policy agendas and in political debates
of countries around the world. It is a theme that runs through discussions of welfare reform, multiculturalism, naturalization and immigration policies, and national security. Nor is it restricted to the national or
domestic arena. Local communities are mobilizing to make demands for
more substantive citizenship rights, and local governments are granting
citizenship rights, such as voting, to noncitizens, often in contradiction
to the policies of the state or federal government. Meanwhile, citizenship policies made at the domestic level by individual states, such as the
decision to allow nationals who emigrate to retain their citizenship,
quickly become issues of international relations once those individuals

move and acquire citizenship in a new state. International organizations and agencies are involving themselves more actively in the protection of fundamental rights typically guaranteed by states. That globalization has had a profound impact on the practice of citizenship and the attention focused on it at various levels and in multiple issue areas is indisputable. The precise nature of that impact is less clear. In some cases, citizenship as membership in a state is declining in importance. In other cases, however, it has taken on heightened significance in an increasingly turbulent world. What is evident from the analysis presented in this chapter is that citizenship is not a static formation, but any predictions about its future configuration are necessarily speculative.

Much of the declining centrality of citizenship as a form of belonging is rooted in the declining autonomy of the modern state. These two sociopolitical formations have been closely intertwined for at least three hundred years; and as globalization weakens the role of the sovereign territorial state, so too does it dilute the need or desire for formal membership in a state. The bond of citizenship has long been premised on the belief that states serve to protect certain socioeconomic, political, and civil rights of their citizens. In each of these arenas, globalization has affected the capacity, willingness, or need for states to act as the ultimate guarantors of these rights. Economic interconnectedness, whether in the form of the growing power and prominence of transnational corporations or the solidification of international economic regimes such as the WTO, limits the capacity of states to meet the welfare needs of their citizens. Meanwhile, international human rights regimes and other forms of international political organization across states offer citizens the opportunity to pursue fundamental rights beyond states; and advances in technology simultaneously expand those opportunities while empowering individuals to pursue them. Finally, human migration is perhaps the most concrete manifestation of the deterritorialization that now challenges the state. If, as Joppke (1999) explained, citizenship is a mechanism for filing every individual into one state, then the unprecedented movement of people across and outside of states is reason enough to question meaning and relevance of citizenship as it has traditionally been understood.

All of this suggests that the filing mechanism of citizenship or the relationship of rights and responsibilities that tie citizens and states together are defunct. Yet, many of the aspects of globalization that tear at the very fabric of citizenship simultaneously raise the stakes of having access to it or not. Globalization results in a heightened sense of insecurity on the part of both citizens and states. Individuals are motivated to seek refuge in a state and to make increased demands upon states. States, for their part, are compelled to guard carefully their threatened autonomy, and acting to maintain control over their borders and their membership is a central mechanism for doing so. Furthermore, the same technology that facilitates the transcendence of states also enhances the capacity of states to control citizens and access to citizenship.

Where then does this seeming paradox of citizenship's simultaneous erosion and invigoration leave us? Clearly, a dogmatic defense of either scenario would be overstated. As Bryan Turner explains: "We do not possess the conceptual apparatus to express the idea of global membership, and in this context a specifically national identity appears anachronistic" (1990, 212). Yet, without question, citizenship as we know it is in a state of flux. As many scholars have suggested, recognizing citizenship's malleability is key to understanding the contemporary context. Charles Tilly cautions that we must "see citizenship and public identities as social relations that remain incessantly open to interpretation and renegotiation" (1995, 12). Ronnie Lipschutz explains that any sense that state and citizen are somehow changeless "flies in the face of long-standing evidence that membership in a political community, and the requirements of such belonging, can hardly be thought of as static elements" (1999, 206). The increasing practice of dual citizenship and the emergence of EU citizenship are contemporary reconfigurations in citizenship practice that illustrate its fluidity. As models for predicting the future of citizenship, however, their implication is less clear.

The most profound shift in citizenship evinced by examples such as dual and EU citizenship is its growing detachment from a territorially delimited nation-state. Based on this, some posit a trend toward a type of world citizenship, but such a prognosis denies the persistent power and appeal of states. As Lipschutz states: "The ties that bound the individual to the territorial state are not completely broken, although they are badly frayed" (1999, 217). For now, the most likely scenario is one in which individuals have access to and maintain multiple and overlapping allegiances— whether to two or more states or to federal-like structures with varied levels of governance. In addition to being aware of the potential staying power of the state in practice, it is also important to be aware of the ways in which the concept of the sovereign state and the notion of a world system made up of individual states is so ingrained in our minds as to preclude thoughtful consideration or recognition of alternative formations of political belonging. This poverty of imagination, and the politics inherent in it, are precisely what Lipschutz refers to when he claims that the state has become "a 'naturalistic necessity' against which all other political actors are treated and evaluated in terms of their (non-natural) inability to replicate the symbolic and functional roles of a state for lack of appropriate (natural) tools" (1999, 219). The following chapter continues the exploration of globalization's implications for a form of belonging related to, but not synonymous with, citizenship—nationhood.

3

Nation-Shaping in a Postmodern World

In the late 1990s, amid bloody struggles between Serbs and ethnic Albanians in Kosovo, Slobodan Milosevic and other Serbian leaders attempted to justify and bolster support for their position through frequent invocations of the Battle of Kosovo Polje in 1389 and the fourteenth-century hero and self-proclaimed "ruler of all Serbs," Prince Lazar (Brown 1999, 1). During that same decade, as South Africa negotiated a fragile transition to a post-Apartheid era, among concerns about the economy and the need to build democratic institutions were references to the absence of a South African nation. Some dissenters questioned the need or desire for nation-building in a "postmodern age" (Degenaar 1994), but its proponents won out and attempted to forge a South African nation through symbols such as a flag, anthem, media slogans, and exclusionary rhetoric directed at non–South Africans (Croucher 1998).

Meanwhile, as Europe proceeded down the bumpy path to full-scale integration, discussion and debate turned increasingly to the question of belonging: how to create a sense of commonality among the peoples of Europe and an attachment to the institutions and ideals of a united Europe. European Union (EU) citizenship, as discussed in chapter 2, was seen as one avenue, but giving form and content to that citizenship turns frequently to invocations of Europe's shared history, culture, and values—

An earlier version of chapter 3 was published as Sheila Croucher 2003, "Perpetual Imagining: Nationhood in a Global Era," in *International Studies Review* 5, no. 1. It appears here with permission from Blackwell Publishing.

what might arguably be described as building a nation of Europe (Guibernau 1996). Italian Prime Minister Silvio Berlusconi's comments in the wake of September 11 offer one of the more hyperbolic examples of the role that culture may play in shaping a sense of Europeaness:

> We must be aware of the superiority of our civilization, a system that has guaranteed well-being, respect for human rights and—in contrast with Islamic countries—respect for religious and political rights, a system that has as its values understandings of diversity and tolerance. ("War on Terror" 2001a, 17)

Each of these cases constitutes a form of nation-building, and each offers a vivid example of what many scholars have already argued about nations: that they provide and/or consist of a potent sense of community and shared consciousness that typically attaches to and serves the interests of a given polity; that this sense of community often reaches far back in historical memory and relies heavily on symbols and myth; that governing elites play a central role in shaping the nation; and that the forging of a national "Us" typically involves differentiation from a "Them." What is peculiar about these examples, however, is that taken as a whole and in the context of the advent of the twenty-first century, they defy the prominent theories of nations and nationalism. This is the case regarding the modernist and postnationalist perspectives that imply or proclaim the end of the era of nations, as well as the primordialist approaches that explain the persistence of nations by reference to their historical and cultural continuity and ethnic potency. In fact, the contemporary perpetuation of nations and nationalism presents a seeming paradox—not unlike the paradox introduced in the introduction to this book of a world that is simultaneously coming together and coming apart, experiencing integration and homogenization via various aspects of globalization while also witnessing fragmentation and differentiation related to the persistence and even resurrection of seemingly ancient and primordial ties.

"the contemporary perpetuation of nations and nationalism presents a seeming paradox—not unlike the paradox . . . of a world that is simultaneously coming together and coming apart, experiencing integration and homogenization via various aspects of globalization while also witnessing fragmentation and differentiation."

This chapter focuses on this apparent paradox as it relates to nations and nationalism. Specifically, what follows is an examination of the implications of globalization for nationhood, or what Benedict Anderson (1991) terms "nation-ness," as a form of belonging. We begin with a discussion of the ambiguity that surrounds the term nation—an ambiguity that itself contributes to the persistence of the national form. Next, and before turning to the question of globalization, the chapter discusses a prominent body of literature that locates nations and nationalism in a context prior to and distinct from the contemporary one—namely, "modernity." A subsequent section assesses a variety of current explanations for why nations persist in a context variably described as postmodern or postnational, and draws upon different empirical examples to illustrate the need for a more refined understanding. The final section demonstrates that by recognizing the contingency of nations, it is possible to locate in globalization both the conditions and mechanisms that support national imaginings. Because nationhood—conceptually and in practice—is malleable, there is no reason to believe that nations will not be perpetually imagined—although they will change in content and form.

The Definitional Dilemma

Globalization and citizenship, as discussed in the preceding chapters, pose numerous conceptual challenges but pale in comparison to the struggle for a clear or widely agreed upon definition of the nation. In 1978, Walker Connor published a seminal article, "A Nation Is a Nation, Is a State, Is an Ethnic Group, Is a . . ." in which he bemoans the terminological chaos that surrounds the study of nations and nationalism. Nor was he alone in acknowledging this definitional dilemma. As early as 1939, a study by the Royal Institute of International Affairs stated that "among other difficulties which impede the study of 'nationalism,' that of language holds a leading place" ("Nationalism," 1939, xvi). In 1977, renowned historian of nationalism Hugh Seton-Watson proclaimed, "Thus I am driven to the conclusion that no 'scientific definition' of the nation can be devised; yet the phenomenon has existed and exists" (1977, 5). Charles Tilly, in his influential work on state-building, characterized "nation" as "one of the most puzzling and tendentious items in the political lexicon" (1975, 6). In the twenty or more years that have passed since these concerns were articulated, little progress has been made. Surveying the state of the field in 2000, Valery Tishkov concludes that "All attempts to develop terminological consensus around *nation* resulted in grand failure" (2000, 627).

Of all these scholars, Connor went the furthest in focusing needed attention on several "barriers to understanding," and foremost among his concerns has been the misguided interutilization of the terms "nation" and "state." States, Connor claims, are the major political subdivisions of the world and are readily identifiable through quantitative criteria. Peru, he writes, "can be defined in an easily conceptualized manner as the territorial-political unit consisting of the sixteen million inhabitants of the 514,060 square miles located on the west coast of South America between 69° and 80° West, and 2° and 18° 21' South" (1978, 379). Nations, on the other hand, have an intangible essence and must ultimately be conceptualized through subjective or psychological criteria.

In addition to concern about the widespread interchangeable use of the terms nation and state, evident, for example, in phrases like inter*nation*al relations instead of inter-*state* relations, or gross *national* product instead of gross *state* product, Connor also challenges the related assumption that the two entities are, or should be, congruent. He correctly cautions that many groups who believe themselves to be a nation do not have a state and/or are spread across different states; and many states contain within them more than one nation. For Connor, these misunderstandings have affected the capacity not only of scholars to understand or anticipate nationalist turmoil and failed states in much of the developing world, but also of policymakers to devise appropriate responses (Connor 1978, 1994). This was certainly the case, as he argues, with regard to the postcolonial world—where social scientists and policymakers assumed that by simply establishing states, for example, Nigeria, a loyal nation would follow.

Connor himself devotes more energy to explaining what nations are not than clarifying what they are, but he comes close to a definition when he draws upon Rupert Emerson's claim that a nation is "a body of people who feel that they are a nation" (cited in Connor 1978, 396). This emphasis on the psychological and subjective nature of nationhood, however unsatisfactory to many social scientists, predominates in the most well-known and respected literature on the topic. Ernest Renan famously described the nation as a "daily plebiscite" (see Bhabha 1990, 19), and Max Weber (1948) stated that nations cannot be defined in terms of empirical qualities—language, religion, blood. Rather, nations must be understood by reference to a "sentiment of solidarity." Some scholars of nations and nationalism have, however, attempted to specify objective criteria. Josef Stalin, for example, declared:

> A nation is a historically constituted, stable community of people, formed on the basis of a common language, territory, economic life, and psychological make-up manifested in a common culture. . . . It is only when all these characteristics are present together that we have a nation. (quoted in Hutchinson and Smith 1994, 20–21)

This definition allowed Stalin to declare that Jews, spread across Russia, Galicia, Armenia, Georgia, and the Caucasus, were not a nation. Many others have also pursued a definition of the nation rooted in objective criteria, but they inevitably run into cases of groups of people who perceive themselves to be and are perceived as a nation, but who do not meet all of the specified objective criteria. Or, they encounter cases that do seem to meet the objective criteria, but lack the sentiment of solidarity to which Weber referred. Ultimately, efforts at objective definitions of nation-ness tend to result in subjective judgments about what the objective criteria are and who does or does not meet them.

Rather than remain tangled in this conundrum, many scholars turn their attention away from the pursuit of a universal definition of nation to classify or categorize different types of nations and nationalisms (Hall 1993). This has often taken the form of describing historical phases, stages, or waves of nationalism that are typically distinguished by type, such as "from above" or "from below," and correspond to the socioeconomic and political context of the time and region (Hobsbawm 1990; Hroch 1985). Many of these efforts at categorization have and continue to be quite illuminating (O'Leary 2001), and all agree with John Hall that "No single, universal theory of nationalism is possible. As the historical record is diverse, so too must be our concepts" (1993, 1).

By far, the most common distinction that has surfaced in the literature on nationalism is that between civic nations and ethnic nations. *Civic* is the term used to refer to national communities that are purportedly rooted in or based upon a shared commitment to a set of political principles and institutions. *Ethnic* nations are those said to be based upon shared ancestry and cultural community. The United States, France, and Canada are frequently cited examples of the former, and Germany, Japan, and countries throughout Eastern Europe of the latter. The distinction has a long history in the works of prominent historians and political theorists, and corresponds to associated distinctions such as Western and Eastern nationalisms, rational and irrational nationalisms, and liberal democratic versus illiberal authoritarian nationalisms. As is evident in the latter descriptions, the distinction is not simply a descriptive or analytical one, but also a prescriptive and normative one. To be civic is good, and to be ethnic is bad.

Historian Hans Kohn was one of the earliest scholars to use this typology. Writing in the aftermath of World War II, Kohn drew a distinction between Western and Eastern nationalisms, with the Rhine River as the divider between the two. Western nationalisms, of which England, France, and the United States were examples, he characterized as rational and voluntaristic. Nationalism in these countries was, according to Kohn, "a predominantly political occurrence," "without too much sentimental regard for the past," and based on the obligation of a social contract. The nation was a free association of rational individuals. Eastern nationalisms, on the other hand (Germany was the prime example), he portrayed as organic and determinist. Group belonging was determined at birth and found its expression in the field of culture, ethnicity, language, and assumptions about the "natural" fact of a community. Of German nationhood, Kohn writes: "Its roots seemed to reach into the dark soil of primitive times and to have grown through thousands of hidden channels of unconscious development, not in the bright light of rational political ends, but in the mysterious womb of the people, deemed to be so much nearer the forces of nature" (1944, 331).

In the decades that followed, countless other scholars would make similar distinctions. Eric Hobsbawm's seminal work on *Nations and Nationalism since 1780* describes the period of 1870 to 1914 as one of significant transformation in the nature of nationalism—from "civic and democratic" as in the case of France, to "ethnic and linguistic" as was the case throughout much of Eastern Europe (1990, 101–30). James Kellas borrowed directly from Kohn's typology to contrast the social, inclusive, liberal, and democratic nationalism of the West with the ethnically exclusive, intolerant, and authoritarian nationalism of Eastern Europe (1991, 73–74). Liah Greenfeld (1992) has drawn a similar distinction between "individualistic-libertarian" and "collectivist-authoritarian" models of nationalism. And in 1992, Rogers Brubaker turned to these different conceptions of national belonging to explain variations in immigration policy in France and Germany. Because national belonging in the former was rooted in territory, the French state developed a civic immigration policy that naturalized immigrants on the basis of residence (*jus soli*). Whereas the German notion of nation, rooted in blood, led the German state to develop a very restrictive immigration policy that tied citizenship to German ethnicity (*jus sanguinis*).

As noted above, many scholars use the civic/ethnic distinction not simply to describe differences in nations or nationalism, but also as a way to prescribe solutions to the problems and conflicts associated with national belonging. In a recent book titled *Blood and Belonging*, Canadian scholar Michael Ignatieff acknowledges, although sadly, that the enlightenment dream of a cosmopolitan world society of rational individuals has and will likely continue to clash with the individual's need to belong. Ethnic nationalism, he argues, is not an acceptable solution to this dilemma because individuals are not free to choose their identity or source of belonging—it is chosen for them by the community into which they are born. Civic nationalism, however, according to Ignatieff, preserves the enlightenment's promise to the individual by allowing him or her to rationally choose an attachment and belonging based on shared values or ideals (1993, 7–11). When applied to the case of Canada, this framework leads Ignatieff to characterize Canadian national identity as civic and Québécois national identity as ethnic.

Jürgen Habermas has struggled with a similar political dilemma as it relates to the reunification of Germany and the threat of a resurgent German ethnic chauvinism. Habermas proposes that the reunification project focus not on the revival of "the pre-political unity of a community with a shared historical destiny," but rather on the restoration of "democracy and a constitutional state in a territory where civil rights had been suspended . . . since 1933" (1995, 256). What he advocates is "constitutional patriotism"—where the community's sense of attachment, loyalty, and pride are focused on political principles and ideals of democracy and the state institutions that protect or uphold them. This same notion of constitutional patriotism is seen as a common characterization of nationalism in the U.S. context. In rejecting philosopher Martha Nussbaum's call for Americans to become more cosmopolitan and less patriotic, Benjamin Barber argues that patriotism in the United States is quintessentially civic or constitutional: "The success of the American experiment [is] in grafting the sentiments of patriotism onto a constitutional frame. . . . Our 'tribal' sources from which we derive our sense of national identity are the Declaration of Independence, the Constitution and the Bill of Rights" (1996, 30, 32).

In whatever ways the civic/ethnic distinction may have been useful for pointing to variations in nations and national belonging, some scholars now contend, and correctly so, that it is vastly overdrawn. Bernard Yack makes this case persuasively in his critique of the civic nation as a myth:

> [T]he civic/ethnic distinction itself reflects a considerable dose of ethnocentrism, as if the political identities French and American were not also culturally inherited artifacts. . . . The characterization of political community in the so-called civic nations as a rational and freely chosen allegiance to a set of political principles seems untenable to me, a mixture of self-congratulations and wishful thinking. (1999, 105)

Anthony Smith shares Yack's view, pointing out that "even the most 'civic' and 'political' nationalisms often turn out on closer inspection to be also 'ethnic' and linguistic" (1998, 126).

Certainly this critique of the civic/ethnic distinction holds up when applied to the U.S. case. The claim, by Barber (1996) and others, that "our tribal sources are constitutional," overlooks the very real, and sometimes tragic, role that race, religion, and language have, and in some cases continue, to play as dimensions of belonging, or not, to the American nation. In this regard, Anthony Smith is correct to conclude that very few national states possess only one form of nationalism. The types frequently overlap and shift within and across historical periods. Although ethnic nations may tend toward exclusivity, he rightly points out that civic nations may be impatient with ethnic differences and tend toward radical assimilation (1998, 212). Not only has the American melting pot often been, in practice, more about Anglo-conformity, but neither does the portrayal of French nationhood as rooted in territorial and political identity likely sit well with the thousands of African Muslims living, in some cases, for generations, in France and still struggling for acceptance as full members of the nation (Hargreaves 1995).

For our purposes, the conceptualizations of civic and ethnic nationhood are important because they relate to and demonstrate the interconnections between other forms of belonging discussed in this book. For example, if nationhood was or could be purely civic in nature, focused solely on political principles and institutions, then how, or would, it need to be distinguished from citizenship—membership in or belonging to a state? Or, if nation-ness is synonymous with ethnicity, then is there a need for both concepts or terms and if so, why? The short answer to these questions is that citizenship, as it has been conventionally instituted, has proven to be too thin to alone satisfy the human need for belonging, and nation is a construction of community endowed with more passion or meaning. Unfortunately, inclusion, even if it attempts to be neutral, inevitably relies on exclusion, and ethnicity, race, religion, language, and so forth are fruitful bases of exclusion. Nonetheless, all nations are not primarily ethnic ones, nor are all ethnic groups necessarily nations. They do not, in other words, all have or aspire to have their own state.

The concluding section of this chapter returns to the definitional dilemma, and the complexities of terminology will continue to be illuminated throughout the book. For now, however, nation does appear to be a particularly slippery concept and term in the lexicon of belonging. The scholarship reviewed above has gone a long way toward clarifying the topic at hand, but it is significant and troubling to note that many of the concerns put forth by Walker Connor and others hold as true today as they did thirty years ago. This has been particularly evident in recent discourse on the war in Afghanistan.

On October 21, 2001, the *New York Times* published an article on the war in Afghanistan titled "After the War, Rebuild a Nation. If It's a Nation" (Schmemann 2001). This title hints at an analysis of the many different ethnic groups that comprise the Afghan population, the historical tensions among them, and the obstacles that this has and will pose to the formation and maintenance of a community with a distinctive consciousness and shared sense of mission, or, a nation. Yet, the article falls short in this regard. Its discussion of the obstacles confronting nation builders in Afghanistan mentions "an array of warring tribes," but focuses primarily on the absence of, and need for, a civil administration and an army. The next day, an editorial by Fareed Zakaria, titled "Next: Nation-Building Lite," appeared in *Newsweek*. In that article, Zakaria expresses concern about the power vacuum that is being created in Afghanistan and commends President Bush for shifting his position on nation-building to support "the stabilization of a future government." Zakaria declares that "We have no option but to create some political order in that country. Call it nation-building lite." The "lite" refers to the limited nature of the goal, which in Zakaria's view is not to turn Afghanistan into a Jeffersonian democracy, "but into a quasi-functioning state, restoring order, roads, bridges and water supplies and ending the famine-like conditions that are producing refugees" (2001, 53).

As central as factors such as a civil administration, an army, roads, and bridges may be to future stability in Afghanistan, in the pristine sense of the terms state and nation (the former referring to a territorial-political unit and the latter to a human collectivity conscious of and in some way committed to its shared identity and mission), the concerns emphasized in both of the above-mentioned articles are issues of state—not nation—building. The distinction might appear subtle, and the two entities are certainly not unrelated; but failure to differentiate nation from state and to clarify the relationship between them weakens our understanding, particularly of the former. Nor is the problem a purely academic one. It has important policy ramifications as well. Zakaria's *Newsweek* article, for example, does recognize that any new governmental structure in Afghanistan will need legitimacy and that the ethnic and tribal diversity and divisiveness of the country will pose a major obstacle in that regard (2001, 53). Yet, Connor's 1978 lament remains just as accurate today: "One searches the literature in vain for techniques by which group ties predicated upon such things as a sense of separate origin, development, and destiny are to be supplanted by loyalty to a state-structure, whose population has never shared such common feelings" (p. 384). In other words, politicians and policymakers interested in or committed to nation-building in the pristine sense of the term, or in accurately assessing its promises and pitfalls, have little to go on.

To further complicate the field, new concepts and terms have emerged recently that have the potential to increase or perpetuate the confusion. "Transnationalism" and "post-nationalism" became buzzwords during the 1990s, and even their proponents acknowledge that the sudden prominence of these concepts has been accompanied by their increasing ambiguity (Smith and Guarnizo 1998, 3). What is often unclear, for example, is what exactly is being transcended in *trans*nationalism and what is being surpassed or superseded in *post*nationalism? Furthermore, it seems that much of the ambiguity continues to be rooted in the interutilization of the terms nation and state, and, fundamentally, in the lack of an agreed upon definition of what constitutes a nation.

> "What is often unclear . . . is what exactly is being transcended in trans*nationalism and what is being surpassed or superseded in* post*nationalism? Furthermore, it seems that much of the ambiguity continues to be rooted in the interutilization of the terms nation and state, and, fundamentally, in the lack of an agreed upon definition of what constitutes a nation."*

The literature on transnationalism, although relatively new, is voluminous (Basch, Glick-Schiller, and Blanc 1994; Portes 1999a, 1999b; Smith and Guarnizo 1998; Vertovec 1999). Analytically, the term refers to a new conceptual model for understanding qualitatively different flows, networks, and practices of people, ideas, and capital. Empirically, emphasis is placed repeatedly on the crossing of borders, the breaking of boundaries, and the transgression of established forms of belonging. What becomes clear in most every discussion of transnationalism, however, is that the borders and boundaries that are being transcended or transgressed are those of states. For example, transnationalism as a concept is closely associated with immigration studies. By the 1990s, numerous immigration scholars began calling attention to an increase in and intensification of links between immigrants' home countries and host countries. In some cases these networks are described as social in nature, characterized by frequent contact as migrants continue to move back and forth between locations, or, for example, by the remittances sent back to the home community by migrants and the community of origin's reliance upon them. In other cases, transnationalism is characterized more by political ties—whether long-distance participation in elections by citizens abroad or dual citizens or the growing incidence of candidates campaigning for and winning elected office in a country where they do not currently reside (Basch, Glick-Schiller, and Blanc 1994; Portes 1999a, 1999b; Smith and Guarnizo 1998; Vertovec 1999).

Basch et al. (1994), for example, write about the Haitian community in New York, and how Haitians have been and continue to be intimately involved socially, culturally, politically, and economically with their homeland. In fact, Haiti itself is divided into nine administrative districts, known as departments, yet Haitians in the United States are commonly referred to as the Tenth Department. Similarly, Alejandro Portes (1986, 1998) frequently uses as an example of transnationalism the efforts of a Mexican enclave in Brooklyn to provide a water purification system for their Mexican village of origin. Luis Guarnizo has inventoried the economic, political, and sociocultural ties that bind Colombians in cities like New York and Los Angeles with their home country (Guarnizo, Sanchez, and Roach 1999).

What this interesting and timely literature highlights is that geographic borders are now less significant and territory less determinant than once was the case, and that crossing borders is a much less permanent, unidirectional, or irreversible process. What is not clear, however, is whether the boundaries that are being crossed or the borders that are being transcended are actually those of nations, as the terminology suggests. The most widely used examples of transnationalism do reveal that the territorial and political borders of *states* have become more porous— more easily and more frequently traversed. Yet, if it is appropriate to speak, for example, of a Haitian, Mexican, or Colombian nation, then what the above examples suggest is not the transcendence of nations, but rather their maintenance or perpetuation; consequently, the more accurate terminology for the phenomena at hand would be trans-state-nationalism.

Similar complexities surround the use of the term postnationalism. This concept also has emerged over the past decade and addresses many of the same circumstances to which the concept transnationalism is applied. One of postnationalism's most articulate proponents, Arjun Appadurai, writes:

> We are looking at the birth of a variety of complex, postnational social formations. . . . The new organizational forms are more diverse, more fluid, more ad hoc, more provisional, less coherent, less organized, and simply less implicated in the comparative advantages of the nation-state. (1996, 168)

Appadurai delineates the contours of a "postnational global order," and in doing so, he identifies various organizations ranging from Amnesty International, to Oxfam, to the Unification Church that act in opposition to, outside of, or around nation-states. Appadurai's decision to use the term nation-state may be a conscious attempt at operationalizing nations as conjoined, by definition, with states. If this is the case, the examples he uses, which are examples of a proliferation of nonstate, trans-state, or antistate actors are illustrative. Still, the global order they suggest would be more accurately characterized as post-state, or post–nation-state, not postnational.

Appadurai and theorists of transnationalism noted above are not being singled out as uniquely sloppy in their use of the terms nation and state, in fact, the contrary. If analysts of this caliber and experience become entangled in the terminological morass, all the more proof that its implications are significant. Furthermore, and to avoid creating a straw-person of the literature on trans- and postnationalism, many of these scholars are well aware of the murky waters into which they tread. Often explicit in much of this scholarship is a keen awareness of contemporary social and political realities for which conventional terms, or conventional understandings of these terms, are inadequate, and new ones do not yet exist.

We will return to these concerns below, but for now, the point is that the question of terminology is not simply a minor issue of semantics. It is related to the theoretical debates about the origins and implications of nationhood and is consequential for understanding the future of nations and nationhood in a global context. Although the search for a firm definition of nation has not yielded definitive results, a great deal of theorizing about nations and nationalism has taken place. Some of this scholarship

provides insights into the meaning of nation, but it also provides a necessary backdrop to examining how nationhood is being affected by contemporary processes of globalization. Particularly relevant, given this
chapter's interest in the implications for nationhood of a context many
would characterize as postmodern, is the large body of literature that
defines nations by reference to the conditions of modernity.

The Modernity of Nations

As is to be logically expected, the lack of a clear or widely accepted definition of what a nation is has had significant implications for theorizing about
the origins, essence, or implications of nations. Identifying the historical
birth of nations or nationhood depends, for example, on how these concepts are defined. How an analyst or policymaker determines the best
course of action, or even the available options, with regard to nationalist
conflict depends upon how he or she conceptualizes nationhood. Finally,
any normative assessment of the promises or pitfalls of nation-building or
nationalist politics is also obviously rooted in the meaning of nation. Given
these constraints, it is no wonder some scholars of nations express disap-
pointment at the current state of theoretical understanding. Nonetheless,
significant insights have accrued, and most have been related to the recognition of nations as distinctly modern, as opposed to ancient, identities and
attachments. This section will review some of the prominent explanations
for nations and nationalism with a focus on those scholars who locate
nations in the context of modernity. There have certainly been dissenters to
this view (J. Armstrong 1982; Greenfeld 1992; Hutchinson 2000; A. Smith
1986), some of whom will be discussed below, but since the 1960s the modernist perspective has become somewhat of an orthodoxy. Furthermore,
given this book's interest in how nationhood is affected by conditions many
would characterize as postmodern, understanding the nation's relationship
to the context or conditions of the modern era is a necessary foundation.

   Prior to the 1960s, most scholars who studied nationalism portrayed
nations as organic entities existing in nature since time immemorial.
Nations were invoked as independent variables to explain international
events and relations, and scholarship on nations typically took the form of
describing the history, symbols, and heroes of the nation. Anthony Smith
(1998) has described this older generation of scholars as both "perennial-
ists" and "primordialists" because of their belief in the persistent and
immemorial nature of nations as seamless wholes stretching back centuries and in their emphasis on nations as deeply rooted in ethno-cultural
and ancestral ties. He also points out that many of these scholars seemed
to adopt, however tacitly, the premises of the nationalist ideologies they
studied (p. 18).

By the 1960s, a new body of thought on nations and nationalism emerged that directly challenged the assumptions and ideas upon which this older school was based. A number of different scholars contributed to this school, and their analyses varied in important ways, but all shared a belief in the historical specificity of nations and nationalism. Specifically, they shared the belief that nations and nationalism are distinctly modern phenomena, and that the context and conditions of modernity both demanded and facilitated the birth of these national phenomena. "Modern," as it was used in this literature, signified relatively recent, not ancient, with most scholars marking the beginning of nations and nationalism at the time of the French Revolution in the late eighteenth century, or, in some cases, the middle of the nineteenth century. Modernity also referred to the modernization process itself, and to the socioeconomic, cultural, and political trends that comprised it—namely, industrialization, urbanization, increased literacy and social mobility, and the consolidation of the modern state (B. Anderson 1991; Gellner 1983; Giddens 1985; Hobsbawm 1990).

In addition to the emphasis on the historical specificity of nations, this school of thought was characterized by a related set of assumptions that contrasted sharply with those of earlier studies. Modernists have and continue to emphasize the recentness and constructedness of nations as social creations engineered by elites in pursuit of political and economic goals and for which objective ethnic or ancestral commonality is not a necessary or a sufficient precondition. Because modernists broke with the earlier view of nations as organic preexisting entities, and instead defined nations and nationalism as products and aspects of the epoch of modernity, they have been left to explain why and how these formations emerged when and as they did. The bulk of scholarship on nations and nationalism focuses on these questions precisely and, despite variations, reaches a general agreement that modernity not only contained within it the conditions that made the formation of nations feasible, but also the conditions that made nations functional or even necessary. In explaining what facilitated and/or made the nation form functional, emphases range from the socio-cultural to the economic to the political, and each of these functions and contexts is recognized as closely interrelated with the others.

"Modernists continue to emphasize the recentness and constructedness of nations as social creations engineered by elites in pursuit of political and economic goals and for which objective ethnic or ancestral commonality is not a necessary or a sufficient precondition."

Ernest Gellner (1964, 1983), for example, is well known for his thesis on nations as sociologically necessary to the era of industrialization. Nationalism, Gellner maintains, "is not the awakening of an old, latent, dormant force. . . . It is in reality the consequence of a new form of social organization, based on deeply internalized, education-dependent high cultures, each protected by its own state" (1983, 48). Nations, for Gellner, do not emerge until the period of industrialization because the conditions that make nations necessary and functional did not previously exist. Modernization, and specifically industrialization, demanded social mobility and a degree of sociocultural homogenization, in contrast to the social stratification and local differentiation that was characteristic of the premodern period. In agricultural societies, for example, culture and language were used to separate elites from peasants, but modern, growth-oriented societies required a literate populous and a high degree of cultural standardization. The modern state provided the mechanism for forging and managing these conditions, and nations were the vehicles or emergent sociocultural and political formations in and through which these conditions were met and maintained (Gellner 1983). Gellner's analysis has been criticized frequently for its functionalism (explaining the existence of nations after the fact by reference to the functions they fulfilled), but his historical account of when nations emerge and his explanations as to why and how were and continue to be widely influential (J. Hall 1998).

Gellner's analysis dealt with the economy, and specifically with the functional demands of a modern capitalist society, but other proponents of the modernist paradigm have made this an even more central focus of their explanations of the emergence of nations. From a Marxist or neo-Marxist perspective, many scholars argue that the nation-state and nationalism are rooted in the rise of capitalism. Immanuel Wallerstein, for example, describes nation as a modal term that hinges on the basic structural features of the capitalist world economy—namely, sovereign states that comprise a political superstructure to the global capitalist economy (1991, 79). Specifically, the state is seen as the political formation necessary for the free movement of goods and the regulation and maintenance of a market economy. Yet, states have problems of cohesion and a need for uniformity. Nations or national communities provide both. In other words, nations are a part of the ideological superstructure that legitimates and reproduces a particular stage of capitalist development. Tom Nairn (1977) developed this argument further, attributing nationalism to *uneven* capitalist development. Nairn locates the emergence of nationalism in underdeveloped societies that are on the periphery of the world economic core. The elite of these societies use nationalism, and typically a shared language and culture, to mobilize the masses around goals of political and economic development. Scottish nationalism, for example, has been fueled by the reality of its regional economic backwardness in contrast to English dominance in Great Britain.

In addition to emphasizing the sociocultural and socioeconomic functions of, and explanations for, nations and nationalism, several scholars focus on the nation as derivative of the modern state. One of the earliest voices of modernization theory, Karl Deutsch (1966), characterized nation-building and nations as the efforts and outcome of a modern state in need of a political community. Charles Tilly's (1975) seminal scholarship on state-building treated states as historically prior to nations, and nations as constructs forged or designed by states. Anthony Giddens has also made a significant contribution to this view of nations as politically functional and politically derived constructs. For Giddens, as for Deutsch, Tilly, and others, modernity represented a revolution in administration, bureaucratization, communication, and state consolidation. The state, Giddens famously argues, is "the pre-eminent power-container of the modern era" (1985, 120), and nations are the necessary accompanying form of human association—a distinctive property of the modern state, or what Appadurai later characterizes as "the ideological alibi of the state" (1996, 159). Scholars operating from this perspective also tend to emphasize that it is nationalism as a political ideology that makes nations, not the other way around (Hobsbawm 1990). These authors recognize, like Walker Connor, that states and nations are distinct entities, but unlike Connor they do not see them as separable.

One of the most influential voices among those tying nations to the modern era is that of Benedict Anderson. His highly influential thesis on nations as *Imagined Communities* (1991) encompasses the range of insights outlined above and pulls these together in a comprehensive analysis of when, how, and why the nation emerges and proliferates as a, actually the, universally salient cultural and political formation of the modern era. Anderson conceptualizes nations as cultural artifacts created toward the end of the eighteenth century as a result of "the spontaneous distillation of a complex crossing of discrete historical forces" (p. 4). These forces include the decline of sacred communities held together by sacred languages, the collapse of the dynastic realm, and fundamental changes in the apprehension of time. These factors comprised the context or conditions for imagining nations, whereas print-capitalism, state functionaries, maps, museums, and the census provided the mechanisms. His book develops this thesis skillfully and succinctly and provides the basis for his famous definition of the nation as "an imagined political community— and imagined as both inherently limited and sovereign" (p. 6).

The nation, according to Anderson, is imagined because the members will never know most of their fellow members. It is limited because it has finite, although elastic, boundaries. No nation, in other words, imagines itself as coterminous with humankind. Nations are sovereign because the concept is born in the midst of the age of the enlightenment, the delegitimation of divine hierarchy, and attainable dreams and expectations of being free. Here, Anderson ties nations directly to states by noting that "the gage and emblem of this freedom is the sovereign state" (1991, 7). Significantly, Anderson also emphasizes, and much of his analysis makes the case that, once created, nations "became 'modular,' capable of being transplanted, with varying degrees of self-consciousness, to a great variety of social terrains, to merge and be merged with a correspondingly wide variety of political and ideological constellations" (p. 4). In this way, Benedict Anderson's scholarship, despite its close association with the modernist paradigm, lays the groundwork for postmodern understandings of nationhood as well.

Postmodern Implications

Much of what makes the present analysis potentially interesting or relevant hinges on whether the world has actually entered or is entering a new historical epoch different in some significant ways from the one preceding it. In other words, has "modernity" indeed come to an end and, if so, what constitutes the epoch that follows it? This is a hugely complex debate that cannot and, fortunately, need not be settled here. As a topic of philosophical and empirical inquiry, the debate surfaces in a variety of disciplines, focuses on realms that range from the socioeconomic (Harvey 1990; Jameson 1984), to the political (J. Rosenau 1990; Strange 1996), to the cultural (Appadurai 1996; Bhabha 1990), and includes a wide spectrum of views, some of which proclaim a fundamentally new world and others that see little qualitative change in the current patterns or processes of the global system. The term postmodern can and has been used in reference to all of these different contexts and occurrences (P. Rosenau 1992).

Most of this discussion and debate referred to above also takes place in relation to or under the rubric of globalization. Globalization, as defined in chapter 1, entails a cluster of related changes occurring in, but not limited to, economic, technological, cultural, and political realms that are increasing the interconnectedness of the world. The theoretical and empirical scholarship about globalization is substantial, and for each thesis generated about fundamental change in the world order, there is a counterargument about continuity. The most useful insights, and those employed here, come from scholars who acknowledge the value of a middle ground position; namely, that although the constituent processes of globalization may not be entirely new, they arguably have intensified in recent decades. As David Harvey wrote in 1990, "we have been experiencing, these last two decades, an intense phase of time-space compression that has had a disorienting and disruptive impact on political—economic practices, the balance of class power, as well as upon cultural and social life" (1990, 284). Harvey acknowledges a "sea-change" but ultimately rejects the emergence of an entirely new postcapitalist or even postindustrial society.

What, then, are the implications of this contemporary context of globalization for nations and national belonging? Different scholars have explored this question, some more systematically than others. Among those who operate within the modernist framework, Eric Hobsbawm has been the most explicit in terms of anticipating the nation's future demise: "Nation-states and nations will be seen as retreating before, resisting, adapting to, being absorbed or dislocated by, the new supranational restructuring of the globe" (1990, 182). Historian William McNeill, in his treatise on *Polyethnicity and National Unity in World History* (1986), also predicted the end of the nation and the withering away of nationalism.

More recently, and writing within the literature on postnationalism discussed above, several analysts have argued that contemporary conditions ranging from technological advancement to the rise of various forms of international political and economic governance have superseded states and diminished the need for or relevance of national belonging. In her research on immigrants and refugees in Europe, Yasemin Soysal (1994, 2000) emphasizes the diminishing centrality of the nation-state as a model of community and attributes its demise to the increasing intensification of transnational discourse and legal instruments, the diffusion of sovereignty, and the emergence of multilevel polities such as the EU (2000). Meanwhile, Homi Bhabha (1990) characterizes the contemporary period as one of fragmentation and cultural hybridity amid which the notions of cultural homogeneity upon which or through which nations were formed have been thoroughly delegitimized. As noted earlier, it is not always clear whether these postnationalist scholars are describing the supersession and destabilization of the nation or of the state. More problematic, however, is that neither the postnationalists nor the modernists who suggest the nation's demise can account adequately for the contemporary persistence, even resurgence, of nationhood as a form of belonging. And, as discussed in the opening paragraphs of this chapter, the allure of nationhood persists not only among established nation-states, but also among new or newly transitioned states—whether in the case of South Africa or in projects of regional integration like the EU.

"neither the postnationalists nor the modernists who suggest the nation's demise can account adequately for the contemporary persistence, even resurgence, of nationhood as a form of belonging."

For some observers and analysts, this persistence and/or resurgence of nations and nationalism comes as no surprise and serves as validation or vindication of the earlier primordialist or perennialist approaches. Nations persist, according to this view, because they are real, historic entities with distinct ethnic cores that naturally or essentially inspire strong emotional attachments and loyalties. Anthony Smith has been a longtime proponent of conceptualizing nations via reference to their ethnic core. Nations, according to Smith, must be understood as historically embedded, "derived from pre-existing and highly particularized cultural heritages and ethnic formations" (1995, viii). In *Nations and Nationalism in a Global Era*, Smith applies his analytical framework to "the paradox of global interdependence and fissiparous nationalism" (p. 5). He argues that both postmodernists and modernists miss the mark in explaining the contemporary rebirth of nationalism. The former approach, according to Smith, is flawed in its insistence on identity, national and otherwise, as hybridized and ambivalent, and the latter in its ahistorical depiction of nations as inevitable products of modernity. Smith writes:

> Only by grasping the power of nationalism and the continuing appeal of national identity through their rootedness in pre-modern ethnic symbolism and modes of organization is there some chance of understanding the resurgence of ethnic nationalism at a time when "objective" conditions might render it obsolete. (p. 7)

John Hutchinson has also examined what he describes as the "vexed questions of relationships between national identity and globalization" (2000, 651). In doing so, he, like Smith, criticizes the modernists' focus on the rationality and novelty of nations and emphasizes instead the ethnic continuity of cultural differences across the premodern/modern divide. Ethnicity, which Hutchinson like Smith views as the core of nations, cannot be dismissed as residual or reactive (p. 653); and, nations must be understood as "long term historical collectivities that structure the forms of modernity" (p. 651) rather than being structured by them. Nations, then, are not mere products or outcomes of something else. They are independent variables in their own right. Although neither Smith or Hutchinson uses Samuel Huntington's (1993) language of civilizational clash, they operate on similar assumptions about the real, basic, and fixed nature of cultural differences.

Despite some meaningful insights, this type of approach, and the assumptions on which it is based, remain open to the same problems that originally gave rise to the modernist paradigm in the early 1960s. Many of the nations that are now capturing attention on the world stage do not constitute, either in content or form, seamless wholes stretching back centuries. President Nelson Mandela and Bishop Desmond Tutu sought not to revive an ancient or preexisting South African nation, but to forge anew a "Rainbow Nation" that would be based in large part on a rejection of the country's divisive past. The symbols, heroes, memories, and myths being invoked by leaders like Slobodan Milosevic may have a long historical past, but the ways in which they are being interpreted, and the populations and circumstances to which they are being applied, are arguably distinct from the history being resurrected. Or, at the very least, so many of the claims put forth by these and other nationalists are contestable and contested; and the blood ties being implied or invoked are of limited credibility. In fact, nationalist claims of shared blood ties, common though they are, rarely, if ever, have much basis in fact. They are, nevertheless, powerful methods of unification and dangerous in their exclusionary implications.

> *"nationalist claims of shared blood ties, common though they are, rarely, if ever, have much basis in fact. They are, nevertheless, powerful methods of unification and dangerous in their exclusionary implications."*

The value of the primordialist view is currently weakened not only by the fact that the number of nations in the world and their individual contours or constituencies are fluid, but by evidence that the form of nationhood as a mechanism of belonging is also in a state of flux. The best example, already mentioned above and seemingly on the rise, is the phenomena of transnationalism—or what would more accurately be described as trans-state nationalism. At first glance, the extension of national community and belonging across two or more states may appear to vindicate the primordialist claims that nations are entities that predate or in any case are not determined by states, and that the bonds of which they are comprised are so strong and so basic as to transcend the political and (from the perspective of the organic nation) arbitrary borders of states. However, the scholarship on transnationalism points not just to the continuation or extension of preexisting or static national ties across states, but also to the emergence of new identities, social spaces, and "transnational localities" (A. Smith 1998). One such example involves the increasing practice and policies of dual nationality (Jones-Correa 2000; Renshon 2001). All of this poses problems for both the primordialist and modernist approaches. If nationhood is a deeply felt essential attachment, how then can it be split simultaneously among two or more different nations, and if nations are created by and attached to states, how is it that they now transcend them?

Finally, the European Union also offers an example of the persistent appeal of nation-ness, but in a reconfigured form that constitutes what might best be described as trans-state nation-building. As Europe's emphasis on economic union has expanded to include efforts at political and social integration, discourse has turned to the need for a sense of belonging to the EU and the possibility of creating a European cultural identity that transcends individual member states (Wiener 1998). Montserrat Guibernau explains that "The engineers of the new Europe will have to look at 'common European trends' and design a myth of origin, rewrite history, invent traditions, rituals and symbols that will create a new identity" (1996, 114). They have done just that and the process, as Anthony Smith notes, has involved the centralized use of the cultural media, student exchanges, the invention and dissemination of pan-European myths, and the reinterpretation and popularization of pan-European history (1992). Writing in 1985, the Commission of the European Communities (CEC) stated that "European culture is marked by its diversity: diversity of climate, countryside, architecture, language, beliefs, taste and artistic style. . . . But underlying this variety there is an affinity, a family likeness, a common European identity" (CEC 1985, 1).

Europe's efforts at imagining a cultural and political community that transcends the limits of a single state represent a significant reconfiguration of some conventional models of membership (as discussed in chapter 2). Yet, what is notable is the continued importance of boundaries—territorial, cultural, social, and otherwise. As Michael Billig observes: "Thus, Europe will be imagined as a totality, either as a homeland itself or as a homeland of homelands. Either way, the ideological traditions of nationhood, including its boundary-consciousness, are not transcended" (1995, 142).

> *"Europe's efforts at imagining a cultural and political community that transcends the limits of a single state represent a significant reconfiguration of some conventional models of membership. . . . Yet, what is notable is the continued importance of boundaries—territorial, cultural, social, and otherwise."*

There is, then, ample evidence that nations and nationhood as a form of belonging persist, but are not unchanged. How and why is this the case? Intended as a critique of the modernist literature, but applicable to the postnationalist and primordialist as well, John Hutchinson writes: "[T]hese interpretations cannot satisfactorily explain the current national revival sweeping much of the globe. Moreover, since this national differentiation is occurring in a period of an allegedly global homogenization of peoples, we need a more nuanced account" (2000, 655). The following section aims to offer such an account.

Perpetual Imagining

If we accept the persistence of nations—a fact that seems currently indisputable—and reject explanations that attribute this persistence to some static, organic, essential nature of nations, then where does that leave us? One possible response is to claim that the national form is indeed a product, or at the very least an aspect, of *modernity*, but that the world is still in, or has not yet moved far enough beyond, that era to witness the ultimate demise of nations and nationalism. Such a response is not without merit. If, for example, the current era is best characterized as "high," "late," or "hypermodern," meaning that the economic, social, and political dimensions and demands of modernity have advanced and/or intensified, then we might reasonably expect hypernationalism as an accompanying social formation.

In fact, many analysts, from opposing ideological positions, make precisely this argument when they suggest, for example, that the contemporary persistence or resurgence of ethnonationalism is a response to the homogenization and sense of anomie that accompanies globalization (Barber 1992; Huntington 1993). Others argue, from a Marxist perspective, that nations, as is the case with other social formations, continue to be reducible to the workings of the world capitalist economy, however altered or intensified those workings may be (Wallerstein 1991). Both responses are problematic. The former risks invoking, implicitly if not explicitly, primordialist assumptions about nationhood by assuming a ready-made, static set of cultural attachments and traits that constitute an automatic and unified source of resistance or response to global change. The latter falls prey, as many Marxist-inspired analyses do, to economic determinism by reducing all social and political realities to the material conditions and structures of capitalism—even if those conditions and structures change. Both explanations fail to recognize that if nations are indeed constructs, then they are by definition malleable, contextual, and capable of persistence and reconfiguration amid socioeconomic and political change. A more promising explanation is one that accepts the modernist thesis that nations are historically contextual formations, shaped by the social and material conditions that surround them, but goes on to recognize that it is the very malleability of nations and nationhood that accounts for why and how they persist. Such is the case both in terms of the content with, or of which, nations are imagined and the form they assume.

Such an explanation, and the one advocated here, takes to heart Rogers

Brubaker's call that we cease treating nations as "stable axioms of being," and recognize them instead as "form, category and event" (1996, 13). The next step entails a fuller understanding of the contemporary relationship between the national form, category, or event on the one hand, and the processes and politics of globalization on the other. Avoiding the issue of how precisely to label the contemporary era or how to determine whether it is fundamentally and qualitatively new, the analysis presented here accepts that at least since the 1970s the world has been experiencing an intensification of global interconnectedness. Corporations, capital, people, and ideas are moving back and forth more freely, rapidly, and at greater distances than at any time in the past. Movement and interchange are facilitated by advances in communications and transportation technology and are also facilitated by (and contribute to) diminishing territorial and political borders. As noted above, states are affected profoundly by these changes—weakened in some arenas and strengthened in others. A careful look at these conditions of globalization, and how they are refracted through the state, can provide valuable insight into the persistence and the contemporary reconfigurations of nations and nationhood.

First, to the extent that the national form is linked to the state (though some analysts debate the nature or degree of this link, few deny that it exists), the persistence of states, however challenged or changed by globalization they may be, offers a partial explanation for the continuation of nationhood as a salient form of belonging. As was argued in chapter 2 with regard to citizenship, certain aspects of globalization that challenge the autonomy of the state serve simultaneously to invigorate the importance or appeal of nationhood. This invigoration stems both from states themselves as well as from the people who comprise a national community or potential national community. In fact, much of what is presented here regarding globalization's implications for nationhood parallels the discussion of citizenship, but with an understanding that the two forms of belonging, while related, are not synonymous.

States have long relied on nations as their raison d'être and in a period of threatened sovereignty tend to use and act to fortify the nation as an ideological alibi. This has been powerfully evident in the United States in the aftermath of the terrorist attacks of 9/11. The attacks exposed the contemporary vulnerability of states, and in particular, the United States. The rhetoric in the wake of those attacks has revolved around and relied heavily on protecting the nation and the homeland. Whether in the form of Homeland Security or the USA PATRIOT Act, what has occurred is a state-led closing of ranks around the nation and a heightened sense of the need or desire to clarify who does and does not belong to the national community. Formal, legal membership in the state, or citizenship, is one boundary that is being invoked, but other cultural, religious, and in the most insidious cases, racial criteria have come into play as well. Despite

President George W. Bush's repeated assurances to Muslim Americans that "we respect your faith," God has been central to the discourse of American nationhood, and it seems clear in most every instance that the "god" being invoked is a Christian one.

Furthermore, since 9/11, the news has been filled with reports of Arabs in the United States, many of whom are U.S. citizens, and individuals that may in some way resemble Arabs, being victims of discrimination, harassment, and violence—by the U.S. government as well as by individual U.S. citizens. In addition to the widespread detention and investigation by the state of innocent immigrants and legal residents who are Arab or Muslim (detentions that have been harshly criticized by Amnesty International and the American Civil Liberties Union), U.S. federal agents have also staged raids on the homes and institutions of what are described as among the "most respected" Muslim leaders and organizations in the United States. Throughout the country, and in other parts of the world as well, mosques have been vandalized and individual Muslim residents report no longer feeling safe in their homes, their schools, or the streets (Dunne 2002). The introduction to this book included examples from the United States, but in the north of England, shortly after 9/11, the phrase "Avenge USA—kill a Muslim now" was spray painted near a mosque (Ford 2001). And in Denmark, an anti-immigrant party that saw its popularity surge after 9/11 created a campaign poster featuring a young blonde girl and the slogan: "When she retires, Denmark will have a Muslim majority" (Finn 2002).

Muslims, and Arabs, are not being attacked and denigrated because they are not citizens, many in fact are, but because they are perceived—whether due to physical appearance, dress, or religious and cultural custom and affiliation—as not belonging to the national community. The rise of post-9/11 xenophobia indicates a distinction between belonging to a national community and possessing formal membership or residence in a state—even in the most civic-minded and purportedly ethnically neutral political communities in the world. Nor is this tendency unique to the post-September 11 context. What is important to note, however, is that the invocation by states of the interests of a national community not only allows states to guard their sovereignty in the midst of globalization, but also legitimizes and maintains the ideological and practical centrality of national belonging in a postmodern world.

Other aspects of contemporary globalization, migration in particular, also compel states to clarify and reinforce the boundaries of the nation. As noted in previous chapters, the world has, in recent decades, witnessed unprecedented human migration—whether in the form of refugees, legal migrants, or illegal aliens—all of which has posed a fundamental challenge to the sovereignty of states—namely, their right to regulate their borders. What is evident, however, is that discourse and policy related to immigration are rarely restricted to the issue of territorial borders or laws surrounding passage across those borders. Instead, state officials typically justify and pursue their border-fortification policies in the name of protecting the nation. In a recent report, *Blueprint for an Ideal Legal Immigration Policy*, former Colorado governor Richard Lamm writes: "Defining who comprises a nation will become more important as commerce becomes more global and less accountable to any one nation or community" (Center for Immigration Studies 2001, 2) The alleged threat to the national community is perceived as not only an economic one (i.e., loss of jobs), but also a cultural one. Witness the frequent references in the United States to the need to preserve American values or the English language. Similar discourse takes place throughout Europe, Australia, Japan, and other parts of the world. The result is that as states respond to encroachments upon their sovereignty, whether in the form of the unprecedented movement of people across international borders or terrorism, they not only invoke the purported interests of a national community and their role in defending it, but, in the process, they also clarify the boundaries and fortify the salience and significance of belonging to a nation.

"discourse and policy related to immigration are rarely restricted to the issue of territorial borders or laws surrounding passage across those borders. Instead, state officials typically justify and pursue their border-fortification policies in the name of protecting the nation."

Furthermore, this occurs not only within and by established states, but within newly formed or forming states as well. The new South Africa provides a telling example. Having made the transition to a post-Apartheid state, South African officials not only confronted the demands of state building, whether in the form of establishing democratic institutions or regulating the economy, but they also perceived the need to build a South African nation. This was no small task given the country's divisive past. How, for example, could the new government unite a population deeply, historically, and sometimes violently divided along lines of race, ethnicity, and class? Immigration, although not as a necessarily intentional or well-coordinated strategy, emerged as one arena in which state officials (most notably Minister of Home Affairs Mangosuthu Buthelezi), politicians, and the media forged a South African "Us" against a foreign or alien "Them." The result is a discourse in South Africa similar to that in the United States and other immigrant-receiving states that blames immigrants for problems that range from unemployment and crime to disease—all the while invoking the interests and needs of the South African nation (Croucher 1998). In 1994, for example, Buthelezi announced, "I am thinking of proposing to Cabinet to consider legislation which will impose severe punishment on people who employ illegal aliens as it is unpatriotic to employ them at the expense of our people" (*Sowetan Comment* 1994, 8). When asked to respond to the charges that South Africa is engaging in xenophobic discrimination against fellow blacks, Buthelezi stated: "I challenge the idea that if one is trying to look after the interests of South Africa, one is xenophobic" (*Economist* 1995, 40).

The South African state, however, is not the sole participant in the nation-formation process. The politics of "Us versus Them" resonates and is perpetuated by individuals in South Africa as well. As Hobsbawm (1990) has explained, nationalism is not simply a top-down process initiated by the state, but also a bottom-up one. In the context of globalization, or what James Rosenau (1990) calls, "turbulence," citizens, as well as states, experience insecurity. Xenophobia among South Africans, black and white, skyrocketed in the mid- to late 1990s. Public opinion polls, letters to the editor in all major newspapers, and political protests conveyed a widespread intolerance of "foreigners." In the most insidious cases, this intolerance took the form of armed gangs of South Africans forcibly removing immigrants from their homes (Minaar and Hough 1996). In each case, disgruntled South Africans declared that the state has a duty to protect South Africans, and that the rights and privileges of the new South Africa belong to the people of South Africa—the nation. States as actors are weakened by globalization, but they may still constitute the best bet for individuals seeking protection from the uncertainties of a changing world. Moreover, claiming membership in a nation is the best way to secure access to the state and exclude others from it—to differentiate an "Us" from a "Them."

Nationhood, then, continues to be a functional, familiar, and legitimate mechanism for belonging. We see evidence of its persistent appeal in the United States in popular support for legislation such as Proposition 187 in California and English-only movements at the local, state, and federal levels. The same is true with regard to popular support for and mobilization around restrictionist and xenophobic politics and policies in other countries as well. Across Europe, public opinion polls and elections results show voters fearful of the dilution of their national identity and of outsiders who do not share or respect their national values or culture (Finn 2002; Ford 2001).

This bottom-up thrust of nationhood is also evident among the many groups who do not currently have a state of their own, seek one, and recognize proclamations of nationhood as the most promising, although by no means guaranteed, pathway. Well-known examples include the Palestinians, Basques, Kurds, and Québécois who are fighting for a state of their own, as well as other groups such as the Catalans, Scots, Welsh, or indigenous peoples around the world who may not be seeking an independent state, but who do desire some enhanced degree of political autonomy and invoke their nationhood to make the case. Repeatedly, these groups articulate and attempt to bolster their political demands by reference to the nation-ness—whether defined by reference to history, culture, language, even blood type.

Finally, not only does globalization create conditions in which nationhood continues to be a valued and functional sociopolitical formation, but it also provides mechanisms that enhance the capacity for constructing, imagining, or maintaining nations. The primary example here points to recent advances in communications technology. Karl Deutsch (1966), one of the earliest and most influential writers on nations and modernity, focused on the central role of communications in nation-building. Similarly, Benedict Anderson's (1991) thesis on imagined communities relies heavily on the role of print media as a precondition for and primary tool of nation formation. Globalization, because it has been accompanied and propelled by advances in technology ranging from the Internet, satellites, fax machines, cell phones, as well as the sophistication and spread of existing technologies such as television, offers new and more effective opportunities for imagining nations. Anderson, himself, in a 1992 essay on "The New World Disorder," warns of the "long-distance nationalist" who "finds it tempting to play identity politics by participating (via propaganda, money, weapons, any way but voting) in the conflicts of his imagined *Heimat*—now only fax-time away" (p. 13).

> *"not only does globalization create conditions in which nationhood continues to be a valued and functional sociopolitical formation, but it also provides mechanisms that enhance the capacity for constructing, imagining, or maintaining nations."*

From the perspective of states, television has proven to be a valuable technological tool for nation-shaping. Although not a new technology, television has spread exponentially over the past decades. As noted in chapter 1, between 1965 and 1996, the number of television receivers in the world went from 192 million to 1,361 million, and the number of televisions per 1,000 people worldwide went from 57 to 236 (UNDP 1999, 4). South Africa again proves to be an illustrative case, this time regarding the use of television in nation formation. As noted above, in the post-Apartheid context, the new South African government turned to signs and symbolism of nationhood in an effort to unite a disparate population. In addition to the exclusionary reliance on an immigrant "Other" to fortify a South African "Us," the state, via the South African Broadcasting Corporation (SABC), mounted a massive public broadcasting effort to promote national unity through cultural diversity. Centered on the slogan *Simunye*—a Zulu word that in English translates into "we are one"—all three SABC stations broadcast repeated images of South Africans with varied skin tones, accents, and attire singing, dancing, and joyfully proclaiming "*Simunye*—we are one." Writing about the South African case, Chris Barker acknowledges that no television slogan, however well intended, will create a utopian nation out of the chaos that has been South Africa: "Yet, success in material terms depends in good measure on how people think about themselves and others, that is, how they are constituted culturally. . . . Imagining 'us' as 'one' is part of the process of nation building and there is no medium which has been able to speak to as many people in pursuit of that goal as television" (1999, 5–6).

Arguments about the role of television in constructing national identity have also been made with reference to broadcasts of national sporting events and *telenovelas* (Latin soap operas) in Latin America (Martin-Barbero 1995). Furthermore, the *telenovelas* broadcast to the U.S. Spanish-speaking market have also been significant in terms of their promotion of a shared sense of Latino cultural identity in the United States (Lopez 1995). In this particular case, television is helping to forge a sense of "nation" that is not tied to any particular state.

Television has also been instrumental in attempting to create a sense of trans-state Europeanness within the European Union. Recognizing the importance of a sense of belonging to the project of European integration, and the difficulty of rooting such belonging in criteria of ethnicity, language, or religion, EU officials turned to public television broadcasting as a means to form a European public sphere and common European culture (Morley and Robins 1995). In 1984, the European Community published a Green Paper on *Television without Frontiers*, noting that "Information is a decisive, perhaps the only decisive factor in European unification. . . . A European identity will only develop if Europeans are adequately informed. At present, information via the mass media is controlled at the national level" (cited in P. Schlesinger 1994, 28). In the years that followed, similar documents were published such as the Council of Europe's *European Convention on Transfrontier Television*; and, in 1991, the EC's *Television without Frontiers* directive went into effect, designed to encourage and facilitate television broadcasting across national frontiers and a market for European audiovisual production. This development of European television has been encouraged via regulatory measures and conventions, and production has been stimulated by various EU-funded ventures—the largest of which was known as MEDIA, and consumed $280 million between 1991 and 1995.

As in the South African case, these efforts at "nation"-building also relied upon an "Other" to forge an "Us"—in this case the United States constituted the "Other." Schlesinger writes: "Characteristically, the role of audiovisual media in constructing a European identity has been officially defined by counterposition to a culturally invasive other, namely the United States" (1994, 28). He also quotes various EU officials and prominent figures in Europe's culture industry who describe a "culture war" with the United States. Of primary concern is the cultural domination of Hollywood and the perceived threat of Americanization. The American share of Europe's film industry hovers, for example, around 75 percent, while in the United States, the non-American share of the box office is a mere 2 percent (Morley and Robins 1995, 18). Europe has imposed quotas on non-European programming, and many Europeans see a common European culture, forged largely through television and cinematic production, as the only form of cultural defense. At a 1989 conference held in Paris, then president of the European Commission Jacques Delors declared: "I would simply like to pose a question to our American friends: do we have the right to exist? Have we the right to preserve our traditions, our heritage, our languages?" (quoted in J. Schlesinger 1994, 29).

The European Union offers only one example of how communications technology facilitates the imagining of community beyond the geographic boundaries of individual states, and television is just one vehicle for nation formation or maintenance. Furthermore, although the examples above point to states, or a suprastate, using technology to shape a national community, technology also offers opportunities for stateless nations or ethnic groups to subvert the control of a state or states. With regard to public broadcasting, for example, satellite dishes and cable networks offer hundreds of channels from which to choose, lessening the impact of state-sponsored programming. Through this and various other forms of globalizing technology—cell phones, e-mail, the World Wide Web—individuals and groups within and across states may resist state-led efforts at nation-building and/or pursue alternative forms of national community. Chris Barker suggests precisely this when he writes that "the globalization of television has provided a proliferating resource for both the deconstruction and reconstruction of cultural identities" (1999, 3).

What these various examples indicate is that aspects of contemporary globalization, whether in the form of international economic interdependence, technological advancement, or unprecedented human migration, create a context in which nationhood as a form of belonging persists and even flourishes. States that find their autonomy and sovereignty under siege turn, in defense, to their role as representatives and defenders of nations. Individuals and groups who inhabit a particular state view membership in that state as a refuge from global turbulence and nationhood as a mechanism for clarifying the boundaries of who belongs to the political community and who does not. Newly emerging polities, whether in the form of states or suprastate organizations like the EU, see the signs and symbols of nationhood as the most promising path for the consolidation of a community identified with and attached to said polity. Groups of people who desire greater political autonomy or a state of their own also recognize that claiming the status of nation legitimizes and hence improves their chances of achieving that goal. And all of these actors make their claims with the aid of new and sophisticated communications technology. Significantly, the content being invoked, whether by states or by nations with political aspirations, is not static or "natural"; nor are the formations of nationhood that take shape consistent or standard.

On the basis of this evidence, then, it seems safe to conclude that the imagining of nations is, can, and likely will continue irrespective of the specific historical epoch at hand. But specific political and socioeconomic conditions will shape and reshape the content, the form, and the process of the imagining. This conclusion is consistent with a recent essay by Alexander Motyl (2002) in which he critiques the artificial and misleading rivalry between constructivist and modernist approaches to nations on the one hand and primordial and perennial ones on the other. Recognizing nations as constructed rather than primordial need not restrict their construction to the modern era. Nor does an acknowledgment of the persistence of nations imply an acceptance of their primordiality. Nations, in other words, can be perennially, or perpetually, constructed. Motyl's essay focuses on how constructivist insights can be extended backward to account for the existence of nations and nationalism in a premodern era. This analysis extends the theoretical reach of constructivism forward to explain national phenomena in a context past or post modernity.

It is important to acknowledge that although the contemporary world context differs in significant respects—economically, technologically, culturally, and politically—from that to which Benedict Anderson attributed the imagining of nations, little of what is now occurring in the world, or what is being presented here as explanation, is inconsistent with Anderson's theorizing. He, himself, wrote in 1983, and saw no need to revise in 1991, that "the 'end of the era of nationalism', so long prophesied, is not remotely in sight. Indeed, nation-ness is the most universally legitimate value in the political life of our time" (1991, 3). Furthermore, the thrust of Anderson's analysis focuses on the historically contextual variations in the national form, and the ways in which the idea of the nation once conceived could be, and was, widely pirated: "nation proved an invention on which it was impossible to secure a patent" (p. 67).

Industrialization and capitalism as they existed in the late eighteenth and nineteenth centuries have clearly given way to a different socioeconomic context—whether we describe it as postindustrialism, post-Fordism, late capitalism, or some other such moniker. In the process, the role of states has been reconfigured, but states continue to be key actors in the world system. This contemporary context does not diminish, and may invigorate, the need for national legitimacy on the part of states, and the need, on the part of individuals, for secure membership in a nation-state. Yet, the interconnectedness that results from economic, political, cultural, and technological globalization also motivates and facilitates new forms of imagining that transcend states. Meanwhile, the mechanisms of imagining have also shifted from print capitalism, as Anderson emphasized, to mass media and the Internet. In other words, the contemporary context of globalization necessitates an updated understanding of the politics and process of national imaginings. This analysis aims to contribute to that understanding.

Conclusion

This chapter maintains that, contrary to the claims of postnationalists and the predictions of some modernists, nations, nationalism, and nation-states have not disappeared. Instead, "nation" continues to be widely available and resonant as a cultural and political category. Nor can the persistence of nations and nationhood be explained by invoking their eternal or organic essence. Rather, it is the very malleability of nationhood, both in content and form, that explains its persistence. Yet, as useful as this emphasis on malleability is for explaining the persistence and reconfiguration of nations and nationhood, it is vulnerable to two related criticisms.

"it is the very malleability of nationhood, both in content and form, that explains its persistence. Yet, as useful as this emphasis on malleability is for explaining the persistence and reconfiguration of nations and nationhood, it is vulnerable to criticism."

The first of these criticisms, and one frequently leveled at the modernist approach to nationalism in general, is the charge of functionalism. Essentially, this chapter maintains that the contemporary conditions of globalization provide the motivation and mechanisms for imagining, and perpetuating already imagined, nations. In short, nationhood persists as a form of belonging, despite significant changes in the social and material conditions of its imagining, because it tends to work. This is not a meaningless conclusion, but what it fails to explain is *why* nations are so functional; or what about the national form is so appealing or effective. One response to these questions, and a response that moves somewhat beyond the mere functionality of nations, suggests that, once imagined, social formations and concomitant social science concepts are not easily unimagined. Nationhood as a form of belonging is deeply embedded in an international system (read: inter-state system) that has long enshrined the dual principles of national self-determination and state sovereignty. Valery Tishkov alludes to this embeddedness when he notes, "*nation* is a metaphorical category that has acquired emotional and political legitimacy" (2000, 640). He also goes on to argue that this vague but "politically alluring" term persists, in large part, because states continue to comprise the most powerful form of human collectivities and possess the resources and legitimacy to be called *nations* (pp. 640–41).

Yet, the term nation has allure not only for practitioners of or participants in nationalist politics, but also for analysts. Basch et al. (1994) recognize this in their book *Nations Unbound*, when they emphasize the need for social science itself to become unbound from static categories and units of analysis—namely, the nation-state. Yasemin Soysal echoes this concern in her critique of Diaspora as an analytical category that is so wedded to the nation-state model that it fails to capture "the transgressions of the national" and "the new dynamics and topography of membership" (2000, 1). These concerns echo those of Thorstein Veblen who warned of "trained incapacity." This refers to the tendency of some concepts or models (in this case nationhood) to become so predominant as to obscure the capacity of analysts to see or think beyond them (quoted in R. Smith 1998, 197). However, as was suggested in the earlier discussion of the terms transnational and postnational, even the scholarship that attempts to transcend or move beyond the conceptual reliance on nations and states gets trapped by both the predominance and ambiguity of these terms. This trap can be attributed in large part to the very malleability of *nation*—the social reality and the terminology—both of which are so poorly defined as to be amenable to widely varied application and interpretation by both analysts and practitioners.

Herein lies a second weakness of the "perpetual imagining" thesis presented here, and one that returns to the definitional dilemma introduced earlier. Namely, of what use is the concept of nation if it cannot be clearly defined and can be so widely applied and loosely interpreted as to lack any degree of analytical precision? In other words, of course nations will be perpetually imagined if any and every form of human association has access to the title and analysts can appropriately apply it to any form of human association. In this regard, Tishkov offers what appears, at least in the theory, to be a promising solution—namely, that we "forget the nation" (2000, 625). Having argued that nation is a "ghost word, escalated to a level of metacategory through historic accident and inertia of intellectual prescription" (p. 625), he proposes that the major clients for being a nation—states and ethnic groups—be prohibited the luxury of the label, and that that prohibition begin with intellectuals mustering the courage to dispense with nation as an academic concept. In other words, neither states nor ethnic groups can any longer defend or justify their actions and existence, or base their legitimacy on claims of nationhood—eliminating simultaneously both civic and ethnic claims to nationhood. Scholars themselves must stop relying uncritically on the concept of nation to explain political behavior. Also critical of the confusion surrounding the term nation, Alexander Motyl suggests that perhaps it is ethnic group, or Anthony Smith's term "ethnie," that should be consigned to the conceptual ash heap (Motyl 2002, 245).

These suggestions are appealing in certain respects, but not likely practical. Whereas it is clear that analysts play a crucial role in constructing that which we seek to explain, it is not clear that simply choosing to ignore the widespread use and appeal of the notion or terminology of nation will advance our understanding of it. This is particularly the case given that globalization has done little to diminish the nation's political, ideological, terminological, or academic appeal, and in many cases has invigorated it. We are, then, stuck with the "nation"—politically and academically, practically and theoretically. Motyl seems to reach a similar conclusion when he writes: "If only because the field is bereft of conceptual contenders, modernity can only continue to breed nationalism" (1999, 113). To argue that nations will be perpetually imagined need not, however, reify their existence as real or static entities. Instead, students and analysts of nationalism are called upon to accept the nation as a social construction, to continue to examine the political implications and applications of the construction, and to ground the content, form, and practice of nationhood in the social and material conditions of their making—particularly as those conditions are now in a state of profound flux. Accomplishing these goals will also require a sound understanding of ethnicity—a topic the next chapter addresses.

4

Constructed Ethnicities,
Global Contingencies

L ong before the results of the 2000 U.S. presidential election were
finalized, Republicans and Democrats began strategizing for the
2004 election. Top among their concerns has been figuring out how
to capture the Hispanic vote—a group identified by the 2000 Census as
the largest ethnic minority in the United States. Party strategists have
been furiously polling Hispanic populations, conducting focus groups,
and calculating outcomes to determine which party's candidate needs
what percentage of the Hispanic vote to win. Meanwhile, potential candidates from both parties have been meeting with Hispanic organizations,
peppering their speeches with Spanish words and phrases, and visiting
Mexico and other Latin American countries from where many immigrants to the United States come and with which many in the United
States continue to maintain close ties (Lester 2002; Malone 2002). Elsewhere in the world, ethnicity also weighs heavily on the minds of political leaders and populations—often in more immediate and destructive
form. Throughout the former Soviet Republics and Eastern Europe, for
example, the collapse of communism ushered in an era of ethnic conflict
bloody and devastating in a way few could have imagined. Ethnic identities that had appeared to be nonissues throughout the Cold War became
the issues in its aftermath—issues of war and peace, issues of life and
death. This has been the case not only in the most infamous examples
from the Balkans, but also in Tajikistan, the Ossetian region of Georgia,
and the breakaway Russian Republic of Chechnya.

These are just a few of the countless places and ways in which ethnicity has and continues to permeate headlines. In fact, if the twentieth century, as has been suggested, was a century of nationalism, the 1990s were a decade of ethnicity. Ethnicity and ethnic politics are not new, but, as Milton Esman points out, "What distinguishes the current era is not the existence of competitive ethnic solidarities but their global political salience" (1994, 2). As the new millennium arrived, there was some indication that ethnicity could be managed. Northern Ireland was at peace, and separatists in Quebec, Canada, continued to mobilize, but not violently. There was and is, however, little indication of ethnicity's demise. The persistence, and in some cases resurgence, of ethnicity is puzzling for at least two reasons. First, ethnic identification and differentiation seem to surge at the same rate that seemingly objective indicators of ethnic difference appear to diminish or decline. Many researchers, for example, have reported classic signs of assimilation among immigrant ethnic groups in countries around the world: native language loss, increases in intermarriages, and declines in traditional religious practices. This creates what Abner Cohen describes as a "sociological paradox" in which ethnic groups can appear to be "rapidly losing their cultural distinctiveness . . . [while] also emphasizing and exaggerating their cultural identity and exclusiveness" (cited in Nagel 1986, 94). Second, and similar to the case of nationhood, the fact that ethnicity continues to hold power and appeal is puzzling in that it defies predominant theories and intellectual frameworks—namely, liberalism and Marxism—that long ago predicted ethnicity's demise.

Interestingly, these two most influential paradigmatic dismissals of ethnicity are closely associated with the two regions of the world that provide the above examples of ethnicity's prominence and appeal—the United States and the former Soviet bloc. Liberal pluralism, which has been theorized largely within and with reference to the West and the United States, predicted that traditional, or parochial, attachments such as those rooted in kinship, clan, or ethnicity would dissipate in the face of modernization. Particularism would give way to universalism, ethnic groups and immigrants would assimilate, and the identities that remained would be functionally specific to the demands of a modern society and economy. Marxism also anticipated the end of ethnicity. For Marx and Engels, ethnicity, along with race, religion, gender, and nationhood, were all forms of false consciousness that masked people's real interest in economic status, or class. Modernization for Marxists meant that the contradictions and crises of capitalism would become so glaring that an international class-consciousness would supplant irrational or primordial attachments such as ethnicity.

As oppositional as liberalism and Marxism might be, both are products of the enlightenment and its emphasis on rationalism and universalism;

neither has had the capacity to deal with the seemingly irrational particularism of ethnicity. To fill this intellectual vacuum, a growing body of scholarship on ethnic identity, ethnic relations, and ethnic conflict has emerged since the 1970s. The bulk of this literature fits within one of two approaches: *primordialism* conceptualizes ethnicity as a deeply felt emotional attachment to ancestral ties; *instrumentalism* portrays it as the result of rational calculation in pursuit of political or economic gain. This chapter operates on the premise laid out in chapter 1 that the most useful insights into ethnicity and other forms of identity come from the constructivist emphasis on fluidity and contextuality. The chapter begins with definitional background on the meaning of ethnicity and a review of the theoretical debates on it origins. The notion of "constructed primordiality" is then presented as the most useful lens for examining ethnic phenomena. The final section combines a constructivist view of ethnicity with an emphasis on the contemporary context of globalization.

> *"As oppositional as liberalism and Marxism might be, both are products of the enlightenment and its emphasis on rationalism and universalism; neither has had the capacity to deal with the seemingly irrational particularism of ethnicity."*

Conceptual Clarification

As with other forms of belonging analyzed in this book, ethnicity is a contested concept. Definitions of ethnicity typically point to a group of people with common ancestry and shared culture. The cultural attributes that an ethnic group is purported to share commonly include language, religion, kinship patterns, and physical appearance. Precise conceptualizations of ethnicity are as varied as the people using them, but German sociologist Max Weber's definition is one of the most classic, widely cited, and representative of the field. Weber writes:

> We shall call "ethnic groups" those human groups that entertain a subjective belief in their common descent because of similarities of physical type or of customs or both, or because of memories of colonization and migration. (1968, 389)

Weber, like many scholars after him, is careful to emphasize that what is most important with regard to ancestry is not the objective fact of common blood ties, but the subjective belief in common descent. This is an important point, particularly in terms of making a distinction between an ethnic group and an ethnic category. Groupness, for example, necessitates some degree of self-consciousness. But, ethnicity is also a category. It is a label that is frequently applied to people, or a series into which people are placed, whether by the state, the media, the academy, or other institutions or groups. In other words, ethnicity, as Cornell and Hartmann (1998) explain, is both asserted and assigned.

For our purposes, what is as important as the wording of the definition of ethnicity or ethnic group is the question of how to distinguish ethnicity from nationhood. As noted in chapter 3, nations are imagined communities and the content of their imagining is quite often cultural, linguistic, religious, racial, and ancestral—in other words, ethnic. In fact, even nation-building projects that claim or set out to avoid ethnic criteria as a precondition for belonging find it difficult to do so. From this perspective, then, ethnicity and nationhood are closely related. They are not, however, synonymous. Weber, himself, makes the distinction when he acknowledges that nationhood shares in common with ethnicity notions of common descent and some degree of cultural homogeneity, but he goes on to emphasize that "the sentiment of ethnic solidarity does not by itself make a nation" (1968, 389).

For Weber and other scholars, the difference between ethnicity and nation lies within the degree of self-consciousness, and, specifically, political self-consciousness that characterizes these attachments. When writing on the "nation," Weber contends that if "there is at all a common object lying behind the obviously ambiguous term 'nation,' it is apparently located in the field of politics." He goes on to explain: "a nation is a community which normally tends to produce a state of its own" (1948, 179). Similarly, Benedict Anderson's famous definition of nation points to an imagined *political* community and emphasizes sovereignty, specifically the sovereign state, as a key dimension of the imagining. When it comes to most definitions of ethnicity, however, the state, or an emphasis on the field of politics, is not a common element and is in fact largely absent. This is not to suggest that ethnic groups do not act politically, or that some ethnic groups cannot or will not seek a state of their own. But once an ethnic group achieves a degree of political self-consciousness that manifests itself as widespread support for or mobilization in pursuit of a state, they have become a nation.

A final distinction of importance is that between ethnicity and race, primarily because the two terms are so frequently conjoined. The literature on race is voluminous and its complexities are much too rich to be adequately captured by this brief overview (see Back and Solomos 2000; Winant 2001). Compared to the other social formations featured in this book, race, in how it is approached and perceived, is the most closely associated with physical characteristics and, although problematically, with biology and genetics. In technical terms, a race is typically defined as "a genetically distinct sub-population of a given species" (Cornell and Hartmann 1998, 21). Yet, as so many scholars have demonstrated, the idea that humans can be classified into four or five distinct races is scientifically untenable, at best absurd, and avaricious at worst (Gould 1996; Montagu 1974).

Races, in other words, like nations, and, as will be shown in this chapter, like ethnic groups as well, are constructed. The construction is not arbitrary, however, and it is far from harmless or inconsequential. In other words, the social definition of racial categories or classifications has drawn upon physical attributes—skin tone or facial features, for example—largely because these are among the most visible markers of difference. Yet, if the goal were simply to identify genetically distinct subpopulations of humans, any number of different combinations are available. For example, humankind could be divided into two distinct subpopulations based on the gene for hemoglobin. Equatorial Africans, Greeks, and Italians would fall into one "sickle-cell" race, while South African Xhosas and Swedes fall into the other. There is also a gene that determines the scooped out shape of the back of the front teeth. Based on this genetic trait, Asians, Native Americans, and Swedes comprise the same race. Humans can also be subdivided by the lactase gene for digesting milk sugar. Norwegians, Arabians, north Indians, and the Fulani of Nigeria have the gene, while other African groups, Japanese, and Native Americans do not. Furthermore, if we were to select any two "black" people at random and compare their chromosomes, they are no more likely to be genetically similar than either would be when compared to a randomly selected "white" person (Begley 1995). The point is, however, that race-making has never been a purely or simply scientific endeavor. Rather, it is a political project that utilizes science, typically pseudo-science, to further specific social and political aims.

> *"Races, in other words, like nations, and, as will be shown in this chapter, like ethnic groups as well, are constructed. The construction is not arbitrary, however, and it is far from harmless or inconsequential."*

How, then, is race different from ethnicity? In addressing the question of whether races are ethnic groups, Cornell and Hartmann offer an honest albeit equivocal response: "sometimes yes, sometimes no" (1998, 25). In other words, the two categories are not mutually exclusive, they can and do overlap. But, they are also not synonymous. As noted above, both formations—ethnicity and race—are social constructions. So, when we examine their differences, we are examining differences in how these categories and/or attachments have been socially defined, responded to, and manipulated. In this regard, there are relevant differences in the two, if only to a slight degree. Race, for example, is and historically has been more closely intertwined with the uses and abuses of power—both in the world system at large and in individual states and societies around the world. Colonialism, slavery, and genocide all turn to race as their legitimating ideologies—whether to justify the exploitation of indigenous peoples, the enslavement of Africans, or the extermination of Jews.

For this reason, and in this way, race has also been deeply imbued with notions of inferiority and superiority, as well as with the belief that race itself and the behaviors or attributes that allegedly flow from it are inherent and unchanging. Racial difference alone has not typically been sufficient to justify exploitation, enslavement, or elimination of one group by another. The victimized group also needed to be seen as ignorant, evil, lazy, untrustworthy, threatening, and the perpetrators as superior, justified in their actions, even benevolent. It was no mistake, then, that when scientists or taxonomists like Carolus Linnaeus identified four distinct races of humans, white (Europeans), red (Native Americans), dark (Asians), and black (Africans), they attached the following character traits: Native Americans were ruled by custom; Africans were indolent and negligent; and Europeans were gentle and inventive!

Linnaeus's categorization scheme is also evidence that racial designation is typically just that, designation. Race, more so than ethnicity, is likely to be assigned from outside or above by a powerful group or institution than to be self-asserted. It is also more likely to rely upon and invoke perceived physical differences (Cornell and Hartmann 1998). Skin color is a common marker of racial difference, but by no means the only one. When Irish immigrants first came to America, they were considered a separate race distinct from and inferior to the Saxon race. American heroes such as Ralph Waldo Emerson described the Irish as "deteriorated in size and shape, the nose sunk, the gums exposed"—evidence of a "diminished brain" (cited in Lind 1995, 29). For Benjamin Franklin, the Spaniards, Italians, French, Russians, Swedes, and Germans "are generally of what we call a swarthy complexion," in contrast to the Saxons and the English who "make up the principal body of white people on the face of the earth" (cited in Lind 1995, 47–48).

Similar characteristics ranging from the shape of the skull, the jaw line, and eye color were used in Nazi Germany to define Jews as a separate and inferior race. And as will be discussed later, many believe that Hutus and Tutsis in Rwanda constitute distinct races largely by virtue of different height and body build. As stated earlier, the notion of humankind as divided into four or five distinct races has no basis in scientific fact. Furthermore, ample evidence exists of the fluidity of race, whether at the level of individuals or groups whose racial identities are ambiguous and shifting. In a study of infant deaths in the United States between 1983 and 1985, the Centers for Disease Control found a surprising number of cases in which the infant had a different race on its death certificate from the one on its birth certificate (L. Wright 1996, 53). A similar fluidity applies to groups whose racial designation has shifted over time. As noted earlier, the Irish, for example were not always "white," nor were other groups such as Italians who are now comfortably considered members of that ambiguous category (Rasmussen 2001). Nonetheless, notions of permanency, physicality, and inferiority have been the building blocks of race, and race has been one of the most powerful, persuasive, and detrimental social constructions of all time.

All of these claims can also be made about ethnicity. It can be closely connected to power and politics, imbued with notions of inferiority and superiority, perceived to be inherent, assigned rather than asserted, and associated with physical attributes. But, although these traits may be present with regard to ethnicity, they are rarely if ever absent from constructions of race. Meanwhile, students of identity must, at some level, take social formations and categorizations as they present themselves— remaining ever cognizant of their constructedness and overlap. Race and ethnicity do continue to operate as distinct social realities. Take, for example, the case of Hispanics in the United States. Hispanic itself is a constructed category, but it is constructed, practiced, and perceived as a distinction of ethnicity. Within that category, race also exists as a separate distinction—Cuban Americans, for example, can be classified (i.e., by the U.S. Census), perceived (by other groups), or self-identified as Hispanic and as black or white. Furthermore, the constructions of race, ethnicity, and other identity formations discussed in this book overlap and intersect in complex ways. Ethnic identity may draw upon race, as nationhood may draw upon ethnicity, and citizenship has relied upon, as well as defined and perpetuated, all of these identities. These intersections will be further elaborated in chapter 5, but, for now, we turn to the theories and frameworks used to explain ethnicity as a form of belonging.

Primordialism versus Instrumentalism

After being generally ignored by scholars on both ends of the ideological spectrum, ethnicity emerged during the 1970s as a topic of substantial interest—primarily to anthropologists and to scholars studying developing societies. It soon became evident, however, that the power and persistence of ethnicity was not confined to the developing world, and that the relevance of ethnicity extended well beyond the discipline of anthropology. Interest in the subject increased dramatically, and by the 1990s, ethnicity was the focus of numerous journals and countless articles, a course offering at most colleges, and the theme of many academic and policymaking conferences. As noted above, until recently the discussion and debate on ethnicity broke down into two competing paradigms—primordialism and instrumentalism—each with a different set of assumptions about the nature of ethnic identity, ethnic mobilization, and ethnic relations.

The primordialist perspective draws much from the work of sociologist Edward Shils and anthropologist Clifford Geertz writing in 1950s and 1960s. Both scholars were interested in the deeply held emotional, natural, and in Geertz's words, "some would say spiritual," affinities or attachments that exist within human groups or communities (1963, 110). Shils rejected specifically the emerging modernization perspective of the time, which asserted that industrialization and democratization would diminish traditional, "irrational" bonds such as kinship or village and give rise to rational, individualized societies based on universal values and utilitarian interests. Instead, he maintained that even the most seemingly "rational" and large-scale of organizations, including modern society, were bound together not by utilitarian calculation, but by personal relationships and the human need for and tendency to commune and interconnect. Modern society, according to Shils, is not soulless, but "is held together by an infinity of personal attachments, moral obligations in concrete contexts, professionals and creative pride, individual ambition, primordial affinities and a civil sense" (1957, 131). Geertz, whose work was heavily influenced by Shils, further developed this concept of primordial ties, which he described as having

> an ineffable, and at times overpowering, coerciveness in and of themselves. One is bound to one's kinsman, one's neighbor, one's fellow believer, ipso facto; as the result not merely of personal affection, practical necessity, common interest or incurred obligation, but at least in great part by virtue of some unaccountable, absolute import attributed to the tie itself. (1963, 109)

Geertz and Shils both emphasized the role of kinship, family, and blood ties as among the "assumed givens of social existence" from which primordial attachments stem (Geertz 1963, 109).

Neither Shils nor Geertz focused solely on ethnicity per se, but a generation of scholars would come to draw repeatedly on their portrayals of the power of primordial ties in order to explain the persistence of ethnicity in a modern world. In 1974, anthropologist Harold Isaacs published an article, and later a book, on "basic group identity" titled "Idols of the Tribe" (1974, 1975). Ethnicity, according to Isaacs, is a form of "basic group identity," which, in his words, "consists of the ready-made set of endowments and identifications that every individual shares with others from the moment of birth by the chance of the family into which he is born at that given time in that given place" (1974, 26). Isaacs broke down basic group identity into eight constituent parts: the physical body, a person's name, the history and origins of the group into which one is born, nationality, language, religion, culture, and the geography of one's birthplace (1974, 26–27). These, according to Isaacs and psychologists such as Erik Erikson and Sigmund Freud, upon whose work he drew, comprise primal dimensions of any individual's sense of being and belonging. Isaacs goes on to argue that "man's essential tribalism is so deeply-rooted in the conditions of his existence that it will keep cropping out of whatever is laid over it, like trees forcing their way through rocks on mountainsides a mile high" (1974, 16).

> *" 'man's essential tribalism is so deeply-rooted in the conditions of his existence that it will keep cropping out of whatever is laid over it, like trees forcing their way through rocks on mountainsides a mile high.' "*

Some scholars, such as Pierre Van Den Berghe, have turned to sociobiology to explain ethnicity. He argues, for example, that ethnic and race sentiments are to be understood as an extended and attenuated form of kin selection (1978, 402). Similarly, Paul Shaw and Yuwa Wong (1989) contend that a consciousness of group affinity is imprinted in the genetic code. Most analysts, however, who proffer a primordial view of ethnicity avoid genetic references and argue instead that it is necessary to grasp the psychological and cultural dimensions of ethnicity in order to explain "the powerful emotional charge that appears to surround or to underlie so much of ethnic behavior" (A. Epstein 1978, xi).

As noted in chapter 1, the primordialist view and the assumptions that underlie it persist—whether among scholars, public officials, the media, or in the public mind more generally. The term primordial may or may not explicitly enter the discourse, but the tendency to attach to ethnicity a primal significance and/or to explain the power and persistence of ethnic identity and ethnic group conflicts by reference to ethnicity's deep embeddedness is common. In his 1993 book *Pandaemonium*, former New York senator Daniel Patrick Moynihan scripts what is essentially a two-hundred-page "I told you so," in which he chastises fellow policymakers for failing to recognize the power and persistent appeal of ethnicity in the former Soviet Union, and, hence, to anticipate ethnicity's role in the USSR's demise. Similarly, when political scientist Donald Horowitz published his analysis of South Africa's pending transition from Apartheid rule in the early 1990s, he urged policymakers and scholars not to dismiss the potency of ethnicity and ethnic identities in a country better known for its racial divisions. He argued that ethnic heterogeneity is real in South Africa and likely to become preeminent in place of race. It is not, Horowitz argues, a mask for something else, such as class, and if participants in or analysts of South Africa's political future ignore ethnicity, they will make the same grave mistake modernization theorists of the 1950s and 1960s made when they failed to anticipate the obstacles ethnicity would pose for nation-state building in much of the rest of Africa (1991, 29–30).

The primordialist portrayal of ethnicity also shows up frequently in media reports of ethnic tensions around the world, as is echoed in the speeches and interviews of prominent leaders as well. In a 1995 interview with Larry King, former President Bill Clinton explained the crisis in the Balkans by noting that "It's tragic, it's terrible, but their enmities go back five hundred years, some would say almost a thousand years." Interestingly, Clinton articulated a different understanding of the crisis months later when he pointed out that "Bosnia once found unity in its diversity." The lives of the groups in conflict were "woven together by marriage and culture" (quoted in Cornell and Hartmann 1998, 144–45). Clinton was not alone in this revised view. Many scholars and observers of the conflict in Yugoslavia came forward to point out that the hatred that was being widely portrayed as ancient was actually quite recent. Prior to the late 1980s, Serbs, Croats, and Muslims in Bosnia, all of whom spoke the same language, had lived side by side as neighbors and friends and had married and shared families. What was now happening was best portrayed as the tragic result of opportunistic political manipulation by nationalist leaders capitalizing on a power vacuum left in wake of the collapse of communism in the region (Woodward 1995). This latter view is representative of the instrumentalist approach to ethnicity, which contradicts, on most every dimension, the primordialist claims.

"Prior to the late 1980s, Serbs, Croats, and Muslims in Bosnia, all of whom spoke the same language, had lived side by side as neighbors and friends and had married and shared families. What was now happening was best portrayed as the tragic result of opportunistic political manipulation by nationalist leaders capitalizing on a power vacuum left in wake of the collapse of communism in the region."

Instrumentalism emerged during the 1970s and rejected primordialism's emphasis on the deep-rootedness, spirituality, or naturalness of ethnicity. Instead, this large and varied body of scholarship attributes the persistence of ethnicity to the functions it fulfills in terms of interest aggregation and group mobilization in pursuit of economic or political gain. In other words, ethnicity is not about spiritual affinity, but, rather, stems from utilitarian calculations and, as many analysts argue, self-serving manipulation by political elites (Bowen 1996). Studies of ethnicity and ethnic politics thus shifted from the masses to the elite, from deeply held values to careful calculations, and from irrationality to rationality (Kasfir 1986).

The instrumentalist literature has taken many different forms. Prominent among them are studies that focus on economic competition and conflict as the source of what is widely, and in their view mistakenly, portrayed as ethnic tension. Inspired by Marxism, much of this literature emphasizes class as the predominant form of social stratification and social conflict. Sociologist Edna Bonacich (1976), for example, uses the concept of a *split labor market* to explain tension between ethnic and racial groups. Employers, or owners of capital, tend to pit workers of different ethnic or racial groups against one another in competition for scarce economic resources—namely, jobs. This scenario is common in immigrant-receiving countries such as the United States, where immigrants who are often willing to work for low wages are hired instead of "native" workers, such as African Americans. From an instrumentalist perspective what appears or is presented as tension between ethnic and racial groups is, at its core, about economic competition or class (Crawford and Lipschutz 1998). This leads scholars studying ethnicity in various regions of the world to conclude, as Stephen Steinberg (1989) does in the case of the United States, that ethnicity is a "myth"; or as Leroy Vail (1989) and countless others do in the case of Africa, that it is a form of false consciousness—an ideology that needs to be explained rather than invoked as an explanation.

In addition to socioeconomic circumstances, instrumentalists also illustrate how politics, the political realm, and particularly the state play critical roles in shaping and defining ethnicity. In an article titled "The Political Construction of Ethnicity," Joane Nagel (1986) argues that within any given state, the structure of political access and the content of political policies shape ethnicity and ethnic mobilization. If, for instance, geographic, political, and administrative boundaries are drawn with reference to ethnicity, then ethnic identification and ethnic political mobilization are likely to occur. Cynthia Enloe makes a similar argument when she writes: "the state apparatus is not merely something that must 'cope with' the mobilization of ethnic groups, but is at times itself a critical factor in generating such ethnic mobilization" (1981, 123). States generate ethnic mobilization and identification, according to Enloe, by, among other things, establishing bureaucracies to deal with certain ethnic groups and by defining ethnic categories and assigning people to them via the census.

Evidence to support Enloe's and Nagel's theses is widespread. Federal systems such as the USSR or Nigeria, for example, established and administered political subunits or constituent republics in ways that fortified and defined ethnic differences. Similar dynamics characterized South Africa's Apartheid-era policies of separate "homelands" for blacks. Groups that may or may not have seen themselves as members of the same ethnic group prior to Apartheid did so after decades of oppression and forced geographic isolation on the basis of a state-assigned ethnicity. In the United States, forced resettlement to reservations, the creation of the Bureau of Indian Affairs (BIA), and other policies toward Native Americans had a similar impact on ethnic definition and subsequent mobilization (Enloe 1981; Nagel 1996).

In addition to the issue of political and administrative boundaries, when states implement political policies that recognize and institutionalize ethnicity, ethnic mobilization will again be the likely result. Nagel uses the example of language policies, arguing that although single official language policies are difficult to establish in linguistically diverse states, "multiple official languages guarantee long-term or permanent linguistic division" (1986, 102). Similar divisions emerge and persist when ethnic designations become the grounds for special treatment or privileged access to political resources. This emphasis on the role of politics, or specifically the state, in creating or fortifying ethnic divisions was also a focus of an influential body of scholarship that Saul Newman (1991) describes as the "conflictual modernization" school. These were scholars writing in the 1970s and 1980s who reversed the modernization thesis to argue that political and economic development would increase rather than decrease ethnic solidarities and tensions because it would create conditions and mechanisms that fuel and facilitate ethnic identification and conflict (Enloe 1973; Newman, 1991).

From this perspective, analysts who invoke the emotional and affective nature of ethnic ties as an explanation of, for example, the implosion of the Soviet Union are misguided. Instead of attributing the collapse of the USSR to the spontaneous surge of ethnic sentiments, instrumentalists maintain that in the midst of a power vacuum, calculating leaders throughout the former Soviet Union and Eastern Europe manipulated ethnicity as a tool for political gain. Furthermore, the fact that ethnicity was widely available as a tool for manipulation had more to do with the policies and practices of communist states than with "basic group identity." The USSR was, for instance, the first federal state to base its political units on ethnicity. "Nativization" policies, supported by Lenin and for some time Stalin, encouraged each ethnic republic to have its own language and culture. Smaller groups without a written language were given an alphabet. As a result, each ethnic republic became over time demographically and culturally more ethnic. It is for this reason that analysts like Ronald Suny (1992) reject what he calls the "sleeping beauty" approach to ethnonationalism in the former Soviet Union—namely, an approach, rooted in primordialism, that assumes that nationalism is the authentic expression of essential ethnic communities. From this perspective, ethnonationalism has a long and deeply rooted history in the Soviet Republics, but lay dormant until awakened by communism's fall. Instead, Suny and other scholars support a view that he labels "the making of nations" (1992, 24).

> Ethnicity in Soviet society was institutionalized both on the individual and group levels. On the individual level, nationality was registered on each person's internal passport, thus establishing a rigid ethnic affiliation for every citizen that passed immutably from one generation to the next. At the group level, the ethnoterritorial basis of political organization established firm links between nationality groups, their territories, and their political administrations. (Goldman, Lapidus, and Zaslavsky 1992, 2)

Suny notes that one of the central ironies of Soviet history is that a regime committed to creating a supraethnic community rooted in attachments to class actually established and fortified potent ethnic solidarities (1992, 24).

Similarly, in the case of South Africa, arguments that portray ethnicity and ethnic identities as givens fail to appreciate the malleability of ethnic identification and ethnic attachments, particularly in a context of intense political uncertainty and maneuvering. Without appreciating the instrumental nature of ethnicity, how, for example, could observers account for the fact that during South Africa's transition from Apartheid, many white Afrikaners supported or joined the predominantly Zulu Inkhatha Freedom Party? Or why did the overwhelmingly white Afrikaner National Party, the architect of Apartheid, reach out enthusiastically for black support? And in reference to the United States, Moynihan, despite his primordial leanings, recognizes a related point regarding the persistence of ethnicity and ethnic politics. Invoking the U.S. Civil Rights Acts of the 1960s, he challenges what he sees as the irony of a body of legislation designed to eliminate racial discrimination and race consciousness that simultaneously dictated an ever more sophisticated system of counting and categorizing people by race and ethnicity (Moynihan 1993, 55). In other words, if assimilation is failing in the United States, the political definition and fortification of ethnicity may be as much the reason as is ethnicity's strong emotional charge (Enloe 1981).

These competing views of ethnicity, primordialism, and instrumentalism have and continue to be pitted against one another, and their strengths and weaknesses are continuously rehashed. Primordialism is criticized for its static and unchanging view of the social world—a world in which ethnic identities and associated enmities shift and change often and with unanticipated ease. Primordialism's treatment of ethnicity as a basic group identity misses, for example, the fact that individuals have many different identities, and at any point in time for any particular individual, ethnicity may or may not be central or salient as a form of identity or belonging. Equally troublesome, however, is the instrumentalists' tendency to reduce ethnic phenomena to purely material motives and, hence, to fail to capture or explain the very real emotion, and even irrationality, that often accompanies ethnic identity and behavior. In this way, instrumentalism fails to explain why ethnicity is the identity or attachment that appears most capable of mobilizing people or evoking passion. Why not class, for example?

Despite some useful efforts at synthesizing these two frameworks (G. Scott 1990), they have generally been treated as irreconcilable. Recently, however, a third framework, constructivism, has gained prominence, and it is an approach that responds directly to Crawford Young's concern: "Both instrumentalists and primordialists need to be stood on their heads; what is problematic is not what drives ethnic group action, but the existence of the group itself" (1993, 23). The next section reviews the constructivist approach to ethnic identity and illustrates how it helps to enhance our understanding of ethnic phenomena.

Constructed Primordiality

In 1992, in what has since become an exemplary and much cited statement of the constructivist view of ethnicity, Kathleen Conzen et al. argue that ethnic identity should not be viewed as ancient, unchanging, or inherent in a group's blood, soul, or misty past; nor be reduced to a rational means-ends calculation of those intent on manipulating it for political or economic ends. "Rather ethnicity itself is to be understood as a cultural construction accomplished over historical time. Ethnic groups in modern settings are constantly recreating themselves, and ethnicity is continuously being reinvented in response to changing realities both within the group and the host society. Ethnic group boundaries, for example, must be renegotiated, while the expressive symbols of ethnicity (ethnic traditions) must be repeatedly reinterpreted" (1992, 5).

What is useful about the constructivist approach is not merely that it turns needed attention to the emergence and maintenance of the ethnic group itself, but also that it combines valuable insights from the primordialist and instrumentalist views without replicating the analytical weaknesses of either. Because the emphasis is on construction, this approach borrows a great deal from the instrumentalists' focus on specific contexts and circumstances—whether they be economic or political, immediate, or structural. In other words, the construction of ethnic identities and ethnic group relations takes place under specific circumstances and can only be understood through a careful examination of those circumstances—for example, who has access to political, economic, and cultural resources, who does not, who lives where, who works where and with whom?

> *"the construction of ethnic identities and ethnic group relations takes place under specific circumstances and can only be understood through a careful examination of those circumstances—for example, who has access to political, economic, and cultural resources, who does not, who lives where, who works where and with whom?"*

Nothing in the constructivist approach, however, necessitates downplaying or dismissing the emotional charge associated with ethnicity. Cornell and Hartmann capture this compromise well with the phrase "constructed primordiality" (1998, 89). Ethnicity is a constructed identity, but its construction relies on appeals to primordial sentiments of belonging. It is constructed, in other words, with reference to kinship, blood ties, shared origins, and common ancestry. As Cornell and Hartmann explain: "'Peoplehood,' 'common origin,' and 'blood ties,' whether asserted or assigned, form in most cultures a uniquely powerful set of interpersonal bonds, but this power is not inherent. It lies in the significance human beings attach to them, a significance that is variable and contingent and altogether a human creation" (1998, 89). Finally, and as noted in chapter 1, what must be clearly understood about the constructivist approach is that an emphasis on social definition, invention, or imagination does not signify superficiality or inconsequentiality of the constructed identities. As Werner Sollors explains, "The forces of modern life embodied by such terms as 'ethnicity,' 'nation,' or 'race' can indeed be meaningfully discussed as 'inventions.'" He cautions, however, that "this usage is meant not to evoke a conspiratorial interpretation of a manipulative inventor who singlehandedly makes ethnics out of unsuspecting subjects, but to suggest widely shared, though intensely debated, collective fictions that are continually reinvented" (1989, x). Empirical applications of the constructivist model are numerous, but Rwanda provides a particularly poignant example for demonstrating the utility of the approach.

Rwanda is a case that illustrates in a stark and disturbing way the persistent power of ethnicity and the paradox of a world that commutes busily along the information superhighway while the bodies of the victims of ethnic cleansing wash up, literally, against the banks of rivers and streams. In 1994, up to one million people were massacred in Rwanda over a three-month period. Television news reports showed piles of dead bodies in the streets of Kigali, Rwanda's capital, and newspapers published horrific accounts of people being stabbed, clubbed, decapitated, and burned. Few today will dispute that what took place in Rwanda was genocide—specifically, ethnic genocide. That, however, is where the agreement often ends.

Rwanda is a relatively small country in east Africa, and home, primarily, to two ethnic groups: Hutus, who make up approximately 85 percent of the population, and Tutsis, who comprise 15 percent. When the slaughter began on April 6, 1994, it was mostly Hutus killing Tutsis, but thousands of Hutus, either opponents of the regime or people in the wrong place at the wrong time, were also among the victims (Uvin 2001, 75). For many analysts and observers Rwanda offers a quintessential example of the emotional charge attached to ethnicity or to a belief in common ancestry and shared blood ties. Hutus killed Tutsis because they hated Tutsis. There were even horrific reports of Hutu husbands killing their Tutsi wives. For other scholars and observers, however, what took place in Rwanda was not the result of the power of primordiality, but rather the outcome of centuries of economic and political competition and conflict between groups of people who share a great deal in terms of culture and history, but who have been pitted against and played off one another for centuries by colonists and calculating politicians.

Primordialist explanations for the turmoil in Rwanda emphasize the very existence of, and seemingly fundamental differences between, two distinct groups. Indeed, the differentiation between the Hutus and Tutsis can be traced to well before European colonization took hold in the late 1800s. The precolonial history of the region is sketchy at best, and as Philip Gourevitch (1998) points out, tends to rely more on legend than documented fact. Nonetheless, convention has it that Hutus, a Bantu people, arrived first in Rwanda, immigrating from the south and west. Tutsis are believed to be a Nilotic people who originally came to Rwanda from the north and east. Hutus were cultivators, and Tutsis were cattle herders. This variation (cattle being a much more valuable commodity) prefigured centuries of inequality between the two groups.

The distinction between cultivators and herders was significant, but what has been as central to the division between Hutus and Tutsis is the accompanying belief in and repeated references to fundamental differences in physical traits. Hutus are characterized as "stocky and round-faced, dark-skinned, flat-nosed, thick-lipped, and square-jawed," and Tutsis as "lanky and long-faced, not so dark-skinned, narrow-nosed, thin-lipped, and narrow-chinned" (Gourevitch 1998, 50). Hutus and Tutsis themselves use these physical archetypes as a means of differentiation, but

Europeans did a great deal to shape and solidify them with the tools of scientific racism. As Gourevitch explains:

> In addition to military and administrative chiefs, and a veritable army of churchmen, the Belgians dispatched scientists to Rwanda. The scientists brought scales and measuring tapes and calipers, and they went about weighing Rwandans, measuring Rwandan cranial capacities, and conducting comparative analyses of the relative protuberance of Rwandan noses. Sure enough, the scientists found what they had believed all along. Tutsis had "nobler," more "naturally" aristocratic dimensions than the "coarse" and "bestial" Hutus. On the "nasal index," for instance, the median Tutsi nose was found to be about two and a half millimeters longer and nearly five millimeters narrower than the median Hutu nose. (p. 56)

And as is typically the case with racism, the differentiation went beyond physical attributes to mental and moral capabilities as well. While Europeans considered Tutsis to be "well-bred" and more aristocratic, the Hutus were characterized as lazy and dishonest.

From this perspective, being Hutu or Tutsi fits within Harold Isaacs's (1974) definition of "basic group identity." Moreover, 1994 was not the first indication of a correlation between ethnic identity and warfare in Rwanda. By the late 1950s, the line between Hutus and Tutsis was a stark one, and ethnic consciousness ran high on both sides of the line. On November 1, 1959, a Hutu political activist was attacked and beaten by Tutsi political activists. Within twenty-four hours, a violent uprising had begun. Hutus torched Tutsis homes and murdered Tutsi officials in a campaign of terror that lasted for months. Thousands of Tutsi were killed, and more than twenty thousand Tutsi were displaced from their homes. The violence ceased only when Belgian colonists intervened and oversaw an illegitimate election in 1960 that placed Hutus in power. Belgium simply replaced one oppressive ethnic regime with another and led a UN commission to report that "some day we will witness violent reactions on the part of the Tutsis" (Gourevitch 1998, 61). Rwanda gained its independence in 1961, and more mass killings took place in the 1960s and 1970s as Hutus consolidated their ethnic domination of the country.

A history of distinct identities dating back centuries, invocations of the body on the part of colonists and the groups themselves, and repeated ethnic bloodshed support a primordialist interpretation of the Rwanda case. However, for every observer who uses primordialism to explain this situation, as many, and typically more, point to Rwanda as the ideal illustration of the instrumentalist origins and essence of ethnicity. Despite the elaborate legends that have come to surround Hutus and Tutsis as distinct peoples, for hundreds of years before the Belgians took over Rwanda these two groups lived intermingled, spoke the same language, practiced the same religion, fought in the same armies, pledged loyalty to the same leaders, and intermarried. As some have pointed out: "It would be extremely difficult to find any kind of cultural or folkloric custom that was specifically Hutu or Tutsi" (Destexhe 1995, 36). Furthermore, through marriage and clientage, Hutus could become hereditary Tutsis and Tutsis could become hereditary Hutus (Gourevitch 1998, 47).

Not only does this history of intermixing call into question the distinctness of Hutu and Tutsi peoplehood, but many observers also challenge the widespread belief that it is possible to distinguish the two groups on the basis of physical appearance. As one journalist reported, "I never saw any evidence in Rwanda or Burundi to support the proposition that Tutsis were lighter skinned than Hutus. Like much else that has been written about the two groups, it appears to be fanciful nonsense" (quoted in Cornell and Hartmann 1998, 41). Similarly, as Laurent Nkongoli, vice president of the Rwandan National Assembly, commented in an interview: "You can't tell us apart. We can't tell us apart. I was on a bus in the north once and because I was in the north where they [Hutus] were, and because I ate corn, which they eat, they said, 'He's one of us.' But I'm a Tutsi from Butare in the south" (quoted in Gourevitch 1998, 50). Tensions persisted in Rwanda after the genocide, and during a 1998 visit to a location of frequent conflict, Rwanda's Minister of Home Affairs, Abdul Karim Harelimana, pleaded with a crowd of villagers: "Do Hutus speak a different language? Do they worship a different God? Do Tutsis not marry Hutus, and don't Hutus and Tutsis live together on the same hills?" (quoted in Santoro 1998, 7).

Finally, in spite of the bloody ethnic conflict that exploded in April 1994 and in 1959, and for which Rwanda is now well known, the past two hundred to three hundred years of Hutu-Tutsi intermingling are characterized more by peaceful coexistence than warfare. With this in mind, Philip Gourevitch cautions:

> the next time you hear a story like the one that ran on the front page of *The New York Times* in October of 1997, reporting on "the age-old animosity between the Tutsi and Hutu ethnic groups," remember that until Mbonyumutwa's beating lit the spark in 1959 there had never been systematic political violence recorded between Hutus and Tutsis—anywhere. (1998, 59)

What then explains the horrific ethnic genocide of 1994 and the only slightly less tragic one that preceded it in 1959? From the instrumentalist perspective, all fingers point to the European colonists and the political elite who they appointed to do their dirty work. Through a familiar, widely employed strategy of divide and conquer, the Germans first and later the Belgians played upon, fortified, and extended the identities "Hutu" and "Tutsi." Tutsis were widely favored by European colonists. They were appointed to positions of power and prestige, given access to economic resources, sent to be educated in Catholic schools; whereas Hutus were relegated to a regime of forced manual labor. Lest the two groups be confused, the Belgians issued ethnic identity cards to all Rwandans. Tutsis willingly participated in this hierarchical structure. In a telling statement to a reporter, a Tutsi elder looking back on Belgian colonial rule described it as "You whip the Hutus or we will whip you" (Gourevitch 1998, 57). The Belgian-Tutsi relationship soured by the late 1950s (related, in part, to Belgium's own ethnic tribalism between the Flemish and Walloon), and when Hutu resentment at decades of exploitation erupted in violence, the colonial power stood idly by before helping to reverse the ethnic pecking order. Once the Belgians left Rwanda in 1961, the practice of ethnic politics was firmly established. In fact, in a review of the scholarship on Rwanda's genocide in 1994, Peter Uvin notes that the most common explanation of the genocide points simply to the desire of the Rwandan elite to stay in power and their willingness to manipulate ethnic identities and affinities in order to do so (2001, 79).

Looking through a primordial lens, Rwanda appears to be a classic case of ethnic clash, rooted in differences that, in Samuel Huntington's terms, are "real and basic." From an instrumentalist viewpoint, Rwanda offers proof of the utilitarian calculations and political manipulation that underlie and determine ethnic conflict. The notion of *constructed primordiality* recognizes that elements of both are present in the Rwanda case. Indeed, Rwanda illustrates well how crass political calculation, whether on the part of colonists or an indigenous elite, gives rise to and shapes ethnic tensions. We also see how economic inequalities and material deprivations foster searing resentment that often manifests itself in an ethnic form. Recall Nagel's (1986) and Enloe's (1981) caution that if you organize politics along ethnic lines, you will get ethnic politics. Yet, the European colonists did not invent Hutu or Tutsi ethnicities out of thin air. They drew upon distinctions and focused attention on differences or perceived differences from which primordial sentiments typically flow—ancestry, names, bodies. There may have been little credibility to the objective fact of shared blood ties, and indeed any genetic differences between Hutu and Tutsi were, or over time, certainly blurred. This does not lessen, however, the significance assigned to the differences or negate the very real passion they were capable of invoking. Otherwise, no amount of callous manipulation could have elicited the blood-curdling behavior that took place during April 1994.

Crawford Young is correct that primordialism and instrumentalism needed to be turned on their heads, but it is also correct that understanding the existence of ethnic groups and the relations between them must incorporate elements of both views. As stated in chapter 1, identities are invented, but the invention process is not arbitrary, it does not make ethnicity or any other identity out of thin air, and it is far from inconsequential. The next section illustrates the applicability and utility of a constructivist lens by turning attention to how the context and conditions of contemporary globalization affect the formation and maintenance of ethnicity.

Global Contingencies

Ethnicity, as noted earlier in this chapter, now consumes a great deal of energy on the part of both the academic and policymaking communities, and prominent among those paying careful attention to ethnicity are scholars and practitioners of international relations and global affairs. It is clear, for example, from the perspective of world politics, that ethnicity matters with regard to conflict both within and between states, to refugee movements and other humanitarian crises, and to political and economic development more generally; and the large and growing number of studies on ethnicity as it relates to these topics has yielded valuable insights. Yet, many of these analyses continue to operate on and perpetuate either strictly primordialist or instrumentalist assumptions about ethnic identity and ethnic group relations and, in doing so, obscure a fuller understanding of ethnic phenomena. The constructivist lens improves upon these two approaches and recognizes that ethnicity cannot be simply taken as a given or conceptualized as an independent variable without also acknowledging its dependent status. In other words, ethnicity, ethnic identity, and ethnic relations are shaped and defined in particular ways and via particular circumstances.

Moreover, globalization constitutes a fundamentally significant set of circumstances for understanding how contemporary ethnic identities and attachments are shaped (Croucher 1999). As outlined in chapter 1, globalization is itself a multifaceted phenomenon. For analytical purposes, this section explores globalization's implications for ethnicity by analyzing the four dynamics of migration, economic restructuring, political integration and reconfiguration, and technological innovation. Cases that range from the decade-long rebellion of Zapatista rebels in Chiapas, Mexico, to ethnic and racial tensions in Miami, Florida—a U.S. city widely associated with the trends of both globalization and conflictual ethnic differentiation—illustrate the varied linkages between globalization and ethnicity.

Migration

Human migration is one significant dimension of globalization and has very direct and seemingly obvious connections to ethnicity. As noted in chapter 1, migration across territorial and political borders has existed since the beginning of time. Over the past several decades, however, the volume, frequency, and distance of transborder human flows have increased. In particular, countries in Western Europe and North America as well as Australia, Japan, and South Africa have experienced not only an increase in the influx of foreign-born—whether refugees or migrants, documented or undocumented—but also shifts in the historical patterns and homeland origins of immigrants. The increase in and direction of global migration are closely related to other aspects or processes of global change, and migration itself is not simply a consequence of globalization, but also a facilitating factor or cause. Migration is, from one perspective, the reason that ethnic identities, ethnic relations, and ethnic politics exist. As Milton Esman writes: "Ethnic pluralism establishes the need for ethnic politics" (1994, 2). In other words, it is partly through movement and/or contact, voluntary or not, with others, with differing language, religion, physical attributes, daily customs, or ancestral origins, that ethnic groups become aware of the similarities among themselves and their differences from other groups. Depending on a wide variety of circumstances, these perceived ethnic similarities and differences can become a source of primary identification and social mobilization as well as a source of ethnic conflict and group tension.

Globalization and ethnicity are, in this way, closely interconnected. What is essential to keep in mind, however, is that whereas international migration brings people from different cultural and historical backgrounds into close proximity, the stratification of these people into various ethnic groups, and the nature of ethnic group identities, does not necessarily or automatically reflect preexisting identities, interests, or attachments, either on the part of the immigrants or the established residents. In other words, neither the content of ethnic identity nor the common concerns around which members of an ethnic group come to unite can be directly traced to primordial givens. They are, as S. R. Charsley explains, "not simply the prolongation of pre-migration customs and patterns, but are the result of an interaction between these and the values and requirements of the receiving

---

"whereas international migration brings people from different cultural and historical backgrounds into close proximity, the stratification of these people into various ethnic groups, and the nature of ethnic group identities, does not necessarily or automatically reflect preexisting identities, interests, or attachments, either on the part of the immigrants or the established residents."

society" (1974, 355). Nor are group identities and attachments manufactured arbitrarily or at will. Ethnic identity formation and differentiation emerge from complex processes of interaction, reaction, self-identification, and institutional categorization—all of which play out in specific economic, political, and sociocultural contexts.

Take as a brief example Cuban American ethnicity among Cuban immigrants and their offspring in the United States. Cubanness in Cuba is not an ethnic identity. To identify as Cuban in Cuba is to signal a citizenship status or membership in the Cuban nation. Cubans in the United States or elsewhere who have left Cuba may, and in fact typically do, share with Cubans in Cuba the same language, religion, and cultural practices, as well as attachments to many of the same symbols, memories, and myths. In fact, it is Cuban culture and an attachment to the Cuban homeland that comprise much of the content of Cuban American ethnic identity in the United States. But the latter identity is also something more and different from the former. The symbols, memories, and myths of Cubanness take on a particular meaning in the U.S. context. Cuban immigrants themselves give form, content, and meaning to their ethnic group identity, but they do so in accord with the specific opportunities and constraints afforded by the immediate context—economic, political, and sociocultural—in which they find themselves. Significantly, these contexts, however local or domestic they may appear, are also influenced by global patterns and trends. Cuban Americans, for example, are an ethnic group well known for their economic and political success in the United States. Yet, this success cannot be understood without recognizing the ways in which Cuban immigrants capitalized on conditions of global economic restructuring in Miami, Florida, specifically, and the Western Hemisphere more generally. Cuban immigrants to the United States also benefited from anticommunist sentiments tied closely to the changing geopolitics of the Cold War (Croucher 1996).

This scenario is not peculiar to Cubans in the United States, but is the case with ethnic groups everywhere who become ethnic groups when they move or come into contact with others who have moved. In some cases the movement of and encounters between different groups is relatively recent (Cubans began arriving in Miami in mass in the early 1960s); in other cases, it dates back centuries (e.g., Hutus and Tutsis in Rwanda). The point being emphasized here is that migration alone is not sufficient to make, invent, or give rise to ethnicity. Nor is migration the only way globalization and ethnicity interrelate.

Economic Restructuring

Of the various dimensions of globalization, economics receives the most attention. Typically, economic globalization refers to global capitalism, to the internationalization of production and exchange, and to the near hegemony of neoliberal ideology that propounds the benefits of economic privatization and free market liberalization. As noted in chapter 1, the economy is also a realm of globalization that invokes heated debate as to its nature and implications. For our purposes, it is sufficient to acknowledge that economic globalization influences access to and competition for resources—jobs, wages, homes, land, and wealth. In some cases, it reinforces existing inequalities; in others, it restructures who competes with whom, for what, and how. Globalization creates both winners and losers, and as several scholars note, has also sharpened group conflict and given rise to defensive forms of collective action (Rodrik 1997). The focus here, however, is on the specific relationship between economic globalization and ethnicity.

Identifying a link between economics and ethnicity is nothing new. In fact, much of the literature categorized as instrumentalist emphasizes the economic origins and underpinnings of ethnic identities and ethnic group relations. In some ways, then, the analysis presented here aims to update that perspective, focusing not on the ethnic implications of economic modernization, industrialization, and "development," as they occurred during or prior to the 1950s, but on global economic restructuring and increasing economic interconnectedness as it currently exists today. But in addition to updating, this discussion bears in mind that ethnicity is never simply a direct outcome of economics, nor a mere epiphenomenon of class. Individual and group identities are not spontaneous eruptions. Conditions (in this case associated with globalization) must be interpreted, grievances channeled, and problems defined; and ethnicity is commonly a mechanism for and outcome of doing so. Meanwhile, few individuals and groups are motivated to act or form attachments on the basis of material interests alone. It is important, in other words, to acknowledge the unique effectiveness of appeals to perceived primordial ties without falling back on objective, organic, or essentialist conceptualizations of ethnicity. The processes and effects of economic globalization are not restricted to any one area or region of the world, yet developing countries, or certain subpopulations within them, have arguably borne the largest burden of global economic restructuring. Mexico offers a significant case in point, and one with illustrative implications for ethnicity.

On January 1, 1994, over three thousand Mayan Indians in Mexico's southern state of Chiapas rose up against the Mexican state. They referred to themselves as the Zapatista National Liberation Army (EZLN) and issued a list of demands that included not only jobs, food, homes, and health care, but also increased autonomy and respect for their cultural beliefs and practices, languages, and indigenous way of life (N. Harvey 2001). It was no coincidence that the uprising began on the same day the North American Free Trade Agreement officially went into effect. From the perspective of the indigenous peoples of the region, NAFTA would perpetuate, in fact, intensify, centuries of economic and cultural oppression and exploitation. In the decades preceding the 1994 uprising, the Mexican economy boomed, by many standards, and the resource rich state of Chiapas was central to an economic expansion rooted in cattle ranching, the growth of cotton and bananas for export, and a lucrative petroleum industry. This growth, however, took place at great environmental and cultural cost. It destroyed precious rainforest lands, replaced traditional subsistence food crops with agricultural exports for the international market, and created huge disparities in wealth and well-being. Writing in 1994, Roger Burbach explained:

> For the past twenty-five years, Chiapas has been convulsed by unprecedented economic transformations that have torn up the traditional agricultural economy and devastated the indigenous cultures. The Mexican state, responding to the interests of the country's emergent bourgeoisie and the demands of the international market place, has treated Chiapas as an internal colony, sucking out its wealth while leaving its people—particularly the overwhelming majority who live off the land—more impoverished than ever. (1994, 115)

The Zapatista movement is a direct reaction against globalization generally, and NAFTA specifically. In fact, one of the Zapatista's early communiqués described NAFTA as "a death certificate for the Indian peoples of Mexico" (Burbach 1994, 122). And every account of the struggle in Chiapas points to the devastating impact of global economic integration on the region and its indigenous inhabitants. This is not, however, a conventional class rebellion or a socialist revolution in Marxist terms. The Zapatistas are not trying to capture the state nor are they calling for state socialism. They are trying to inspire a broad-based movement to end victimization of Indians and destruction of their way of life by centuries of Western modernization. Subcomandante Marcos, the movement's charismatic leader, emphasizes the cultural basis of this struggle and attributes the Zapatistas' success to a convergence of indigenous peoples own stories of exploitation, humiliation, and racism with a Marxist critique of Mexican history (N. Harvey 2001).

The violence in Chiapas has subsided, somewhat, but paramilitary units continue to threaten the security of the indigenous people, and until recently, the government maintained seven military bases in the region occupied by thousands of soldiers. Meanwhile, the Zapatistas continue to pressure the Mexican state and their local government leaders for economic and political reforms and protections against the perils of globalization. In March 2001, the Zapatistas organized a two-week tour of the country to promote Indian rights that culminated in an appearance before Mexico's congress to plead for the passage of an

Indian Rights Bill, which includes provisions for greater local autonomy and the promotion of Indian languages, customs, and systems of justice (W. Patterson 2001, 7). Meanwhile, a recent and growing globalization-related threat to the Mayan people and culture is that of tourism, specifically what is now being termed "revolutionary tourism." Europeans and Americans enamored with the legendary Zapatista movement now mill about the capital city of San Cristóbal de las Casas in large numbers, competing with locals and vendors for coveted space on the narrow streets. The good news, at least from the perspective of preserving a distinctive indigenous culture and lifestyle, is that the city recently staved off the arrival of a Sam's Club, the U.S. wholesale warehouse chain, to its city center (LaFranchi 2000a, 7).

The Zapatistas represent just one of many indigenous movements throughout the Americas and the world that are reacting to or resisting the impact of economic globalization. These movements are both motivated and shaped by ethnic identities and attachments—which in turn invigorate and reshape those identities and attachments. In Ecuador, a powerful indigenous movement has emerged in recent years to protest the country's imposition of a neoliberal economic model. As in Mexico, Ecuador's indigenous groups have been hit hard by privatization, agricultural modernization, and currency devaluations—particularly a 2000 decision to "dollarize" the economy by pegging the local currency to the U.S. dollar. In all of these measures, the Ecuadorian state is responding to demands of an increasingly competitive and interconnected global economy. In a 2000 interview, Raul Lopez, the Roman Catholic bishop of the Andean town of Latacunga, explained: "The situation is truly tragic. The government has cut the budget for everything in the social sector in order to satisfy the demands of the International Monetary Fund and to make payments on our foreign debt" (Rohter 2000, A14). The indigenous response focuses on issues of land, jobs, and abject poverty, but as is the case with the Zapatistas, also emphasizes resentment at widespread cultural repression—namely, the lack of respect for indigenous languages, religious practices, and distinctive ways of life.

"The Zapatistas represent just one of many indigenous movements throughout the Americas and the world that are reacting to or resisting the impact of economic globalization. These movements are both motivated and shaped by ethnic identities and attachments—which in turn invigorate and reshape those identities and attachments."

Melina Selverston characterizes the indigenous movement in Ecuador as one of the country's most important social movements. She attributes the success of the movement to the formation and spread of an indigenous ideology that has influenced not only how the dominant culture sees Indians, but also how Indians perceive themselves. Selverston points out that although concerns of economic exclusion and access to scarce material resources such as land are central to the grievances and demands of the indigenous movement, it is not simply a class struggle. Rather, ethnicity and cultural dignity are also key aspects and concerns. In fact, and as was also the case with the Zapatistas, it is the convergence of the two that best characterizes the indigenous struggle. One of Ecuador's indigenous leaders explains: "There were two visions: the indigenist cultural vision, focused on bilingual education, and the class vision, focused on land conflicts. The two merged when we realized that we could not have our culture without land" (quoted in Selverston 1997, 176).

The role of economic globalization in fueling ethnic mobilization or conflict is not restricted to indigenous movements. There is also evidence, for example, that factors associated with the global arena exacerbated the Rwandan conflict discussed earlier. Some analysts point to the drop in international coffee prices (a key commodity export for Rwanda) as a precipitating factor in the 1994 genocide, as well as to structural adjustment programs imposed by international community (Chossudovsky 1996). Some studies even assign blame to the numerous international aid and development agencies, including the Catholic Church, operating in Rwanda which was at best blind to the political and social dynamics destroying the country and, at worst, complicitous (Uvin 1998). Similar arguments are advanced about the ethnic turmoil in Bosnia and its relationship to international economic factors and processes (Woodward 1995).

In the scenarios described above, globalization intensifies economic competition and deprivation, which inspires ethnic mobilization; but, this is not the sum total of the linkages between economic globalization and ethnicity. Globalization has also helped to make ethnicity a valuable economic resource in an increasingly integrated and competitive world system. This is evident in the extent to which corporations have sought to commodify ethnicity as a lucrative marketing device (Klein 2000). It is also apparent among states, particularly advanced industrialized states and large urban areas within them, that increasingly compete for corporate businesses and contracts by emphasizing and advertising their cultural and linguistic diversity. Furthermore, remittances from ethnic kin who have migrated to other states (movement that is itself related to patterns of global economic change) have become valuable sources of income for the relatives and governments that they left behind. In Mexico, for example, remittances from Mexicans working abroad, primarily in the United States, totaled more than $9.8 billion in 2001—an amount equal to tourism, which is Mexico's third-largest source of foreign income and a dramatic increase from the $700 million in remittances Mexico received in 1980 (*Associated Press* 2001b).

Political Integration and Reconfiguration

Economics and the world marketplace constitute a fundamental dimension of globalization, but neither the constituent processes of economic globalization nor their impact on ethnicity exist in isolation from the global political realm. Just as there are profound changes occurring in the international economic system, so, too, in the realm of politics, political organizations, and governance structures. The end of the Cold War marked one important example of global political reconfiguration, mainly because it ended a decades-long rivalry of East versus West that had come to permeate all aspects of international relations. But even in decades prior to the end of the Cold War and intensifying in decades since, there is evidence of increasing interconnectedness and interdependence in the international political system (Keohane and Nye 1977). In some cases, this takes the form of increased contact and cooperation among sovereign states; but, more notable is the rise of suprastate forms of global governance as discussed in chapter 1. IGOs like the UN or WTO are comprised of member states, as are the EU, NAFTA, and other regional organizations, but the very act of membership in these bodies requires that states give up some degree of sovereignty to the organization itself. And many of these organizations, the United Nations in particular, focus substantial attention and energy on recognizing and empowering nonstate actors, trans-state actors, or subpopulations within states—such as indigenous peoples or women. Alongside the IGOs exist a large and growing number of INGOs. The combined activities of these organizations have produced an array of international conventions, standards, guidelines, and regimes for protecting and promoting various individual and group rights. Although scholars disagree on the extent to which these international regimes have or will diminish the role of the sovereign state, all agree that as a result of global governance structures, states are under increasing pressure to comply with international rules related to democratization and human rights protection. Meanwhile, individuals and groups within states have increased political access and resources beyond or outside of states (J. Rosenau 1990; Scholte 2000; Soysal 1994).

The implications for ethnicity of what is described here as political globalization are multifold. With regard to the end of the Cold War, to the extent that the United States and the USSR tended to pit ethnic groups in countries throughout Africa, Asia, and Latin America against one another in an ideological tug-of-war, its demise should allow some ethnic tensions to subside (Nagel 1993). On the other hand, as has already been argued, the end of the Cold War, and the collapse of the Soviet Union in particular, left in its wake a power vacuum, as well as decades of political manipulation along ethnic lines, which has contributed to the resurgence of ethnic mobilization and ethnic conflict throughout the former Soviet Republics and Eastern Europe. The New World Order quickly turned into one of disorder, and the post–Cold War era appears likely to be more unstable, at least with regard to ethnicity, than the previous decades of Cold War. More important, however, just as instrumentalists have demonstrated that the policies, organizational structures, and political practices of states in both the communist and noncommunist worlds defined and maintained ethnic identification and fueled ethnic mobilization, the same may now be said of the governance structures and ideational regimes that make up the international political system. In other words, the organizations, treaties, conventions, and networks described above provide access and incentives, or in the language of social movement theorists, create a *political opportunity structure*, for ethnic group identification and mobilization (Tarrow 1994).

The United Nations, its constituent bodies, and related organizations are critical in this regard. Take for example the indigenous movements described above, as well as countless others. These movements have relied heavily upon, worked through, and, in fact, been shaped by the practices, policies, and resources of various IGOs and INGOs. For years, a working group within the UN's Commission on Human Rights has been preparing a Declaration on the Rights of Indigenous Peoples. They have completed a final Draft Declaration that includes countless recognitions of and provisions for protecting the rights of indigenous peoples—their human rights, their rights to land and resources, and also their cultural rights as distinct peoples. Repeatedly, the document guarantees indigenous peoples a collective right to maintain and strengthen their distinct cultures (Draft Declaration, Part I, Articles 3–7). Similarly, in 1992, the United Nations promulgated a Declaration on the Rights of Persons Belonging to National or Ethnic, Religious and Linguistic Minorities. That declaration mandates that states "protect the existence and the national or ethnic, cultural, religious and language identity of minorities within their respective territory and shall encourage conditions for the promotion of that identity" (United Nations 1992). Both of these developments are significant in that the practice and guarantee of some of these rights are likely to conflict with the sovereignty of the modern states in which indigenous peoples reside. Second, the emphasis on collective and cultural rights departs notably from the hegemonic Western liberal ideology that rights inhere within and are the sole purview of individuals, not groups.

The UN working group and its resulting Declaration on the Rights of Indigenous Peoples is just one of countless examples of international bodies and documents that now recognize the rights of indigenous groups. The International Labour Organization, the World Bank, and the Organization of American States all maintain instruments for safeguarding the rights of indigenous peoples (Sambo 1994). In 1994, the U.S. State Department, which delivers an annual Human Rights Report to Congress, added "rights of native peoples" as a new category for assessing the human rights records of countries throughout the world (Barber 1994). In 2001, the United Nations sponsored the first-ever World Conference Against Racism, held in Durban, South Africa. The UN commissioner of human rights and conference organizer Mary Robinson explained the goal of the conference: "Whilst individual societies have embarked on processes of reflection and reconciliation [about racism], we as a global community have never attempted it before" (quoted in E. Armstrong 2001, 8). The conference provided a forum not just for indigenous peoples, but also for migrants victimized by hate crimes in host countries throughout the world, and groups ranging from the Roma in Eastern Europe to the Dalits (low caste persons) in India. Any hopes that the conference would produce significant changes were dashed by the consuming controversy over calls for reparations and apologies for slavery as well as demands for equating Zionism with racism (Armstrong 2001, 8). Nonetheless, the conference itself provided an important venue for mobilizing and increasing the solidarity among numerous ethnic groups around the world.

Certainly the existence of the documents, conferences, and commissions described above result in part from concerted lobbying efforts on behalf of indigenous groups and their supporters. Yet, at the same time, the existence and availability of these political resources and points of access create incentives for ethnic identification and mobilization. Recall once again Joane Nagel's (1986) and Cynthia Enloe's (1981) theses on the political construction of ethnicity. Referring specifically to politics within states, but applicable to the international realm as well, both authors argue that if you organize political access and the distribution of political resources along ethnic lines, ethnic mobilization and ethnic politics will be the result. One implication of globalization for ethnicity as a form of belonging is that this insight is now relevant at the international or suprastate level as well. Moreover, similar dynamics also play out at the level of regional integration and interconnectedness.

Many analysts have noted the paradox of resurgent ethnonationalism throughout Europe, coinciding with increasing integration within the European Union. Yet, what appears at first glance to be a paradox seems less so when one acknowledges the many ways in which the institutions and apparatuses of the EU have opened up political space beyond and outside of the member states for ethnic groups to mobilize and demand recognition and respect for their distinct ethnicities, languages, and cultural practices. In fact, the EU maintains a very active Committee on the Regions, which provides valuable political access, voice, and recognition for substate and trans-state groups within Europe, and EU charters encourage minority language use in government and education. Meanwhile, prospective members of the EU are expected to meet certain standards regarding the treatment of ethnic and cultural minorities within their borders. These standards often involve guarantees for the protection and promotion of minority languages and other cultural practices (Csergo and Goldgeier 2001; Jones and Keating 1995).

Finally, political globalization also entails demands and expectations for democratization. Specifically, contemporary international institutional and ideational regimes mandate that states throughout the world are and should be becoming more democratic—operationalized as guaranteeing basic civil and political rights. The extent to which this is happening varies widely and is open to debate, but the impact with regard to ethnicity is that political opening on the part of states creates space for ethnic mobilization within and across states. Deborah Yashar (2002), for example, attributes the rise and success of various indigenous movements throughout Latin America to the wave of democratization sweeping the region during the 1980s.

Technological Innovation

For all these reasons, it seems safe to conclude that ethnicity will persist in a globalizing world, but not in any static or predictable form. Contributing powerfully to the persistence and reconfiguration of ethnicity, whether by international organizations, states, or groups and individuals, is technology. Again, this dimension of globalization is closely intertwined with the processes of economic and political interconnectedness and migration outlined above. For some scholars such as Anthony Giddens, communications media have been "the leading influence in the globalization of society over the past 20 or 30 years," and one that has been accompanied by the resurgence of religious, nationalistic, and ethnic fundamentalisms (1995, 10). Other scholars have even more directly linked the two trends of technology and ethnicity. As early as 1976, Abdul Said and Luiz Simmons stated that "The dominant causal agent behind the emerging international political system is the technological revolution in communication that permits previously isolated ethnic groups to become more visible and, in certain cases, interact across national boundaries" (1976, 18). John Stack also maintains that the world political system has been transformed by technological advancements that facilitate transnational ties among ethnic groups around the world. This global penetration of the domestic arena provides ethnic groups with a greater opportunity to exchange ideas, information, wealth, and political strategies. Moreover, it results in what Stack describes as a powerful "demonstration effect," whereby one group in one part of the world is inspired and informed by another group's ethnic success or failures in another part of the world (1981, 20).

There are countless interesting examples of ethnic groups using communications technology, whether to fortify ethnic identifications, further political mobilization efforts, establish or maintain links with ethnic brethren across state borders, or nurture and support ethnic solidarity within a new homeland or host country. The Zapatistas, for example, have become well known for their skillful use of the Internet and e-mail to publicize and gain international support for their cause (Froehling 1997; Robberson 1995). So, too, have other indigenous groups. In a front page article titled "Indians Hear a High-Tech Drumbeat," the *Christian Science Monitor* reported: "Using cell phones, fax machines, and the Internet, a national native American movement is coalescing, helping disparate tribes communicate, educate, mobilize, and stand up for themselves." The article goes on to quote Tom Goldtooth, founder of the Indigenous Environmental Network: "We are seeing the result of years of coalition-building coming together with the aid of new ways to communicate to very remote, rural populations" (quoted in Wood 1998, 1).

Among countless other examples are a "cybercommunity" of Chinese students in the United States who use computer-mediated communication to strengthen their cultural identity as well as to smooth their acculturation process (Wu 1999). Diasporic Jews celebrate Passover transnationally with the help of contemporary satellite communications (Braman and Mohammadi 1996). A digital radio network in northern Scandinavia is preserving, in fact, reviving, the language, culture, and ethnic solidarity among the Sami people spread across Norway, Sweden, Finland, and Russia (Varis 1999). And in his studies of transnational linkages between Mexicans in the United States and Mexico, Robert Smith (1998) emphasizes the importance of technology, specifically telephones, airplanes, and videotapes, in forging and maintaining increasingly close ties among ethnic brethren spread across different states and locales. Finally, David Elkins makes the case that in addition to strengthening existing groups or constructing new ones, technology is also paving the way for virtual ethnic communities, which, in his words, "have the potential to be just as fundamental to the identities of some people as the existing ethnic communities whose existence we have taken for granted for decades or even centuries" (1997, 141).

What Elkins and others interested in technology and ethnicity illustrate is that access to information and to groups or individuals who share interests, ethnic or otherwise, is now much less mediated by political gatekeepers or restricted by the confines of territory as a result of innovations in the media of communication. Hence, neither ethnic group formation nor ethnic solidarity requires proximity or density of population (Elkins 1997, 145). Yet, what is important to remember is that technology, like other aspects of globalization, is not simply uniting existing, predetermined ethnic groups or igniting existing ethnic passions; rather, it is contributing to the continual shaping and reshaping of both.

Conclusion

As we begin a new millennium, ethnic conflicts rage in every region of the globe. Even where tension is low, ethnicity continues to play a significant role in social, political, and economic life, and from all indications it persists as a salient form of belonging for individuals and groups throughout the world. Much of the development literature of the 1950 and 1960s, both liberal and Marxist, failed to anticipate the power and persistence of ethnicity, assuming instead that it would give way to more rational identifications with modern interest groups or class. By the 1970s, it became clear that ethnicity would not disappear, and evidence of that reality has mounted ever since. In recent decades, two competing explanations for ethnicity—primordialism and instrumentalism—have vied for prominence. But this chapter has argued that a third, constructivism, offers a more compelling account by combining insights from both and exploring more deeply how ethnicity comes to be.

Paying careful attention to context is one of the key tenets of the constructivist approach to ethnicity, and a primary goal of this chapter has been to treat globalization as a context fundamental to understanding contemporary manifestations and reconfigurations of ethnicity. What should be clear from the preceding discussion is that globalization gives rise to conditions that affect both the need and capacity for ethnic belonging. Globalization creates incentives for individuals and groups to cling to or form ethnic attachments and provides mechanisms that facilitate doing so. The incentives to attach to or identify with an ethnicity may be both psychological and emotional on the one hand, or instrumental and carefully calculated on the other. As has been argued in this chapter, they are usually some combination of both.

> *"Globalization creates incentives for individuals and groups to cling to or form ethnic attachments and provides mechanisms that facilitate doing so. The incentives to attach to or identify with an ethnicity may be both psychological and emotional on the one hand, or instrumental and carefully calculated on the other . . . they are usually some combination of both."*

As a composite of forces that are restructuring economic, political, and sociocultural life in fundamental ways, globalization is arguably unsettling. For the thousands of people migrating across borders each year to unfamiliar terrain, the process of resettlement is difficult and demanding. For the countless individuals or groups who perceive that their familiar patterns of life are being altered or disrupted by an influx of newcomers, the process or prospects of adjustment may also be unsettling. In addition to demographic changes, globalization also entails economic changes that affect the material well-being or lack thereof for individuals around the world. Economic globalization may privilege or disadvantage some groups more so than others, or result in ethnic groups being pitted against one another in heightened competition for scarce resources. In this way, global capitalism may use existing ethnic identities to further its aims of profit-making, but the conditions of economic deprivation as in Chiapas, or economic competition as in cities like Miami, which result from globalization, also provide incentives to attach to and organize around ethnicity.

Globalization, then, can be both psychologically and materially disruptive, and ethnicity offers both a refuge and a strategy for coping with the disruption. Yet, globalization not only creates conditions that help explain the need for or utility of ethnicity, but it simultaneously entails factors that facilitate identification and mobilization along ethnic lines. Politically, globalization involves the emergence and growing prominence of international organizations, treaties, and structures, many of which recognize, even reward, ethnic belonging and foster ethnic political mobilization. Whether or not ethnic identification and mobilization are channeled through international organizations, technology is an important dimension of globalization that eases the formation and maintenance of ethnic identities and the organization of ethnic interests.

Two important caveats are in order before concluding this examination of globalization's implications for ethnicity. The first is that globalization itself is not a behemoth with a universal, all-encompassing power to dictate social realities at will. The forces of globalization are powerful, but not unidirectional, not deterministic and not irreversible. To the extent that globalization shapes ethnicities, it does so through individuals and groups acting and reacting to the circumstances of their lives. This, then, leads to the second caveat, which is foregrounded by the constructivist approach. Ethnicity is not some ready-made set of endowments that globalization awakens intact. Immigrants, for example, re-create rather than transplant the ethnic identities they assume in a new homeland. Nor is ethnicity an automatic and easily predictable response rooted solely in a rational calculation of the costs and benefits that result from globalization. The Mayan Indians in Chiapas responded to deprivation associated with globalization, but they did so through leaders who helped to crystallize the grievances and catalyze the response, and via ideologies that linked the material concerns to cultural identities and beliefs. Ethnic identities and ethnic relations are, in other words, complex constructions—constructions that must be situated within the context of global change.

5

Gendering Globalization, Globalizing Gender

On September 4, 1995, more than fifty thousand women from across the globe gathered in Beijing, China, for the fourth UN World Conference on Women. Many came as official delegates for the 189 UN-member states represented at the conference. Others came as members of the 2,500 NGOs from around the world who were granted observer status at the conference. They came from Africa, Asia, Europe, North and South America, from rich countries and very poor ones, and from authoritarian regimes, monarchies, and democracies. As a group, these participants comprised an impressive panoply of different social, cultural, religious, racial, linguistic, sexual, political, and ideological backgrounds. Yet, they all came with some degree of hope for and commitment to improving the lives of women. The conference itself, the events that led up to it, the themes that comprised it, and the politics that surrounded it illustrate the close and complex connection between globalization and gender as an identity or form of belonging.

Some aspects of the conference called into question the notion of "woman" as a universal category, or the idea that women as a group automatically share common interests or experiences. At the same time the numerous topics that brought together women from around the world, and the widespread agreement that existed and was codified in the final Platform for Action, indicate that women as a group do indeed share common concerns. The conference focused on a range of topics that included poverty, education, health care, violence, armed conflict, and the environment. Not only do these topics have significant implications for women, they are also closely related to globalization. In fact, each of the issues focused on at the conference connects closely, albeit differently, to global change. Moreover, the growing knowledge of and awareness about these issues on the part of women, as well as women's capacity to act on or resist them, are also linked to global change. This chapter examines the relationships between globalization and gender. Specifically, it illustrates how globalization relies upon and perpetuates gender ideologies and stereotypes that have particularly troubling implications for women; and how globalization creates opportunities and resources that facilitate women's transnational political mobilization. The chapter concludes with a brief look at how gender intersects with citizenship, nationhood, and ethnicity.

What Is Gender?

Like many of the concepts examined in this book, the terminology associated with gender appears, at first glance, simple and straightforward. When people are asked about their gender, it is likely that they will respond by identifying as female or male. Yet these are categories of sex, not gender. They connote an anatomical, biological, or genetic distinction. To respond to the question on the basis of gender, an individual should identify as either feminine or masculine. These are categories that suggest behavioral, attitudinal, or physical characteristics. Masculine, for example, typically signifies toughness, strength, or aggression. Feminine, on the other hand, tends to convey tenderness or passivity. Assuming that the individual was aware of the distinction between sex (a biological category) and gender (a social one), it is still likely that a woman, or female, would identify her gender as feminine and a man, or male, as masculine. Doing so is perfectly consistent with assumptions and beliefs widespread across space and time that women are feminine and men are masculine. Nevertheless, a great deal of confusion and debate exists around the precise nature of the relationship between sex and gender. If women are indeed feminine (soft, tender, timid) and men are masculine (strong, tough, aggressive), is this because genetics, or sex, biologically determines distinct social behaviors and attitudes? Or, do women tend to be feminine and men masculine because society and culture teaches and requires them to be so?

Many individuals believe that gender behaviors and attitudes are the natural outcomes of, or biologically determined by, sex. If women are more likely than men to cry, for example, and men more likely to engage in physical violence, these tendencies are believed to be somehow hard-wired into an individual's brain or psyche as a result of her or his genetic sex makeup. When young boys behave aggressively on the playground, the common refrain "boys will be boys" implies that this behavior is inevitable given the chromosomal or hormonal makeup of the male sex. Similarly, many assume that if a young girl prefers the color pink, or dolls instead of toy trucks, this choice is predetermined by her biological makeup. In some cases, these assumptions and their related stereotypes are seemingly harmless. In other cases, they are used to explain, justify, and perhaps even perpetuate dangerous actions and behavior.

An adult variant of the "boys will be boys" refrain often surfaces, for example, in reference to male sexual behavior and violence in the context of war. Mass rapes and sexual torture of women are common occurrences in wars, but the bloody conflicts in the Balkans in the early 1990s brought international attention to the gender-specific tragedies of war. Camps were established for the explicit purpose of raping women, and the number of women raped in the region during the war reached beyond sixty thousand. Explanations for this type of male violence toward women in the context of war vary, but one of the most common is what Ruth Seifert (1996) describes as the "sexual urge" argument. From this perspective rape is a consequence of testosterone, which creates in men a powerful need to have sex. Because male soldiers are away from wives and girlfriends during war, rape and sexual aggression become the mechanism for satisfying this innate biological urge.

Empirical and theoretical evidence to contradict this explanation is abundant. Countless studies have determined that rape is not a crime of sex, but one of aggression. It fulfills not sexual desire, but a male perpetrator's need to dominate and humiliate the woman (Brownmiller 1975). Studies have also shown that rape is not equally common across cultures and time. In many cultures, particularly in the West, rape is a relatively widespread occurrence. In other societies, however, it is largely nonexistent. Moreover, evidence indicates that even in the West, sexual violence occurred less often during earlier historical epochs (Tomaselli and Porter 1986). If rape were indeed rooted in a biological urge for sex, these variations would be less prevalent. Finally, scientific research has left biochemists uncertain about the precise nature of the relationship between testosterone and aggression—namely, which is cause and which is consequence. Studies of primates, for example, found that aggressive behavior, stressful situations, and social status produce testosterone, not the reverse (Seifert 1996, 36).

Despite evidence to the contrary, these genetic interpretations of gendered behavior persist, as many people, academics among them, insist that there are fundamental differences between women and men—differences in attitude, behavior, emotion—and that these differences are rooted in genes. Specifically, evolutionary psychologists such as Robert Wright (1994) and others turn to Darwinian theories of evolution and natural selection to explain gender relations and observed differences in gender roles (Buss

1994; Daly and Wilson 1983). Using the example of sexual attitudes and behavior, Wright claims that human males, like male members of other species, are the sexual aggressors or wooers, as well as the more promiscuous sex. Men, according to Wright, "are naturally inclined to cheat on their mates," "never feel 'violated' by sex with a woman," and are, in his words, "by nature oppressive, possessive, flesh-obsessed pigs" (1994, 42–44). Women, on the other hand, are less sexually eager and less promiscuous. Unlike men, women can and do experience anguish or violation as a result of uncommitted sex. Not only do these personality traits constitute a general rule among the human species, Wright argues, but they are linked directly to genes. Women's sexual reserve is rooted in the fact that because they are saddled with the responsibility of giving birth, they can reproduce much less often than men. Therefore, women must guard their eggs much more carefully than men do their sperm. For males, reproduction is, according to Wright, a frequent and low-cost affair: "the more sex partners, the more chances to get genes into the next generation" (p. 36).

Views such as Wright's have been widely rejected and discredited among most of the scholarly community. More pervasive is the argument that gender is a socially learned, not genetically determined, behavior. V. Spike Peterson and Anne Sisson Runyan maintain that "gender is not a physiological concept but a social one that refers to sets of culturally defined character traits labeled 'masculinity' and 'femininity'" (1999, 257). It is "an acquired identity learned through performing prescribed gender roles" (p. 5). "Gender," Maria Patricia Fernández Kelly writes, "is a process woven into the economic and political fabric of society. It is therefore not a characteristic of individuals nor a static phenomenon but a continuously evolving sequence of interactive events" (1994, 143). Similarly, Robert Connell (1987) defines gender as an active process that creates divisions of labor, power, and emotions between men and women as well as modes of dress, deportment, and identity. Joan Scott writes that gender is "a primary way of signifying relationships of power" (1986, 1,067). Finally, Marianne Marchand and Anne Sisson Runyan emphasize that gender operates not only at the level of social relations, but also ideologically, "especially in terms of gendered representations and valorizations of social processes and practices" (2000, 8).

From this perspective, if men are more aggressive than women, it is because they are taught or socialized to be. And if women are more passive or tender than men, it is because they, too, are trained as such—encouraged, for example, to be "lady-like." This socialization process occurs at home, in schools, and through the media and is firmly entrenched in social institutions and structures ranging from religion to business to politics. From the moment a child enters the world, she or he is taught the rules of gender. Some parents may seek consciously to avoid imposing gender norms or enforcing gender stereotypes on their children;

yet the social pervasiveness of these rules and roles is daunting. In fact, of the myriad of sociocultural identities an individual acquires or lives in a lifetime, gender is arguably one of the most ubiquitous. As Cynthia Epstein writes: "No aspect of social life—whether the gathering of crops, the ritual of religion, the formal dinner party or the organization of government—is free from the dichotomous thinking that casts the world in categories of 'male' and 'female'" (1988, 232).

> *"'No aspect of social life—whether the gathering of crops, the ritual of religion, the formal dinner party or the organization of government—is free from the dichotomous thinking that casts the world in categories of "male" and "female."'"*

For analysts or observers who consider gender to be the product of biological sex, the ubiquitousness and persistence of gender roles is proof of its genetic roots. Yet, beneath the pervasiveness of gender lies ample and compelling evidence of its fluidity. At the most individual and anecdotal levels, girls and boys, or women and men, possess both feminine and masculine traits and characteristics in varied degrees or combinations. Moreover, all individuals can identify experiences in school, work, or play where they have been conditioned or trained to behave according to an assigned gender and been sanctioned, however subtly, for not doing so.

The ambivalence of gender is also evident at a broader or more universal level. The admonition "act like a man," for example, does not mean the same thing in the United States as it does in Papua New Guinea, nor does it mean the same thing in the year 2003 that it meant in 1640, 1011, or 500 B.C. (Peterson and Runyan 1999). Masculinity, in other words, has a long history as a sociocultural category, but its form and content vary across space and time. Contrary to their contemporary significations, the color pink once conveyed power and was, as such, worn proudly by men. Blue connoted passivity and was more commonly associated with women. Moreover, in spite of the widespread belief that the world is comprised of only two genders—feminine and masculine—some cultures recognize the existence of a third gender (Nanda 2000).

This emphasis on the social constructedness of gender is in no way meant to suggest that gender distinctions are meaningless, arbitrary, or inconsequential—quite the contrary. Gender is deeply imbued with power, politics, and hierarchy. Not only does masculinity and femininity constitute a near-universal dichotomization, but the traits and characteristics defined as or associated with masculinity are, with few exceptions, more highly valued than those associated with femininity. Traits such as aggressiveness, competitiveness, and rationality, for example, are among the most valued in fields such as politics or business. Notably, these characteristics are also widely associated with masculinity. Women who wish to succeed in fields or occupations typically thought of as men's or male, are expected to behave "like men" and are criticized or professionally constrained for not doing so. During a speech in which she withdrew from the 1988 U.S. presidential primaries, Congresswoman Patricia Schroeder publicly shed tears of emotion and regret. The fact that she did so was, for many, proof that she was unfit to hold such high political office. Meanwhile, men or boys who are perceived as acting like women or girls are typically disparaged. Contrast, for instance, society's reaction to a woman in a business suit with reactions to a man wearing a dress (Peterson and Runyan 1999, 44). As with all generalizations, there are exceptions to these patterns, but they are just that, exceptions. In some societies, such as that of the United States, sensitivity is increasingly valued in men. Meanwhile, women in some societies are encouraged to adopt more masculine traits in order to succeed in politics or business. They must do so, however, without sacrificing their femininity. Failure on a woman's part to walk this fine line typically invites further attempts at social sanctioning, such as being labeled a lesbian.

Societies, then, not genes, decide the form and content of gender roles and identities. They do so in the context of and through processes associated with economics, politics, and culture—contexts and processes now heavily influenced by globalization. Part of this analysis focuses on how globalization and gender interrelate. Central to that examination, however, is the recognition that gender, although socially defined, is highly significant and consequential for humankind. Moreover, contemporary globalization seems to ensure that it will continue to be so. Gender, as ideology and identity, and the manner in which globalization relies upon, perpetuates, and reconfigures gender significantly affects both women and men. Women, however, tend to suffer the most extreme consequences of gender ideologies and exploitation. A 1997 Human Development Report by the United Nations made this painfully clear by concluding that "no society treats its women as well as its men" (UNDP 1997, 39). In 1999, Lois West, political analyst and participant in the UN World Women's Conference in Beijing, agreed: "Social change for women is happening rapidly and globally, but there is still no society where women enjoy the same opportunities as men" (1999, 177).

Aggregate data and statistics are readily available to prove the inequity between women and men throughout the world in terms of wealth, health, education, and political power. Women are the greatest and fastest growing share of the world's poor; they own only 1 percent of the world's land, are significantly underrepresented in the higher paid, higher status sectors of the workforce, and earn universally lower wages than men for the same work. In some countries, women employed in industry and services earn as little as 50 percent of what men earn (UNIFEM 2000). Two out of every three illiterate people in the world are women. Domestic violence is a leading cause of injury and death to women around the world, and in almost every culture, boy babies are preferred over girl babies. Female infanticide has been reliably documented in China and India, and a 1994 survey in the United States found that 86 percent of men and 59 percent of women would prefer a male child over a female if they were to have only one (Seager 1997). In only eight countries in the world has women's share of seats in parliament reached a level of 30 percent: Denmark, Finland, Germany, Iceland, the Netherlands, Norway, Sweden, and South Africa. In the governing bodies of some countries, women's representation is as low as 0 to 4 percent. In many others, such as Burundi, Eritrea, Moldova, Tajikistan, and the United States, it hovers around only 14 percent (UNIFEM 2000; UNDP 2002).

Neither gender nor globalization is, however, universal or homogenous in its effects. As already noted, the specifics of gender identities and gender relations vary across cultures, as does the impact of globalization. In other words, although all women around the world are affected by gender ideology, globalization, and the intersection of the two, they are not affected equally or identically. Failure to acknowledge the particularities of women's lives has hindered not only analysis, but also social and political mobilization on the part of women worldwide who aim to resist or reconfigure aspects of global change (Bhavnani 2001).

During the 1970s, Robin Morgan, an American writer, feminist activist, and editor of an anthology on the U.S. women's movement turned her attention to compiling an International Women's Movement Anthology. Published in 1984 and titled *Sisterhood Is Global*, the volume sets out to document the situations, concerns, and responses of women around the world to problems of women's subordination, sexual exploitation, and gender-based oppression. The project's stated assumption is that women across the globe share common concerns because of their status as women. Addressing those concerns, Robin Morgan writes, necessitates that "we act now—speak to one another as women, listen to one another as women, and pass on what we have learned" (1984, xxiii). Morgan goes on to credit feminist political philosophy with providing a new approach to international affairs that moves beyond diplomatic posturing or abstractions to focus on concrete, unifying realities of human existence and strategies for their betterment. She writes:

[T]he historical, cross-cultural opposition women express to war and our healthy skepticism of certain technological advances (by which most men seem overly impressed at first and disillusioned at last) are only two instances of shared attitudes among women which seem

basic to a common world view. Nor is there anything mystical or biologically deterministic about this commonality. It is the result of a
common condition which, despite variations in degree, is experienced
by all human beings who are born female. (1984, 4, emphasis in the
original)

Morgan's view is just one illustration of a perspective shared by many
participants in an international women's movement that began to burgeon
in the 1970s. But her assumptions and assertions about women's worldwide commonalties have also been put forth by feminist academics. In a
1994 analysis of "Gender Inequality and Cultural Differences," political scientist Susan Okin maintains that women around the world suffer grave
inequalities in comparison to men in the areas of income, economic opportunity, education, and health care. She feels that gender as an ideology is to
blame. Okin acknowledges some variations in gender roles and women's
lives throughout the world, but she insists that the differences between
women in poorer countries and women in richer countries are not qualitative ones, but are differences of degree. She focuses on women's unequal
access to power and resources in regions around the world and concludes
repeatedly that poor women in poorer countries suffer circumstances that
are "similar but worse" than those of richer women in richer countries.
Arguments like Okin's, that women around the world share the experience of discrimination based on their membership in the sexual category of "female," support the view that sisterhood is, or at least could
and perhaps should be, global. Her argument might also be read as
reflecting or contributing to a welcome awareness on the part of more
privileged women in wealthy countries, such as the United States, that
their "sisters" in the developing world are at an even greater disadvantage than they are. Nevertheless, views like Okin's and Morgan's have
been criticized on a number of important counts. First, the tendency of
many feminists, particularly in the Western world, to treat women's
issues, situations, or concerns as universal fails to appreciate the very real
qualitative, not just quantitative, differences in women's lives and their
struggles around the world. Beginning in the 1980s, and evident, for
example, in many of the meetings and events related to the UN Decade
for Women (1975–85), some women from countries in the less-developed
South argued that the "international" women's movement advanced, in
effect, a "particular" view and experience—namely, that of women in
North America and Western Europe—masking it as a "universal" one.
Related to that critique was the charge that many women from advanced
industrialized countries of the North or West were failing to recognize or
acknowledge their own complicity in the oppression and exploitation of
women in countries throughout Central and South America, Africa, and
Asia. In the United States, for example, the clothes that many women

wear, the food we eat, and the child care we rely upon are available and affordable as a result of other women's underpaid, and in some cases unpaid, labor.

One outcome of having a better understanding of the differences or particularities of women's lives is realizing that gender is not the only, and perhaps not even the primary, source of women's oppression. For some Palestinian women, for example, Zionism and U.S. militarism may be as oppressive, if not more so, than male interpretations and invocations of Islamic fundamentalism. For women working in the many hundreds of export processing zones (EPZs) throughout the developing world, capitalism and Western consumerism may be more fundamental sources of exploitation than sexism. Furthermore, when some Western feminists do acknowledge differences in women's lives, or that gender is experienced in particular ways (as does Okin with her refrain of "similar but worse"), they run the risk of portraying some women, and typically Third World women, as poor, backward, victimized "Others," while Western women, in contrast, are implicitly represented as modern, educated, and independent (Ang 1995; Mohanty 1991).

"For some Palestinian women . . . Zionism and U.S. militarism may be as oppressive, if not more so, than male interpretations and invocations of Islamic fundamentalism. For women working in the many hundreds of export processing zones (EPZs) throughout the developing world, capitalism and Western consumerism may be more fundamental sources of exploitation than sexism."

The impact of such cultural stereotypes is far from inconsequential as evinced in the controversy surrounding the issue of female genital cutting (FGC), as well as in the practice of veiling among Muslim women. The former issue has captured widespread international attention over the past decade or so, due in part to the globalization of the women's movement, the related emergence of an international human rights regime, the advances in communications technology, and the migration of women and men from countries who practice FGC. Today, few people throughout the world have not heard or read about the painful and in some cases dangerous procedure, practiced in more than two dozen countries across Africa, that involves removing all or part of a young girl's clitoris. During the 1990s, films and publications such as *Warrior Marks* (Walker and Parmar 1993) and countless other exposés in the U.S. print and visual media publicized the issue among American audiences. As a result, FGC became somewhat of a cause célèbre among some Western feminists.

The cultural history and politics that surround FGC are complex. In many societies it is a tradition that a girl or her family shun only at great social and economic risk. As one father in the Ivory Coast explains: "If your daughter has not been excised, the father is not allowed to speak at village meetings. No man in the village will marry her. It is an obligation. We have done it, we do it and we will continue to do it" (Dugger 1996, 4). Because women in many of these countries have few options for survival without a husband, genital cutting is an important guarantee of marriageability. Furthermore, some young girls welcome the rite of passage to womanhood (some do not), and some families take pride in the honor and celebrations that accompany the event (Dugger 1996). That FGC is painful is not generally in question, nor is there any reason to doubt the sincerity of the women and men from outside countries who have mobilized to stop the practice. The problem is this: too often Western activists fail to educate themselves fully about the historical, cultural, social, political, and economic contexts and complexities about which they protest. There is also a tendency to overlook the existence of, or a failure to seek, the expertise and cooperation of indigenous groups who are seeking to address the issue from a more immediate, informed, and often personal perspective (Honig 1999).

The same has been true with regard to veiling. Many women outside of Muslim countries, and certainly some within, view the practice of veiling as oppressive and designed specifically to restrict and control women. In some cases this may be accurate, as it was in the example of the Taliban in Afghanistan forcing women to wear the *burqua*—a heavy wrap that covers a woman's body from head to toe, leaving only a small screened opening at the eyes—which severely restricts women's mobility, and threatens their physical and psychological well-being. There are, however, many variations of veils and many reasons for wearing them. Some Muslim women wear the veil with pride in their culture and with respect for their religion and contend that it is a symbol of honor for women, not of oppression. At a 2000 forum on Women in Islam held in Gaza City, a young graduate student, covered from head to toe in a black veil, stood up to proclaim, "I represent the free, modern, Muslim woman!" Referring to her dress she explained: "This way, I'm not defending myself against the looks of other people. I express the genuine face of the true Muslim, who comes out into the world not as a woman, but as a human being." Outside of the conference, a local woman shop owner made the following distinction, "In Europe and America, they dress for the outside. In our culture, women dress for themselves" (Prusher 2000, 8–9).

The inability or unwillingness of some women to acknowledge and respect the differences among women led many activists and scholars to question the very category of "woman." Chandra Mohanty writes:

The assumption of women as an already constituted, coherent group with identical interests and desires, regardless of class, ethnic or racial location, or contradictions, implies a notion of gender or sexual difference or even patriarchy which can be applied universally and cross-culturally. (1991, 55)

Similarly, Elizabeth Spelman warns:

The notion of the generic "woman" functions in feminist thought much the way the notion of generic "man" has functioned in Western philosophy: it obscures the heterogeneity of women and cuts off examination of the significance of such heterogeneity for feminist theory and political activity. (1988, ix)

These critiques have and continue to pose significant challenges to an international women's movement and to feminist scholarship. For practical, political, ethical, and analytical reasons, it is essential to remain aware of the differences in women's lives whether related to nationality, ethnicity, race, class, sexual orientation, or religion. Nonetheless, women throughout the world do share some similar concerns as women, and as the next two sections show, globalization affects and exacerbates these concerns and women's ability to mobilize around them.

Gendering Globalization

Incorporating women into economic and political analyses of the world system is not new. During the 1970s a growing number of scholars interested in development began to focus on women's roles in economic development and the differential impact development policies had on women compared to men. "Women in Development" emerged as a prominent field, as scholars, many of them women, emphasized factors such as the economic importance of women's unpaid labor, the role of women in agriculture and subsistence farming, and the particularly harmful effects of some development strategies for women's well-being (Boserup 1970). As interest in the topic of women in development expanded, an emerging literature, preferring the label "Gender and Development," began to offer a more structural critique of the inequalities between women and men. From this perspective, it is not sufficient to simply add women to existing models or frameworks for development, and stir. Instead, gender asymmetries must be recognized as deeply rooted in fundamental structures of thought (Fernández Kelly 1994).

Marianne Marchand and Anne Sisson Runyan's recent volume on *Gender and Global Restructuring* continues in this vein: "Gender figures prominently in the globalization problématique, not only because global restructuring tends to reinforce and exacerbate existing gender inequalities, but also because it is embedded in highly gendered discourse" (2000, 11). This section first illuminates the various ways globalization exacerbates hardships and inequalities for women, then turns to gender ideology and discourse to explain how and why. The focus is on women, but globalization affects and involves men in highly gendered ways as well. As noted earlier in this chapter, gender works through the dichotomization of masculinity and femininity and the characteristics or traits assigned to each. In the process of globalization, as Charlotte Hooper explains, "different 'elements' or ingredients of masculinity and femininity are co-opted in new or old configurations to serve particular interests and particular gendered (and other) identities are consolidated and legitimated or downgraded and devalued" (2000, 60). Some of the results include the undermining of men's personal authority in the family and a reduction of the value of so-called masculine attributes in the labor market. In fact, for each of the ways, described below, that globalization and gender affect women, there is typically a related implication for men. This leads Linda McDowell to conclude that "gender is being used to divide women's and men's interests in the labor market in such a way that both sexes—at least among the majority of the population—are losing out" (cited in Hooper 2000, 60).

As described in chapter 1, the economic dimensions of globalization, fueled by neoliberal ideology, entail the liberalization of markets, the privatization of capital, and the flexibility of labor. New actors emerge and gain prominence, while others are weakened as the patterns and processes of economic production and exchange are restructured in significant ways. Transnational corporations have gained power and importance in the international system, illustrating and furthering the mobility and increased autonomy of global capital. Myriad IGOs, including the World Trade Organization, the World Bank, and the International Monetary Fund, now function to promote and protect the effective functioning of the international economic system. Meanwhile, states, once the predominant if not the unitary actors in the international system, have seen their capacity to manage or regulate domestic economic affairs diminished by the liberalization and globalization of the marketplace and by the IGOs to whom they have ceded a significant amount of autonomy and control.

Workers have also been profoundly affected by globalization, but not in uniform ways. Some workers in some parts of the world benefit from global restructuring, but many others suffer from the increased competitiveness and fluidity of the international economy. Corporations have been downsizing, outsourcing, and decentralizing production in ways that demand a flexible labor force and result in the relative growth of informal, temporary, underpaid, and insecure employment. Moreover, weakened states are less able or willing to safeguard the well-being of their residents when corporations eliminate jobs or relocate manufacturing plants to take advantage of less expensive labor overseas.

All of these processes are problematic in various ways, but they are particularly so for women. To begin, one significant and widely noted aspect of economic globalization is the dramatic rise in free trade areas (FTAs) and export processing zones (EPZs). The number of countries in the world with EPZs increased from twenty-four in 1976 to ninety-three in 1998. As significant as the increase in the number of these production facilities is, the fact remains that the overwhelming majority of workers have been and continue to be women, and particularly young women between the ages of eighteen and twenty-five. In many countries, including Malaysia, Mexico, Philippines, and Sri Lanka, women comprise 80 percent or more of the employees in EPZs (Pyle 2001, 62–63). From one perspective, the emergence and spread of these EPZs have opened up new employment opportunities for women, and indeed many women have been able to improve their life conditions by earning an independent wage. By all accounts, however, the working conditions associated with these factories range from bad to horrendous. Women endure long hours (often ten to twelve hours per day), low pay (as little as 50 cents per hour), forced overtime, and no benefits. They work in physically dangerous conditions, including excessive heat and noise, hazardous materials, and unsafe equipment. As a result, many women suffer long-term health problems (Enriquez 1999; Pyle 2001).

"the working conditions associated with these factories range from bad to horrendous. Women endure long hours (often ten to twelve hours per day), low pay (as little as 50 cents per hour), forced overtime, and no benefits. They work in physically dangerous conditions, including excessive heat and noise, hazardous materials, and unsafe equipment."

In spite of the view that EPZs provide women workers with needed income, studies show that while the wages paid by some EPZs are higher than the wages at similar jobs locally, the pay in other EPZs is worse (Joekes and Weston 1994). There is also evidence of the habitual underpayment of wages earned by women in EPZs. Furthermore, women workers are often forced to live on-site in high-cost, but substandard, housing, and without access to medical facilities or child care (Pyle 2001). The latter is a particular problem given that the rapid incorporation over the past several decades of women around the world into wage labor has not been accompanied by a decline in women's domestic work or women's share of the responsibility for house and child care. Finally, women workers in EPZs also endure perpetual harassment on the job and coming to and from work. Some women describe sexual harassment by male supervisors in terms of a policy of "lay down or be laid off" (Peterson and Runyan 1999, 144). International awareness of the working conditions in EPZs and women's resistance to them has grown steadily, but a recent study of the U.S.-Mexico border region, an area very heavily populated by EPZs, concludes that living standards have not improved for a large proportion of the population, and women's working conditions have improved little, if at all (Fussell 2000).

EPZs and FTAs offer powerful examples of how global economic restructuring has led to what Saskia Sassen (1996) terms the "feminization of the proletariat." Also contributing to this process is the increase in informal jobs as well as temporary and part-time employment—what scholars of the global economy label the informal economy or informal sector. As Peterson and Runyan explain, the informal sector includes "a whole range of legal and extralegal economic activities that lie largely outside national accounting, labour legislation, and social protection mandates and are typically performed in the contexts of self-employment, family businesses, and insecure wage work" (1999, 140). Petty trading of handicrafts and foodstuffs are examples of informal sector activity as is the increasingly common subcontracting by large firms to small workplaces, "sweat shops," or home-based workers who do piecework or "homework" for long hours at dismal wages.

Between 1980 and 1990 the relative weight of informal sector employment increased substantially in all areas of the world (Benería 2001, 35). A 1999 UN report found a notable increase in home-based work in both industrialized and developing countries, but a particularly sharp increase in lower wage countries. Employment in subcontracting is estimated to involve between twenty-two and thirty-three million people in developing countries, and a very high percentage of these employees are women. In many countries, women comprise 80 percent or more of home-based workers (Benería 2001; Bullock 1994). Women are over 89 percent of home garment workers in Brazil, Peru, and Thailand, and over 90 percent of home-based workers in half the European countries. In addition to the garment industry, women predominate in shoe sewing in Italy, Spain, Colombia, Uruguay, and Mexico, and in carpet weaving in Turkey, Nepal, and Iran (Pyle 2001, 65). The result is that in many countries women's informal sector activities account for 50 percent or more of the GDP (Benería 2001, 39). Analyses of the informal sector uniformly characterize it in terms of very low earnings, unstable working conditions, absence of job contracts or benefits, poor access to social services, and illegal or quasi-legal work. In fact, some scholars conclude that the risk to women's well-being in these informal networks is even greater than in EPZs (Pyle 2001, 65).

Globalization not only affects women's lives in their home countries, but has also increased the number of women migrating across state borders. As Jan Pettman states, an estimated "50 million people [are] 'on the move' internationally each year," half of whom are women (1996, 66). Women constitute a majority of the world's refugees fleeing political, economic, and environmental crises, and an increasingly large proportion of migrants who leave home in search of work (Sassen 1996). Two burgeoning industries exemplify, often tragically, the intersection of economic globalization, migration, and women's exploitation—the "international maid trade" and international sex trafficking.

Domestic work, including household labor and child care, has long been a sector dominated by women, and for many women around the world, it offers one of few opportunities for employment. In Brazil, for example, 20 percent of employed women work as domestic servants (Benería 2001, 51). In recent years, however, the industry has gone global. Accurate data on the international maid trade are hard to come by because many of these women migrate illegally and their work is undocumented. But as Geertje Nijeholt notes, the international domestic service industry is "a multimillion-dollar transnational business which is closely related to other agencies that facilitate the migration process, such as banks, money-lenders, hotels, airlines, illegal money-changers, translation services, medical clinics and training institutions" (1995, 59). During the 1990s, Asian women became the fastest growing category of the world's migrant workers. In the 1970s, for example, women were only 15 percent of the migrant labor force in Asia. They are now more than half. The Philippines, Indonesia, and Thailand are primary sending countries, and an estimated 1.5 million Asian women are now working abroad (Pyle 2001, 61).

Wages for these domestic workers are very low, often no more than U.S.$100 per week, and working conditions can be treacherous. In 2000, many in the United States were shocked by a rash of cases that exposed an industry that amounts to a form of modern-day slavery (Bales 1999). Lakireddy Bali Reddy, one of the largest landowners in Berkeley, California, was indicted for luring dozens of women to the United States from India with the promise of jobs. Yet, when they arrived, he forced them to work as unpaid maids in his many buildings and as his personal sex slaves. Rene R. Bonetti, a satellite engineer in Gaithersburg, Maryland, was indicted for trapping a Brazilian maid in his home for twenty years with no pay and insufficient food. By the time neighbors discovered the situation, the maid, Hilda Rosa Dos Santos, had repeatedly been beaten, burned, and had an untreated tumor in her stomach the size of a soccer ball. Months later, another family was also arrested for illegally transporting a teenage girl from Cameroon and forcing her to work for no pay. She was made to care for several children, rarely permitted to leave the townhouse, and never allowed to see a physician or dentist (France 2000).

Countless others, a majority of whom are young girls, suffer similar fates, having been trapped or tricked by promise of jobs and education. Cautious estimates place the current number of slaves in the world at twenty-seven million (Bales 1999, 8).

Alongside growth in the international maid trade is the burgeoning sex industry that is global in scope and highly gendered. While a substantial number of men profit from the sex trade and benefit as consumers from the sex industry, its commodities and victims are overwhelmingly women. Jan Pettman discusses the confluence of the sex industry and globalization in terms of "the international political economy of sex" (1996, 197). Sex tourism and militarized prostitution in the form of brothels, massage parlors, and bars, and a booming Internet bride business create the demand for women. In Thailand, sex tourism was actually adopted as a form of economic development in the 1970s and now flourishes thanks to thousands of male travelers each year from Europe, North America, and Japan. By some estimates, as many as 1.5 percent of the total female population in Malaysia, the Philippines, Thailand, and Indonesia work as prostitutes (Lim 1998). The United Nations reports that thousands of Burmese women are trafficked every year into brothels in Thailand, and more than two hundred thousand Nepalese women and girls are forced to work in brothels in India (UNIFEM 2000). Between 1991 and 1998, more than five hundred thousand Ukrainian women were trafficked for the purposes of sexual exploitation to countries in Europe, North America, and the Middle East (Hughes 2000).

Overall, the value of the global trade in women as sex commodities is estimated to be between U.S.$7 and $12 billion annually (Hughes 2000, 625). It has become, as Peterson and Runyan explain, "a major pillar of the global economy, erected literally on the bodies of women" (1999, 139). The United States plays a significant role in the demand for women for sex. During 2000, U.S. law enforcement officials and the INS cracked down on prostitution rings in Atlanta and Chicago that were smuggling women from Asia. They identified 250 other brothels in twenty-six different states suspected of using unwitting immigrant women as prostitutes (France 2000). The mail-order bride business has also become a multimillion-dollar transnational industry.

"The United States plays a significant role in the demand for women for sex. During 2000, U.S. law enforcement officials and the INS cracked down on prostitution rings in Atlanta and Chicago that were smuggling women from Asia. They identified 250 other brothels in twenty-six different states suspected of using unwitting immigrant women as prostitutes."

Peterson and Runyan cite estimates of more than 250 companies in the United States alone that specialize in marketing women from Asia, Latin America and the former Soviet Union as brides for American men who are willing to pay as much as $15,000 for the company's services (1999, 140).

The available supply of women to service the booming global sex industry is rooted in a variety of factors including unemployment and impoverishment, both of which are caused, in part, by global economic restructuring and poorer states' desperate need for foreign exchange. In some countries, the sex sector contributes up to 14 percent of the GDP. In Thailand, for example, sex tourism pumps an estimated $27 billion a year into the economy, and in Indonesia, it accounts for $3.3 billion annually. This is a substantial sum of money for income-strapped countries, and it helps to explain why many governments actually support the illicit trade in women and many others look the other way. The collapse of communism in the Soviet Union initially brought grave economic hardship to the region and opened up a pool of millions of unemployed and desperate women upon which traffickers have and continue to prey. Moreover, privatization and market liberalization have allowed, and in some cases necessitated, the emergence of an informal, and in this case illegal, economy. By 1995, the informal sector accounted for 50 percent of Russia's GDP, and the sex trade contributed substantially. In fact, so much money was tied up in prostitution that some Russian government officials advocated legalizing it in order to collect taxes on the lucrative trade (Pettman 1996).

Perhaps it goes without saying that the conditions for women in the international sex trade are not good. The abuse takes many forms—economic, physical, and psychological. Traffickers can receive as much as U.S.$5,000 per woman, and pimps who own or control women can earn between U.S.$50,000 and $100,000 per year. Women see little if any of the profits from the sex industry, despite the fact the some are lured into it by the promise of lucrative wages. Women sex workers are expected to turn 50 to 75 percent of their earnings over to pimps, to pay for the cost of their room and board, and are often forced to work off the expense of their smuggling as "debt." They are routinely raped and physically abused, suffer emotional trauma, and are at a high risk of contracting sexually transmitted diseases, including the growing incidence of HIV/AIDS (Hughes 2000; Kempadoo and Doezema 1998; Lim 1998). Lest the analogy between sex trafficking and slavery seem overdrawn, in 1997, police in Milan, Italy, uncovered a gang of traffickers auctioning off women from the former Soviet Union. The women were stripped, displayed, and sold to the highest bidder for an average of U.S.$1,000 (Hughes 2000).

What may not be as obvious as the poor working conditions is the fact that although some women are aware they are entering into the sex trade, many others are tricked or trapped into it. They are lured by the promise of jobs as waitresses, dancers, or bartenders, and made to believe that a better life awaits them in a faraway place. The story of Irina, a seventeen-year-old Moldovan girl, is tragic and typical. Enticed by the guarantee of good wages as a waitress in Milan, Irina left for Italy in 1999 with a Moldovan couple and four other young women. The trip quickly took an unexpected turn. The young women were taken to Albania. Their passports were confiscated, and they were delivered to two men whom they were told had "purchased" them. Irina and the other girls were raped by a succession of Albanian men at all hours of the day and night, apparently as a form of psychological conditioning for a life of prostitution. Irina was then informed that she must work for a year as a prostitute in Milan to pay back her smuggling debt. Upon arrival in Italy, she managed to escape and ended up at a Catholic Refugee Center with forty other women, most of whom were also victims of sex trafficking. She, like the other women, arrived beaten, bruised, and emotionally traumatized (J. Smith 2000).

All of these are examples of how economic globalization and related patterns of migration or trafficking have and are affecting women around the world. But three important points remain in unraveling the relationship between globalization and gender. The first is the reminder that globalization is not simply economic in nature or scope. Second, documenting globalization's impact on women is only part of the story. It is also necessary to incorporate an understanding of how gender as ideology and identity influences patterns of globalization and their differential impact on women. Third, and the topic of the subsequent section, is the fact that globalization not only creates and perpetuates conditions that are harmful to women, but it simultaneously fuels and facilitates women's political mobilization and social activism.

Globalization, as has already been stated, is a multifaceted phenomena; and none of the economic trends or outcomes described above would be occurring as they are without advancements in communications and transportation technologies or changes in the global political realm. Technologies ranging from the Internet, to fax machines, to jet airplanes have and continue to be indispensable to the integration of a global marketplace and to the decentralization and informalization of production. It is these same technologies that make possible the transnational marketing, export, exchange, and exploitation of women. Conversely, technology, as will be evident in the next section, enhances the capacity of women around the world to challenge, resist, and reconfigure the harmful effects of global change. Globalization in the political realm also has ambiguous implications for women. It involves both the rise of transnational organizations and the decline in the power of states. The former trend supports, as can technology, women's resistance in ways that will be discussed in the next section, but the latter generally leaves women without needed support.

One example of how globalization's pressure on states has detrimental implications for women concerns structural adjustment programs (SAPs).

As a result of global interconnectedness, organizations such as the IMF have come to impose SAPs upon poorer or less developed countries. SAPs require states who wish to receive loans and assistance from international development organizations to adjust their economies in ways that conform to the dictates of neoliberal economic theory—namely, they are forced to shrink their public sector payments and employment, privatize state ownership, and reduce social service or welfare benefits to citizens. These SAPs have particularly deleterious effects on women (Peterson and Runyan 1999). Women are typically overrepresented in public sector jobs and depend more heavily on social services than do men. Nor are the negative impacts of economic restructuring for women restricted to the developing world. Between the mid-1980s and the 1990s, for example, the United States also instituted various measures to reduce welfare payments, and from all indications women have and continue to bear the brunt of this political response to global economic change (Deen 2000).

Globalization demands not only that states make certain adjustments in the economic realm, but many supporters of globalization maintain that it has also led to much needed democratization and political liberalization in various states throughout the world (Fukuyama 1989; Pye 1990). If democratization indeed entails political opportunities as opposed merely to economic liberalization and free markets, as is often the case, then in few cases can this trend be viewed as harmful to women. As the next section indicates, democratization can open for women important political space that did not previously exist. One notable exception involves Eastern Europe and the former Soviet Union, where the transition to democracy and away from communism, a system that guaranteed, in fact insisted, that women participate in the political organs or institutions of the state, has sharply reduced women's formal political presence. Under Soviet rule, women's representation in national governing bodies was as high as 29 percent during the 1980s, but dropped precipitously to an average of 7 percent in 1995 after the collapse of communism. Similarly, in Bulgaria, the percentage of parliamentary seats held by women dropped from 21 percent in 1987 to 13 percent in 1995. In Romania the percentage fell from 34 to 4; and in Slovakia from 30 to 15. Women's political gains in national parliaments have continued be slow since then (UNIFEM 2000).

Democratization, generally, has not been harmful to women, but what is notable and troubling is the creeping pace at which women are advancing into positions of political power, even in the most established democracies. As noted above, women in the United States, for example, currently hold less than 15 percent of the seats in Congress. In France the total is 11 percent, 7 percent in Japan, 18 percent in the United Kingdom, and 21 percent in Canada (UNIFEM 2000). Furthermore, it is a sad irony that just as some women in some countries are beginning to gain greater political voice in their governments, the power and sovereignty of states are said to be in decline. The United Nations recently called attention to this dilemma in reference to the commitments that governments made at the fourth UN World Conference on Women in Beijing:

> The commitments reflect an expectation that governments are responsible for implementing policies to improve the well-being of women, especially poor women, but they do not effectively address the ways in which market liberalization and privatization may undermine the capacity of governments to discharge these responsibilities. There is a need to refocus attention on gender equality and macroeconomic policy, in the context of globalization. (UNIFEM 2000, exec. summary)

Documenting the realities and hardships that women endure in an era of globalization is critical not just for women's rights, but for human rights more generally. Equally critical, however, is understanding how gender stereotypes and ideologies underlie many of the patterns and processes outlined above. Why, for example, do women comprise the majority of the labor force in EPZs or the low-wage informal sector? Why is it that the phrase the *"feminization* of the labor force" is used to refer not simply to the growth of female employment, but also to a downward shift in the job market toward unstable and low-wage (read: inferior) jobs? How, and why, has international sex trafficking mushroomed into such a lucrative trade, and why are women overwhelmingly its victims? And why is it that so few women hold political office in countries around the world? In a poignant statement about the phrase "cheap labor," Cynthia Enloe sheds light on these questions. She writes:

> It's an analytically dreadful phrase. It hides politics. To casually (lazily) say "cheap labour" was what lured Nike to South Korea is to tempt us to imagine the labour of a Korean woman stitching a sneaker is automatically ("naturally") cheap—as if it takes nothing to cheapen her labour. More politically accurate is "cheapened labour." It prompts you

> *"Documenting the realities and hardships that women endure in an era of globalization is critical not just for women's rights, but for human rights more generally. Equally critical, however, is understanding how gender stereotypes and ideologies underlie many of the patterns and processes outlined above."*

to ask what and who does it take, operating in concert, to cheapen labour?" (2000, 240)

Enloe and other scholars explain the impact of globalization on women by pointing to gender as a set of ideological constructions that defines women not only as different from, but also lesser than or inferior to, men. Women are portrayed, for example, as the most appropriate workers for low-wage, low-status, tedious, or monotonous occupations because of their presumed physical and psychological traits, and restricted from employment in some higher paying jobs on the premise that they must be protected from dangerous equipment or settings. Winifred Poster (2001) captures the essence of these gendered discourses, widespread in the industrial world, with the phrase "nimble fingers and dangerous places." Small, nimble fingers, for example, and a passive dispossession are said to make women uniquely suited for EPZs. From her research on EPZs, Maria Patricia Fernández Kelly cites various statements typical of maquiladora managers:

> [Because of] their mothering instincts, women are . . . more responsible than men; they are raised to be gentle and obedient, and so they are easier to deal with. They are also more nimble and meticulous and they don't get tired of doing the same thing nine-hundred times a day. . . . We hire them because we know we'll have fewer problems. (1994, 158)

She also cites a manager of a plant in Southern California that subcontracts much of its work to immigrant women:

> [I]t's not just the fact that they are women, it's also the culture. Mexican women, especially the foreign-born, will do anything for their families. They work hard and they don't ask for much, they don't give you any hassles. So men could do the same job but men are more ambitious and what we have is handiwork; that's women's work. (p. 160)

Low wages and limited benefits for women are also justified by ideological constructions that define women's paid employment as supplemental to men's. In a study of the microelectronics industry in Silicon Valley, California, Karen Hossfeld (1990) confirmed that women, and particularly migrant women, form the majority of the workforce in low-paying production and assembly jobs. Her primary interest, however, was in analyzing the gender logic that plant managers used to justify women's low pay compared to men's and their confinement in low-skilled jobs. Employers repeated the familiar refrains heard in the EPZs about women's hand-eye coordination and patience as uniquely qualifying them for manual assembly line work. In no case, however, did these "special" skills warrant "special" pay. Instead, managers repeatedly explained that higher wage jobs and promotions rightly belong to heads of households which, according to their logic, meant men. In fact, 70 percent of the employers Hossfeld interviewed stated that a woman's primary jobs are wife, mother, and housekeeper, even if she works full time in the paid labor force (1990, 163). Around the world, this same ideology of male as breadwinner and female as caretaker also has and continues to justify social welfare policies that disadvantage women (Sainsbury 1994). Hence, women remain more dependent upon states and more threatened when states constrict social services in response to global restructuring and demands for the privatization of the public sector.

"70 percent of [those] interviewed stated that a woman's primary jobs are wife, mother, and housekeeper, even if she works full time in the paid labor force."

Gender ideologies and their implications for women reverberate well beyond the realm of formal employment and are also indispensable in accounting for the existence and nature of the international sex trade. Poverty is certainly part of the explanation for the ready supply of women to be recruited or forced into the global sex industry; but it is only part of the explanation. Gender norms, strategies, and hierarchies determine why women are typically the poorest of the poor, and in countries undergoing painful economic transitions, the hardest hit. Under such circumstances, some women understandably perceive the sex trade as one of few available options for survival. But, the demand side of the international political economy of sex—and the conditions of and mechanisms by which it functions—also relates to gender and in particular to the very low status of women in countries throughout the world and the ease with which women are treated and perceived as sexual commodities.

In the international sex industry, sexism and misogyny work in combination with widespread cultural stereotypes and persistent racism. Asian women, for example, are perceived and marketed as submissive, nonthreatening, and extremely responsive, and Russian mail-order brides are advertised as "traditional," "family-oriented," and untainted by Western feminism (Peterson and Runyan 1999, 140). The latter, in Lena Sun's words, plays into "men's desires for women who are white—yet exotic" (1998, 10). Trafficking and prostitution are "highly gendered systems that result from structural inequality between women and men on a large scale. Men create the demand, and women are the supply" (Hughes 2000, 643). To attribute this simply to sex difference, hormones, or Darwinian evolutionary psychology is both politically naive and socially irresponsible.

Finally, gender norms and ideologies also contribute to the relative absence of women in political office. The perception that politics is a man's world has and continues to be widespread, but particularly startling is the fact that such attitudes persist even in countries and among age groups often assumed to be among the most "advanced." In a recent study of U.S. college students, Kathleen Dolan (1997) compared men's and women's attitudes toward female political candidates. Her survey revealed that among students from a representative sampling of U.S. colleges and universities, only 54 percent of males would support a woman candidate for president. Among female students, the percentage was 80. Dolan concludes:

> This evidence suggests that women may have more to overcome than just structural barriers. If indeed some voters are expressing a reluctance to consider supporting women as candidates for higher office, women will still be faced with convincing voters that they are legitimate, qualified candidates for office. (1997, 36)

Women continue to struggle for full equality with men, and globalization poses and perpetuates countless hardships for women, but it also opens up opportunity structures for women to mobilize in response to these challenges. The next section examines the transnationalization of women's mobilization and some ways in which women have capitalized on aspects of global change to become actors in the global world, not merely those who are acted upon.

Globalizing Gender

What James Rosenau (1990) and others have identified as "turbulence" in the international system not only describes the rise of transnational governing institutions and structures but also the emergence and invigoration of transnational civil society—of movements, organizations, and actors operating across and outside of states. Women's organizations and a growing international women's movement are particularly important dimensions of the latter. The previous section focused on how processes of globalization, supported by gender ideologies and hierarchies, serve to perpetuate and exacerbate inequalities and hardships for women around the world. This section examines how gender, as a basis for sociocultural attachment and political mobilization, has become more internationalized.

Women activists and women engaging in activism across political and territorial borders are not new (Stienstra 1994). For centuries women have mobilized in pursuit of peace and various forms of political, social, or economic justice; and they have done so in ways that are global in scope. As early as the fifth century B.C., a well-known Greek play, *Lysistrata*, told the story of women refusing to sleep with men who went to war. Interestingly, during 2000 peace talks on the conflict in Burundi, Nelson Mandela made reference to this play as a strategy that Burundi's women might employ if Burundian men began fighting again (Hunt and Posa 2001). In the 1840s, women's rights advocates in North America and Europe shared strategies; and in the pre–World War I era, a number of international women's groups formed to advocate for peace. These organizations included the International Council of Women, International Women's Suffrage Alliance, International Association of University Women, and the International YWCA (Zinsser 2002, 165). In 1915, after World War I had begun, 1,136 women delegates from twelve countries traveled to the Hague to protest the war at the International Congress of Women. This congress also marked the founding of the Women's International League for Peace and Freedom, which continues to exist today (West 1999). Throughout the Cold War era, countless women also mobilized locally and globally to protest the arms race and the testing and deployment of various forms of nuclear weapons (Peterson and Runyan 1991, 180–84). In all of these endeavors, women have drawn upon and emphasized their shared concerns and experiences as women. Frequently they have invoked Virginia Woolf's now famous quotation: "As a woman I have no country, as a woman I want no country, as a woman my country is the whole world" (1938, 234).

Among the most well-known examples of an international women's movement are the UN World Conferences on Women. The 1995 conference in Beijing, although the most recent, is the fourth in a series. The three previous conferences took place between 1975 and 1985—a period designated as the UN Decade for Women. The first conference was held in Mexico in 1975. Prior to this gathering the United Nations had acknowledged women's concerns. The UN Charter, for example, lists women alongside men as deserving of equal rights. A UN Commission on the Status of Women (CSW) was established in 1947; and subsidiary organizations of the United Nations such as the International Labour Organization and the World Health Organization had sponsored initiatives that affected women directly. Yet, as historian Judith Zinsser maintains, "despite these ideological and structural acknowledgments of women's separate needs, the condition of women worldwide was never a priority for action in any part of

> *"Each of the four UN women's conferences was distinct in terms of the themes that predominated, the atmosphere that prevailed, and the outcomes that were generated. Yet . . . the four conferences, spanning a twenty-year period, illustrate well the evolution of an international women's movement that has grown larger, stronger, more sophisticated, and less fragmented."*

the United Nations system" (2002, 139). This began to change in 1975. Each of the four UN women's conferences was distinct in terms of the themes that predominated, the atmosphere that prevailed, and the outcomes that were generated. Yet, as most analysts, observers, and participants agree, the four conferences, spanning a twenty-year period, illustrate well the evolution of an international women's movement that has grown larger, stronger, more sophisticated, and less fragmented (Simpson 1996, Stienstra 2000; West 1999).

A total of 133 government representatives and 6,000 participants from a range of INGOs and NGOs attended the Mexico City Conference in 1975. The 6,000 participants not attending as government delegates organized an alternative meeting known as the Tribune. This marked the beginning of a lively NGO counterpart to the official governmental meetings that persisted and grew more powerful with each of the subsequent conferences (West 1999). Development was the key theme at the conference as it was in the practice and study of world politics generally at this time. In fact much of the success of the CSW in securing broader UN support for the conference lay in presenting discrimination against women as a central impediment to development. By doing so, women secured as valuable allies the male leadership of less developed countries actively involved in and committed to the UN's development efforts. Still, the CSW was given a very limited budget and little time to prepare for the conference. Many of the documents that emerged from the conference avoided challenging the structural hierarchies of the international system. There was little, in other words, in the way of a gender critique. The conference was also plagued by divisions between a U.S.-led Western bloc, a Soviet-led Eastern bloc, and a third bloc comprised of a group of developing countries known as the Group of 77. "In the end," as Zinsser writes, "the delegates enshrined rather than reconciled their ideological differences" (2002, 147).

Despite these challenges, one particularly notable outcome of the Mexico conference was the Convention on the Elimination of Discrimination

Against Women (CEDAW). The CSW had been working on the convention since 1967, but the Mexico conference and the declaration of Decade for Women facilitated its adoption by the UN General Assembly on December 19, 1979. Unlike the nonbinding agreements negotiated at the UN conferences, the CEDAW is a binding treaty that obliges signatory governments to end discrimination against women. The formal signing took place at the opening ceremonies of the second UN World Conference in Copenhagen, Denmark, and the agreement is widely heralded as a landmark in the history of women's human rights.

The second conference, held in Copenhagen in 1980, was considered a mid-decade review of the UN Decade for Women 1975–85. A total of 145 governments were represented at the official conference and over 8,000 women attended the NGO Forum. Analysts characterize the Copenhagen meetings as the most conflictive of the UN Conferences on Women. They point to the predominance of various nationalist causes that drowned out the official conference agenda. The Palestinian cause was highlighted and resulted in a clause in the final Programme of Action equating Zionism with racism. Apartheid in South Africa was condemned, and Iranian women revolutionaries called for a return to veiling as a symbol of anti-colonialism. According to some observers, such as Conference President Lise Østergaard, the UN conference had been "politicised" by "special situations"; and Lois West noted that the international women's movement was "split between those who felt that women were being used by male-dominated political and revolutionary movements to further masculine agendas and women in those movements who, like the PLO's Leila Khaled, felt that they could not separate their national struggles from their feminist ones and should not be asked to do so" (West 1999, 181). These divisions at the Copenhagen conference revealed the emergence within the international women's movement of the debate over the universalism versus the particularism of women's issues and lives—a debate that would persist for much of the rest of the decade.

As was the case in Mexico, the documents that came forth from Copenhagen continued to reflect the competing ideologies and political agendas of the West, the East, and the Group of 77. Nor did Copenhagen produce any overt or sustained critique of the structures—local, national, and international—that define women as inferior and constrain them in subordinate roles. Nonetheless, in a detailed analysis of the language and discourse of the Copenhagen meetings, Zinsser finds evidence of improvements in how women are portrayed and how their interests are articulated. Specifically, generalized images of women defined largely in terms of motherhood are replaced by "a multiplicity of images that describe and applaud women's autonomous activities in the economy and in the family" (Zinsser 2002, 153). And although the documents from Copenhagen were not outwardly or systematically critical of the structures and ideologies of the world system, they consistently linked the achievement of broader economic development goals to the elimination of inequalities between women and men and identified practices specifically harmful to women (p. 156). They emphasized, for example, women's dual burden as primary caregivers in the home and wage earners outside of the home. The Programme for Action also called for improvements in the UN's database on women and the collection of data on women's unpaid work ("Programme" 1980, 17–18).

The third UN women's conference was held in Nairobi, Kenya, in 1985. One hundred fifty-seven governments sent a total of 1,899 representatives (81 percent of whom were women) to the official conference. Attendance at the parallel NGO forum nearly doubled from five years prior to fifteen thousand participants (Patton 1995, 65). From all indications, this conference continued and improved upon the focus and strategies established in Copenhagen. The meetings, however, were not without controversy, especially during the discussions of sexual preference and same sex relationships, and many of the more fundamental structural critiques and alternative economic proposals generated in the NGO forum never made it into the official conference document, "Forward Looking Strategies" (Patton 1995). Moreover, the opportunities for women from North America and Western Europe to tour Kenya and witness the challenges that characterize the daily lives of many women in Kenya—securing safe and adequate water, food, and housing—highlighted the differences in women's lives around the world.

Still, the conference and final document were transformative in many respects. The language of the document was redirected to focus on a women's agenda in a way that made women central, not peripheral, to the broader goals of the United Nations. Much of the class division that was influential in shaping the Mexico documents was subsumed by a broader understanding and critique of patriarchal practices and attitudes that hinder the advancement of all women. As Zinsser explains: "Though few would have described themselves as 'feminists,' the majority of delegates in Nairobi were committed to approving a document that presented an image of women's global solidarity, not their division and fragmentation" (2002, 163). West sums up the Nairobi conference as follows: "By the end of the UN women's decade, feminist issues that had been invisible ten years before had become mainstreamed" (1999, 181).

Ten years after the Nairobi conference and the close of the UN Decade for Women, the fourth UN World Women's Conference was held in Beijing, China. As noted above, 189 governments were represented at the official conference, and over 30,000 women attended the NGO forum—five times the number in Mexico and double the attendance in Nairobi. The preparatory process was informed by a review of the implementation of recommendations from Nairobi's "Forward Looking Strategies," and the 1995 conference was shaped in part by the recognition that women's global status was improving slowly, if at all. The Beijing conference was also shaped significantly by the proliferation as well as the capacity, skill, and tenacity of women's NGOs around the world (Dunlop, Kyte, and Macdonald 1996, 156). As Secretary of State Madeleine Albright, U.S. Ambassador to the Beijing conference, stated in a speech at the NGO forum:

> Since the first Women's Conference 20 years ago, opportunities for women have expanded around the world. This is no accident. It is because women did not wait for governments to act on their own. It is because you—the NGOs—created a global network that shares information, provides counseling, lobbies for change, and reaches out to women who need help or who are abused. (Albright 1996, 149)

All of this was facilitated by profound advances in communication and transportation technologies and women's skill in utilizing the new technologies for global networking. At the conference itself, several web networks were set up to disseminate information and facilitate communication. At the NGO forum, a computer center staffed by Apple, Hewlett Packard, and the Women's Networking Support Program provided e-mail accounts, access to the World Wide Web, and electronic conferencing (West 1999, 192). Finally, the Beijing conference also reflected, as Dunlop et al. argue, "a re-examination and re-shaping of governments' understanding of the role of the international community" (1996, 155).

Again, the conference was not without controversy. West (1999) and others describe a conservative backlash on issues of reproductive rights and sexuality, with opposition coming mainly from conservative Islamic countries, the Vatican, and some Latin American countries—or what came to be known by many as "the unholy alliance" (Dunlop et al. 1996, 16). In general, however, assessments of what took place in Beijing were overwhelmingly positive (Simpson 1996). Dunlop et al. state that Beijing represents "the coming of age of the international women's movement, with women playing key roles in the inter-governmental negotiations as delegates, advisors, and advocates." They go on to claim that "When the negotiations ended, governments had agreed to the strongest international document ever detailing the reality of women's lives and which called for sustained and precise action" (1996, 154–55). Madeleine Albright agreed: "Although those attending represented virtually every cultural and political system on earth, a remarkable consensus emerged around a number of basic principles" (1996, 145).

The UN conferences offer examples of women mobilizing globally to deal with global issues, but women's substate and trans-state activism in response to globalization also takes place at the local or regional level. In a recent volume on *Gender, Globalization, and Democratization*, several authors focus on how globalization, by disrupting established economic, political, and social structures, opens up political space for women's mobilization in a variety of specific regions and locales; and how, in capitalizing on that space, women help to effect globalization in ways that enhance or further democratization (Kelly et al. 2001). Particularly interesting are the case studies of Chiapas and the mobilization along the U.S./Mexico border. In these cases, the authors focus on the intersection of global restructuring, specifically NAFTA, and women's political mobilization in two strategic sites of globalization. As discussed in chapter 4, the 1994 uprising of the Zapatista rebels in Chiapas, Mexico, was intended to coincide with and publicize the damaging effects of the implementation of NAFTA. The Zapatista revolution has received widespread attention, but what is often less well known is the significant role of women in the movement.

Women comprise 30 percent of the Zapatista army and hold important military and political leadership positions in the organization. In 1992, the Zapatistas initiated a grassroots "women's equality campaign" during which several women traveled through the countryside interviewing other women about their challenges and concerns. The outcome was the ten-point "Revolutionary Laws of Women," which addressed issues ranging from women's right to participate in the revolutionary struggle and occupy positions of leadership in the organization and the army to women's rights to control their reproduction, choose their partners, and be safe from physical harm (Bayes and Kelly 2001). The Zapatista movement, as was outlined in chapter 4, has been helped immensely by networking across borders and with other NGOs to gain international recognition and support. By the late 1980s, over 365 international organizations maintained branches in the capital of Chiapas, San Cristóbal de las Casas. And in 1996, the National Commission for Democracy in Mexico created a National Women's Commission, headquartered in Tucson, Arizona, "to support the resistance of women against the devastation of neo-liberal restructuring, especially in Mexico and the US, by combating the low-intensity warfare being directed at women in Chiapas" (cited in Bayes and Kelly 2001, 162).

In addition to the active role of women in Chiapas, the Zapatistas also had a U.S. spokesperson, Cecilia Rodriguez, who, throughout 1996, conducted speaking tours on college campuses throughout the United States to give voice to the Zapatista cause and to the remarkable role of women in the struggle against global economic oppression. Rodriguez explained that the "patriarchal culture brought by the Spanish is still present and powerful in Mexico. . . . So, for Indian women to take up arms as Zapatistas is a profound event. . . . It was these terrible living conditions that prompted the women to decide to change" (quoted in Bayes and Kelly 2001, 162).

NAFTA has a significant impact on the Chiapas region of Mexico, but has also led to the expansion of the EPZs and maquiladoras along Mexico's northern border with the United States. The harmful implications for women of the maquiladoras in Mexico have already been described, but Bayes and Kelly (2001) illustrate how globalization generally, and NAFTA specifically, served as an impetus for the trans-state mobilization of women working in factories along the U.S./Mexico border. In June of 1989, an international coalition of NGOs, the Coalition for Justice in the Maquiladoras (CJM), was formed at a meeting in Matamoros, Mexico. The coalition brought together religious, labor, environmental, and women's groups from the United States and Mexico, and declared its mission "to pressure US transnational corporations to adopt socially responsible practices within the maquiladora industry" (Bayes and Kelly 2001, 165). After the passage of NAFTA, the coalition grew significantly, the executive board that had been dominated by representatives of U.S. NGOs became 50 percent Mexican, and three different workers centers were established along the U.S./Mexico border. This and the case of women Zapatistas are just two of countless examples of women organizing locally and transnationally to take control over the forces, increasingly global in scope, that affect their daily lives (Marchand and Runyan 2000; Kelly et al. 2001).

If progress is measured in terms of profound changes in the daily lives of women throughout the world, the impact of the international women's movement has been gradual, and substantial work remains to be done—particularly with regard to the implementation of the countless agreements and plans for action arrived at during the four international women's conferences. Yet, from the perspective of the spread or globalization of the women's movement, the progress has been truly remarkable. The numbers of women participating have soared, and the networking and organizational capacity of women's groups has improved dramatically. Women have gone from tentatively requesting entry into the male-dominated world of economics and politics to demanding equal access and asserting themselves as active agents at the local, national, and international levels. In the process, women around the world have come to better understand and respect their differences while simultaneously appreciating the common interests and concerns that unite them. Writing about transnational women's organizing and the United Nations, Deborah Stienstra explains:

> The women's caucuses that formed to act at these conferences brought together women active in community-based, national, regional, and international networks and organizations. They denounced governmental restructuring frameworks and practices. They contested the discourses and assumptions upon which restructuring was established. They shared strategies for resisting restructuring at the local and international levels. (2000, 209)

Globalization, operating with and through gender discourses, ideologies, and biases, not only creates conditions that threaten women's well-being, but also heightens women's awareness of those conditions and of their shared interests with women in other parts of the world. In other words, the growing global mobilization and solidarity of women has been fueled by the distinct challenges that globalization—global economic restructuring in particular—poses for women. Yet, the international women's movement has also capitalized on the opportunities afforded by the increased inter-connectedness of the world. Technological advancements have proved indispensable to women in sharing information and building coalitions. So, too, have transformations in sovereignty and global governance that, as Saskia Sassen describes, opened political space for "women (and other hitherto largely invisible actors) to become visible participants in international relations and subjects of international law" (1996, 15).

"Globalization, operating with and through gender discourses, ideologies and biases, not only creates conditions that threaten women's well-being, but also heightens women's awareness of those conditions and of their shared interests with women in other parts of the world."

Conclusion

Gender, like ethnicity and nationhood, is a social and political construct. It is a category or mechanism of assignment and control as well as a source and site of belonging. It is also an identity whose formation and articulation intersect with other forms of identity and belonging such as those already discussed in this book. As noted in chapter 1, identities are, among other things, multiple and overlapping. Any one individual will not only be situated in the world as a particular sex and gender, but also as a member of a particular state, nation, and ethnic group (not to mention the related and very salient categories of race, religion, and sexual orientation that are not covered in this book). Any one of these identities may be more or less central as a form of belonging at any particular time. A Palestinian woman, for example, lives her life as female, Arab, belonging to the nation of Palestine, and, because Palestine is not an official state, with citizenship or formal membership in a recognized state. As a consequence of globalization, the rigidity of many of these categories has, for some people, lessened. It is possible, in other words, to have formal membership in two or more states, to maintain active membership in a national community outside of or different from your state of residence, and to gain, lose, or change an ethnic affiliation. The intersection and overlap of identity and belonging play out not only at the micro level of the individual, but also at the more macro level of political and sociocultural practices and discourses that give form and content to belongings such as citizenship, nationhood, ethnicity, and gender. Citizenship, for example, often draws upon notions of nationhood for its symbolic content. Many national communities emphasize shared ethnicity as a criterion of membership; and gender is shaped by and shapes each of these other categories and formations of belonging.

> *"The intersection and overlap of identity and belonging plays out not only at the micro level of the individual, but also at the more macro level of political and sociocultural practices and discourses that give form and content to belongings such as citizenship, nationhood, ethnicity, and gender."*

Many feminists have argued, for example, that the very concept of citizenship is inherently gendered, and was, from its conception, constructed in terms of the "Rights of Man" (Pateman 1988). In other words, women's exclusion was not an accident or a cultural oversight to be rectified through the course of history. Instead, excluding women was part and parcel of the construction of the entitlements of men (Yuval-Davis 1991). This is why, in 1995, it was still possible to conclude that "women, regardless of race and class, rarely enjoy the physical and economic independence available to men and thus are excluded from full citizenship" (Staeheli and Clarke 1995, 15). Women's exclusion is not just from formal, legalistic dimensions of citizenship such as the right to a passport or to vote—although women have and in some cases continued to be excluded in this regard as well. They are also excluded from broader or more substantive dimensions of citizenship as discussed in chapter 2.

The justification and perpetuation of gendered citizenship practices is rooted in the distinction between the public and private realms. Gender, itself, as a social construction typically takes the form of dichotomization—masculine/feminine, hard/soft, soldier/mother, and in this example, public/private. The public realm refers to the realm of the state, of politics, and, by extension, of citizenship practice. The private realm, on the other hand, generally refers to the household, or as Mary Dietz writes: "marriage, family, housework, and child care. In short, the liberal notion of 'the private' has included what has been called 'woman's sphere' as 'male property' and sought not only to preserve it from the interference of the public realm but also to keep those who 'belong' in that realm—women—from the life of the public" (1992, 4). One of the primary tenets of political liberalism is that the private realm is to be secure from state intervention. It is for this reason and in this way that women have had less access to the state and less capacity to wield its power and resources to their benefit. This is why, for example, for years in the United States and some countries still, there could be no such thing as rape in the context of marriage. Nor is the state neutral or the boundaries of what constitutes the private realm pregiven or natural. Rather, it is the state, typically controlled by men, that structures and determines what is to be considered the "private" realm (Yuval-Davis 1991, 63).

As with the construction of citizenship as a form of belonging, nationhood (in both its civic and ethnic dimensions) also relies upon and reinforces gender. Women, like men, participate in and are affected by nationalism and nationalist conflicts, but the nature of their involvement and the implications are typically gendered. Some women are direct participants in nationalist struggles as soldiers, revolutionaries, and even terrorists. Women soldiers play an active role, for example, in the Israeli military. The Zapatistas are only one of many examples of women participating directly in revolutionary struggles, and Palestinian women in the West Bank have begun to join the ranks of suicide bombers. Yet, it is still the case that women are more often expected to be, and perceived as, mothers and wives who support their sons and husbands, holding down the home front while boys and men wage war at the battlefront (Enloe 1989).

This is not, however, an indication of women's exclusion from nationalist projects or from the shaping of national communities—quite the contrary. The gendering of women as mothers, homemakers, and beings in need of protection is closely related to the biological and symbolic roles women play in nation-building and nationalism. As was discussed in chapter 3, nations are not born, but made. They are made in large part by states or state elite, through policies and practices such as immigration or the census, and in the context of specific social and cultural relations. Gender relations permeate all of the above and lead scholars such as Nira Yuval-Davis and others to conclude that "it is women and not just the bureaucracy and intelligentsia who reproduce nations—biologically, culturally, symbolically" (1993, 622).

Nations are collectivities of people whose sense of community often relies upon a myth of common origin. For this reason, population policies, and by extension, women, become central to the construction and maintenance of national boundaries. Migration policies are one method by which nations seek to control the size and "purity" of their membership. Policies related to biological reproduction are another. The latter may take the form of the forced sterilization of a group the nation wishes to exclude or prohibition against sexual relationships with outsiders (Yuval-Davis

1993). One of the pillars of Apartheid legislation in South Africa was a prohibition against miscegenation between whites and blacks. Racism was clearly underlying this policy, but so too was a fear on the part of white Afrikaners for the future of their nation—a nation founded on a notion of common origin and already a very small numerical minority in the majority black South Africa. The United States, in an effort to preserve the whiteness of the American nation, had similar prohibitions against sexual relationships between the races until as recently as the 1960s. The Israeli Fascist Party has proposed laws forbidding sexual relations between Jews and Arabs. Women obviously do not reproduce in isolation from men, but women are the predominant focus and the primary targets of reproductive policies.

In many cases, the intent of reproductive policies in nation-shaping is not to limit or restrict biological reproduction, but rather to encourage and facilitate it. Around the world, women have been encouraged to contribute to various nationalist struggles by having children, or through slogans such as "have a child for the revolution." In Hitler's Germany, many young German women took seriously their duty to reproduce in order to preserve the strength and purity of the Aryan race. A popular Palestinian saying has boasted that "The Israelis beat us at the borders but we beat them in the bedroom" (Yuval-Davis and Anthias 1989, 8). As the birth rate of French-speaking Canadians grew during the 1960s, Québécois separatists referred proudly to the increase as "the revenge of the cradle." Meanwhile, state support, or lack thereof, for maternal benefits and child care can also be traced to concerns about the size and "purity" of the national stock (Yuval-Davis 1993).

The gendering of women as mothers and homemakers relates not only to the biological reproduction of nations, but also to their symbolic and cultural construction. As imagined communities, nations rely heavily upon cultural symbols, practices, and beliefs to define the meaning and boundaries of belonging, and women and gender are central to the process. Nations, for example, are often referred to or represented as mothers or the motherland, and among the most powerful symbols of nationhood and for mobilizing nationalist sentiments are women in danger or mothers who have lost sons in war. In France, for example, the defining symbol of the

> "Nations, for example, are often referred to or represented as mothers or the motherland, and among the most powerful symbols of nationhood and for mobilizing nationalist sentiments are women in danger or mothers who have lost sons in war."

revolution was *La Patrie,* a figure of a woman giving birth (Yuval-Davis 1993); and many wartime posters and slogans around the world focus on the threat to or security of women and children.

Women's actual bodies and behaviors also become signifiers of the nation and mechanisms for marking the boundaries between nations. Women wearing or not wearing the veil often becomes a political tool or strategy in nationalist politics. Turkey's secular nationalist leader Ataturk beseeched women to remove the veil in order to symbolize Turkey's modernization and independence, while various groups from Hizbullah in Lebanon to Hamas in Palestine to the Taliban in Afghanistan have resurrected the veil as a statement against Western colonialism. Women's sexual behavior can also be deemed reflective of the nation and, hence, tightly monitored. This is the case, for example, in countries that allow "honor killings" or the murder of a woman whose alleged sexual infidelity or promiscuity—even if she is a victim of rape—is considered a disgrace to the culture and community (Feldner 2000). Moreover, because women are made the embodiment of the nation, they also become the targets of violence against that nation. Maja Korac explains: "rape in war, ethnic-national war in particular, becomes a powerful symbolic weapon against the 'enemy.' As women are seen as precious property of the 'enemy,' women and their bodies become territories to be seized and conquered." She goes on to state that "rape is an effective implement of territorial 'cleansing' as men will not return to the place where they have been humiliated by the rape of 'their' women" (1996, 137).

Finally, women and gender are also implicated in the construction of ethnic identity and belonging. The form and content of ethnic group identity, like nationhood, is not pregiven, but socially defined, and gender roles and relations help shape the definition. Referring to the example of Cuban American ethnic identity in the United States, and the emphasis on the Cuban enclave economy as evidence of the ethnic solidarity and entrepreneurial character of Cuban immigrants, Lisandro Perez (1986) points out that so much of the Cuban economic miracle has been dependent upon women's unpaid labor. Without understanding gender, then, it is difficult to grasp the workings of citizenship, nationhood, or ethnicity. Although the preceding chapters have separated these identities or categories of belonging as analytically distinct, each is closely implicated in the construction and maintenance of the others. This and preceding chapters have also emphasized the need to understand how globalization is affecting these political and sociocultural attachments. But beyond the needed analysis of globalization's implications for belonging, the relationship between the two also provokes normative and philosophical debate. The concluding chapter touches briefly upon these questions.

6

Belonging to the World

At the turn of the new millennium, globalization is in full swing. A composite of economic, technological, political, and cultural processes is increasing the interconnectedness of the world. Although interconnectedness in the world system is not, in itself, new, contemporary manifestations of globalization are compressing time and space in ways that profoundly affect social, political, and economic relations and realities. The turn of the millennium also gives witness to the power and pervasiveness of identity and belonging. From violent ethnonational conflicts to transnational social movements to growing demands for cultural recognition and respect, identity has taken center stage. The goal of this book has been to explore the relationship between these two contemporary realities—globalization and the politics and practices of belonging. The purpose of this concluding chapter is to summarize briefly insights from the preceding exploration, but also to acknowledge some of the normative and philosophical questions that arise in relation to globalization's implications for belonging. If globalization reinvigorates allegiances and attachments to states, or weakens them, what are the respective implications for democracy? If nations are destined to persist as primary forms of sociocultural attachment, must they always be rooted in exclusion? Can the demands of some ethnic groups for collective rights or recognition be reconciled with political liberalism's emphasis on the individualism and universalism? And how might gender and women be implicated in and affected by all of the above?

The four preceding chapters examine how a particular form of belonging is affected by, and related to, global change. As noted in the first two chapters, both globalization and belonging are complex and multidimensional phenomena. Hence, the relationships between them will, by definition, also be complex and multidimensional. Indeed, each chapter, whether it focused on citizenship, nationhood, ethnicity, or gender revealed that the linkages with and implications of globalization are diverse and, in some cases, contradictory. As a result of contemporary globalization processes, the centrality of citizenship as a form of belonging is being both diminished and invigorated. Despite predictions to the contrary, globalization has not meant the end of nations or nationalism, but it has altered in significant ways the form and content of national imaginings. Advanced communications technology has, for instance, expanded opportunities and capacities for shaping or maintaining nations. Meanwhile, the ethnic identities and ethnic politics that now capture headlines cannot be fully understood outside of the context of globalization, but the relationship between these two phenomena is not static or determinant. The processes of globalization do not simply impinge upon already existing ethnic groups and patterns of ethnic relations, but also contribute to the construction and reconstruction of ethnic identities and the nature of ethnic interactions. Finally, globalization relies upon and perpetuates gender hierarchies and inequalities, but it simultaneously opens space for women to mobilize transnationally to resist, shape, and rechannel global forces and gender ideologies.

The results from the preceding examination of how globalization affects belonging are not, in other words, definitive. Some identity formations in some situations provide support for one hypothesis about globalization's impact on belonging, others for another. This indeterminacy reflects, in part, the variable nature of globalization itself. Globalization is powerful and widespread, but its impact is not experienced equally or identically in all parts of the world or for all people. Globalization's tendency toward homogenization and standardization is strong, and few regions, locales, or individuals escape its reach. But, still, it must and does work through, with, and around an array of distinct local, state, and regional contexts—all of which shape and reshape the otherwise uniform patterns and processes of globalization in particular ways. The same is true of identity and belonging—which is by definition particularistic and individualistic. Whether globalization increases or decreases the salience of citizenship can be discussed structurally at the level of states or suprastates, but it also depends on individuals—on where and how any particular person or group lives and responds to the surrounding world. One person or group might respond

"One person or group might respond to a set of circumstances or events, such as 9/11, by clinging more tightly to membership in a state, while others might choose to embrace the importance and meaning of world citizenship."

to a set of circumstances or events, such as 9/11, by clinging more tightly to membership in a state, while others might choose to embrace the importance and meaning of world citizenship.

From the perspective of social science, these conclusions might seem frustrating or unsatisfying. Nonetheless, what the preceding discussion provides is an analytical foundation that can generate more focused hypotheses about globalization and belonging and from which further comparative empirical investigation can proceed. Meanwhile, what also warrants further analysis is the question of how to assess or evaluate from a more normative perspective the trends and relationships identified above. Chapter 1 discussed the evaluative debates surrounding globalization. Does globalization increase, for example, or decrease equality, democracy, and diversity? Adding the politics of belonging to the equation opens up a different set of questions regarding the impact of globalization. Many of these questions are not new, but are being highlighted and in some cases given greater urgency by processes of globalization. What follows is a sampling of some broader philosophical debates now taking place with implications for the intersection of globalization and belonging

Chapter 2 discussed the fact that the meaning and importance of formal membership in a state is both increasing and decreasing. For some individuals, citizenship or state membership is now and always has been nothing more than a legal arrangement, a formal category, or a response to a blank space on a customs form. For others, membership in a state provides a powerful source of identity and belonging and evokes emotions of pride, loyalty, and devotion. Moreover, as explained in the preceding chapters, the salience of any type of belonging varies not only across but within individuals across time. For a college student in the United States, the identity of "American" may not be particularly central while she or he is attending class at a university somewhere in Ohio. But when that student is watching the Olympics, traveling overseas, or witnessing a terrorist attack on the World Trade Center, her or his sense of being a U.S. citizen may be heightened. With few exceptions, all individuals in the world have formal membership in a state (in some cases more than one state), but many also experience and exhibit a meaningful and deep-seated attachment to that state. This is patriotism.

Scholars and philosophers around the world have long debated the virtues and vices of patriotism. Where should our most central loyalties and attachments lie: with family, the state, God, the neighborhood, the tribe? In 1996, philosopher Martha Nussbaum and several fellow intellectuals contributed to a collection of essays that explores these issues in a provocative way. Focusing on the value of attachment to and identification with a particular nation-state versus with humankind more generally, the contributors to *For Love of Country: Debating the Limits of Patriotism* bring into focus the politics of belonging in a global era.

The United States, and specifically the American education system, is Nussbaum's primary reference point. She argues that patriotism is a problematic sentiment and may, particularly in the case of the United States, be ultimately subversive of some of the worthy goals it sets out to serve such as justice and equality (1996, 4). Americans are typically taught to think of themselves as above all citizens of the United States and are encouraged to give central importance to the emotion of national (state) pride. While the moral ideals for which America stands are laudable ones, there is no reason, Nussbaum argues, why those ideals should extend only to the borders of the United States. In place of patriotism, she proposes cosmopolitanism, or world citizenship. Cosmopolitanism advocates allegiance not to a local community of birth (determined essentially by accident), but to the worldwide community of human beings. From this perspective, Americans should be taught that "they are, above all, citizens of a world of human beings, and that, while they happen to be situated in the United States, they have to share this world with the citizens of other countries" (Nussbaum 1996, 6).

Several respondents in the book agree with Nussbaum's assessment, but others raise important objections. According to some, the dichotomy between cosmopolitanism and patriotism is an artificial one. Not only can these two sentiments comfortably coexist, but learning and experiencing loyalty and devotion to one's own community or inner circle (patriotism) may be a prerequisite to extending those same emotions and attachments to the whole of humanity (cosmopolitanism) (Appiah, Barber, Bok, and Walzer in Nussbaum 1996). Also at issue are the democratic implications of world citizenship. Although Nussbaum does not advocate a world state, some contributors interpret her argument as one that opposes a world system based upon the sovereignty and centrality of separate independent states. As such, many respondents defend the modern state as central to the protection and promotion of democracy. Anthony Appiah maintains that "because the cultural variability that cosmopolitanism celebrates has come to depend on the existence of a plurality of states, we need to take states seriously" (quoted in Nussbaum 1996, 28). Amy Gutmann writes: "We can truly be citizens of the world only if there is a world polity. Given what we now know, a world polity could only exist in tyrannical form" (quoted in Nussbaum 1996, 68). And Gertrude Himmelfarb cautions that the "principles and policies that Nussbaum presumably cherishes . . . depend not on a nebulous cosmopolitan order but on a vigorous administrative and legal order deriving its authority from the state" (quoted in Nussbaum 1996, 76). In other words, states serve a valuable function and any effort to dismantle or undermine the modern nation-state model may prove not only impractical, but dangerous.

Respondents to Nussbaum's plea for world citizenship express concern not only for preserving the administrative functions of the state, but also for the sentiments of loyalty and devotion to a state—patriotism. Benjamin Barber, for example, criticizes the "thinness" of cosmopolitanism as a source and the abstraction of the world as a site, of belonging, and advocates "civic patriotism rather than abstract universalism" (quoted in Nussbaum 1996, 31). He views the yearning for concrete community and particular identity as natural and wholesome, and offers the United States as an example of healthy patriotism. The sentiments of American patriotism are, according to Barber, directed toward civic ideals and institutions—the Declaration of Independence, the Constitution, and the Bill of Rights. In this way, American patriotism is not incompatible with, but is a celebration of, cosmopolitanism (p. 33). Charles Taylor also defends patriotism, stating bluntly that "we cannot do without patriotism in the modern world" (quoted in Nussbaum 1996, 119). Democracies require strong identification and allegiance on the part of their citizens, according to Taylor, or "a special sense of bonding" (p. 119). From this perspective, patriotism supports, rather than subverts, values of justice, equality, and the very functioning of democracy.

The sentiments of patriotism and cosmopolitanism are not new, nor are the debates over their respective merits. Globalization, however, heightens the prevalence and significance of the issues and concerns discussed by Nussbaum and her colleagues. In many respects, globalization intensifies the need for cosmopolitanism, or for an awareness of being citizens of the world. As the world becomes more interconnected, the need to take seriously the rights and dignity of all human beings, regardless of state membership or national identity, becomes more immediate. Although distinct states and societies have rarely existed in complete isolation from others, they do so even less now. The pollution of air and water and the spread of disease, for example, know no state or national boundaries. "Like it or not," Nussbaum correctly asserts, "we live in a world in which the destinies of nations are closely intertwined with respect to basic goods and survival itself" (1996, 12). The habits and practices—whether economic, political, cultural, or ecological—of some societies and states, particularly the most wealthy and powerful, have profound implications for other states and their inhabitants. This is what Nussbaum refers to when she points to the injustice underlying the exceptionally high living standards enjoyed by Americans. Extravagant by global standards, the American lifestyle is sustained, in effect, at the expense of other countries, and could not possibly be universalized without global ecological disaster. By what moral standards, for example, can Americans, who make up less than 5 percent of world's population, justify consuming 25 percent of the globe's resource (Barber 1995, 294–95)? For those Americans who believed in or desired some degree of separation from the rest of the world, 9/11 went a long way toward shattering those delusions.

For those who embrace cosmopolitanism, globalization not only increases the reality and awareness of human interconnectedness across borders, it simultaneously enhances the capacity for individuals to imagine themselves members of a global community. Sophisticated communications and transportation technology allow what was once foreign to become easily familiar. As a result of the Internet, satellites, CNN, BBC, air travel, and so forth, a growing number of individuals have the capacity, if they so choose, to be better aware of a range of human suffering and human triumph around the world and the role their own governments may play in both. Moreover, as a result of political globalization greater opportunities exist for people to participate in an emerging "global civil society"—a dense network of social movements and interest groups who organize and mobilize across and outside states. This reality challenges the claims by opponents of cosmopolitanism that the leap from the local, immediate allegiances to more global ones is too large. In other words, globalization affects not only the need for, but also provides unprecedented opportunities to belong to a community of world citizens.

> *"globalization not only increases the reality and awareness of human interconnectedness across borders, it simultaneously enhances the capacity for individuals to imagine themselves members of a global community."*

While cosmopolitanism is one possible response to or outcome of globalization, as the preceding chapters have shown, so too are xenophobia, ethnic nationalism, and brutal sexism. Global interconnectedness and the vulnerabilities and challenges it poses are for many individuals, societies, and states a reason to cling more tightly to particularities, not to embrace universals. Moreover, just as globalization can enhance the capacity for world citizenship, it can also facilitate the maintenance and flourishing of particularistic identities and attachments. None of the respondents to Nussbaum's essay advocate chauvinism—ethnic, racial, gender, or otherwise—but several do propose that patriotism, when civic or constitutional in form, is not only defensible, but even laudable. Globalization, however, poses two notable challenges for this perspective. First, the political units—namely, states—that are being held up as the mechanisms or vessels for protecting and promoting democracy are themselves in a period of crisis due to global restructuring. Second, both states and their members are responding to globalization in ways that are decidedly not civic. If states, in other words, are the only or the best vehicles for democracy, democracy's future may be a shaky one. Furthermore, it is not clear that strong allegiance to a state, or what Taylor describes as a "special sense of bonding," can ever remain purely civic or constitutional.

As noted in chapter 3, Barber's portrayal of the United States as a country that derives its national or "tribal" identity solely from sources such as the Declaration of Independence seems naive. It seemed so prior to 9/11 and notably so afterward, as examples in preceding chapters indicate. Throughout U.S. history, the moniker *American* has, in practice, typically assumed a particular color, gender, sexual orientation, and religion. Several examples pre- and post-9/11 reveal that truly belonging to America is not purely or simply a matter of adherence to a set of political ideals. A particularly prominent marker of difference after 9/11 has been religion, although ethnicity is certainly central to belonging to America as well. The same has also been shown to be true in other nominally civic nations. There is little indication, for example, that Habermas's (1995) call for Europe to pursue "constitutional patriotism," based not on shared traditions, cultures, and languages, but on principles of justice and democracy, has been widely heeded.

Chapter 3 pointed out that the distinction between civic and ethnic belonging is never as firm in practice as it is portrayed in theory; and globalization seems likely to perpetuate the blurring of the distinction. From the perspective of polities who define their commonality or sense of community with reference to ethnicity, globalization—namely, migration and technological sophistication—fuels an array of substate and trans-state attachments and identifications that challenge any state's capacity to draw upon cultural homogeneity as a basis of identity or belonging. In other words, myths about or efforts to preserve the ethnic and cultural homogeneity of states have become increasingly impractical in a globalized world. At the same time, globalization also complicates state commitments

> *"myths about or efforts to preserve the ethnic and cultural homogeneity of states have become increasingly impractical in a globalized world."*

to civic neutrality. As discussed in chapter 2, many states now struggle to reconcile demands for cultural recognition on the part of the diverse ethnocultural groups with a commitment to individualism and universal human rights. In this regard, cosmopolitanism and patriotism must both contend with multiculturalism.

Debates about multiculturalism are widespread and varied, but in many cases relate directly to the normative implications of globalization and belonging. The United States and Canada, as large immigrant receiving societies, have been centrally, though by no means exclusively, involved in these debates. In 1992, author and former special adviser to President John F. Kennedy, Arthur Schlesinger Jr., issued a somber warning about U.S. multiculturalism in his book *The Disuniting of America*. A proud supporter of America's melting pot, Schlesinger attributes America's success as a cohesive nation to the principle of *E pluribus unum*—from many into one. By developing a unique national character based not on ethnicity, but on common political ideals, America has, in Schlesinger's view, avoided the fragmentation or *balkanization* taking place in so many countries around the world. His concern, however, is this: "A cult of ethnicity has arisen both among non-Anglo whites and among nonwhite minorities to denounce the idea of a melting pot, to challenge the concept of 'one people,' and to protect, promote, and perpetuate separate ethnic and racial communities" (1992, 15). Other recent works such as John J. Miller's *The Unmaking of Americans* (1998) echo Schlesinger's concerns. Whether because of bilingual education, affirmative action, or multicultural curriculum, America is, according to this view, decomposing or disuniting—changing from a nation of individuals to a loose conglomeration of groups.

Schlesinger uses Canada as an example of a country without a strong national identity and suffering ethnic fragmentation as a result—an example, in other words, of what he fears America will become. Author and Trinidad-born Canadian Neil Bissoondath agrees. In *Selling Illusions*, Bissoondath criticizes what he calls "The Cult of Multiculturalism in Canada." He writes:

> Multiculturalism, with all of its festivals and its celebrations, has done—and can do—nothing to foster a factual and clear-minded vision of our neighbours. Depending on stereotype, ensuring that ethnic groups will preserve their distinctiveness in a gentle and insidious form of cultural apartheid, multiculturalism has done little more than lead an already divided country down the path to further social divisiveness. (1994, 238)

For these authors, a healthy dose of patriotism or "civic" nationalism is the antidote for what they portray as cultural fragmentation and divisiveness.

While writers such as Schlesinger and Bissoondath portray multiculturalism as wholly incompatible with liberal democracy, Canadian scholar Will Kymlicka has written extensively about the reconcilability of the two (1989, 1995). Kymlicka recognizes that the essence of liberal democracy is the protection of individual rights, but goes on to explain that if an individual is also a member of a distinct cultural community, then recognizing that individual's rights may entail respecting the importance and centrality that he attaches to his cultural heritage. In this way, Kymlicka rejects the juxtaposition of individual versus group rights, because for many individuals their selfhood is inextricably bound with their membership in a group. Respecting and recognizing cultural rights is not, then, necessarily incompatible with a commitment to individual liberties.

Kymlicka also rejects the notion that cultural recognition inherently leads to national fragmentation. In fact, many multicultural demands reflect a desire on the part of an individual or group to join the mainstream, not remain separate from it. Take for example the controversy over Canadian Sikhs who wished to join the Royal Canadian Mounted Police but who, because of their religious requirement to wear turbans, could not do so unless they were exempted from the usual dress code. It was a special right they were requesting, Kymlicka acknowledges, but they did so in pursuit of membership in the larger community and via participation in a quintessentially Canadian institution (Kymlicka and Norman 1995, 306). The same might be said of ethnic or racial groups in the United States who desire the redrawing of electoral districts in a way that allows them to have a fair and equal voice in the American political system.

The critics of multiculturalism value a unifying national identity over the promotion of or identification with ethnic identity. Multiculturalism's supporters defend ethnocultural attachments as central to individual rights and compatible with national community. Neither group, however, has been particularly concerned with the implications of national identity or ethnic community for women. As explained in the preceding chapter, identity is intersectional. Citizenship as a sociopolitical formation of belonging draws upon nationhood and ethnicity for its content, as ethnicity and nationhood draw upon each other. Gender plays a role in all three, and vice versa.

> *"Citizenship as a sociopolitical formation of belonging draws upon nationhood and ethnicity for its content, as ethnicity and nationhood draw upon each other. Gender plays a role in all three, and vice versa."*

Chapter 5 discussed ways in which nationhood, citizenship, and ethnicity rely upon gender identity. More recently, some scholars have begun to debate multiculturalism's impact on women. In 1999, Susan Okin published an essay arguing that although feminism and multiculturalism are often seen as related movements and ideals working toward similarly progressive goals, multiculturalism, when defined as promoting or protecting the cultural rights of groups, can actually harm women. As was the case with Nussbaum's volume on patriotism, several fellow scholars pen a range of responses and replies (Okin 1999).

Okin, like Arthur Schlesinger, is concerned with a shift from individual rights toward group rights. Her concern, however, is not the demise of a unifying national identity or the disuniting of America, but the potential damage to women of protecting the rights of groups whose cultural norms and practices do not entail respect for the equal rights of women. She uses examples that include female genital mutilation (FGM), honor killing, veiling, polygamy, and cultural groups who are willing to accept and perpetuate unequal access to health and education for women and men. Based on these examples, she concludes that "It is by no means clear, then, from a feminist point of view, that minority group rights are 'part of the solution.' They may well exacerbate the problem" (Okin 1999, 22).

Some of Okin's respondents agree with her concerns, but many others are quite critical of her ethnocentrism—specifically, her assumption that Western feminism is supreme—and her inability to recognize that cultural practices such as veiling, even polygamy, may not be oppressive to women (Honig, Al-Hibri, Gilman, and Parekh in Okin 1999). Some respondents also caution her against taking certain practices (such as FGM, which is a complex and often controversial social and political issue even within the cultures where it is practiced) as characteristic of a whole culture (Pollit and Bhabha in Okin 1999). Much of the debate that takes place in Okin's book illustrates the persistence of some of the obstacles to global sisterhood that have divided the international women's movement in the past.

Kymlicka is a contributor to Okin's text and writes in defense of multiculturalism, rejecting Okin's claim that respect and recognition for the cultural rights of groups are incompatible with women's rights:

> I accept Okin's claim that we need a more subtle account of internal restrictions which helps us identify limitations on the freedom of women within ethnocultural groups. But it still seems to me that the basic distinction is sound—i.e., liberals can accept external protections which promote justice between groups, but must reject internal restrictions which reduce freedom within groups. (quoted in Okin 1999, 32)

None of these debates about rights, equality, or democracy invite easy or unequivocal answers, as is evinced by the array of viewpoints expressed by the scholars above. Many of these issues and ideals have formed the content of political and philosophical discourse since at least the fifth century B.C. debates between democrats and aristocrats in ancient Greece. Contemporary globalization, however, has given new urgency, or at least a new twist, to these debates. It has done so, as the preceding chapters illustrate, by altering the psychological and material context of identity formation—specifically, the need for and mechanisms of belonging. The point of this concluding chapter is to suggest that not only do we need to continue exploring the precise and varied ways globalization affects the politics of identity and belonging among different groups and in different locales, but we also need to be open and cautious about assessing the promise and peril of these trends. Benjamin Barber's analysis of "Jihad and McWorld" conveys doom, as does Samuel Huntington's "Clash of Civilizations." Both authors place rather fixed forms of ethnic and cultural identity at the heart of the turmoil.

The past decade indeed offers ample reason for pessimism, but primordial or essential conceptualizations of identity are crumbling in the face of pervasive fluidity—social, political, economic, and cultural. Belonging and identity will certainly not go away; nor, however, will they remain static in their content or form. To cling too tightly to states as the preferred vehicles for democratic belonging seems to reflect a certain poverty of imagination with regard to the meaning and possibilities of world citizenship. Put into historical perspective, the era of the modern nation-state model is a relatively short one. There is no reason to believe that it is the best one or the only possible democratic one. Moreover, world citizenship does not necessitate a world state. Much of what cosmopolitan philosophers like Nussbaum advocate focuses not on the specifics of global governance regimes, but on how individuals think and live their daily lives.

Nonetheless, in that it advocates belonging to the world, cosmopolitanism must contend with a planet characterized not by homogenous, universal values and ideals, but by a rich and sometimes conflicting array of particularities—ethnic, national, and gendered. Emphasizing and embracing these particularities is often perceived as a call for complete and baseless cultural relativism—a mentality of "anything goes." In fact, in the aftermath of 9/11, some critics went so far as to hold public intellectuals and activists who they perceive as relativists partially responsible for the tragedy. This included the hyperbole of Jerry Falwell who blamed pagans, abortionists, feminists, and gays and lesbians; but also included more mainstream voices who chastised multiculturalists, cultural relativists, and anyone who, in their view, fails to embrace the existence of objective moral truths (Fish 2002, 27–28).

Stanley Fish, dean of the College of Liberal Arts and Sciences at the University of Illinois, is one of those "relativists" upon whom criticism is often heaped; but, a closer look at Fish's relativism suggests an alternative assessment.

> If by relativism one means the practice of putting yourself in your adversary's shoes, not in order to wear them as your own but in order to have some understanding (far short of approval) of why someone else—in your view, a deluded someone—might want to wear them, then relativism will not and should not end because it is simply another name for serious thought. (2002, 31)

From this perspective, not only is sensitivity to cultural diversity compatible with Martha Nussbaum's call for cosmopolitanism, but it seems particularly sound advice for all of us across the planet who are faced with both the promise and potential peril of negotiating belonging in an increasingly globalized world.

References

Albright, Madeleine K. 1996. "The Fourth World Conference on Women." *SAIS Review* 16, no. 1: 145–51.

Albrow, Marlin. 1990. *Globalization and Society*. Newbury Park, Calif.: Sage.

Aleinikoff, T. Alexander. 2000. "Between Principles and Politics: US Citizenship Practice." Pp. 119–74 in *From Migrants to Citizens: Membership in a Changing World*, edited by T. A. Aleinikoff and D. Klusmeyer. Washington, D.C.: Carnegie Endowment for International Peace.

Aleinikoff, T. Alexander, and Douglas Klusmeyer. 2001. "Plural Nationality: Facing the Future in a Migratory World." Pp. 63–88 in *Citizenship Today: Global Perspectives and Practices*, edited by T. A. Aleinikoff and D. Klusmeyer. Washington, D.C.: Carnegie Endowment for International Peace.

Anderson, Benedict. 1991. *Imagined Communities*. London: Verso.

———. 1992. "The New World Disorder." *New Left Review* 193: 3–13.

Anderson, Perry. 1974. *Lineages of the Absolutist State*. London: New Left Books.

Ang, Ien. 1995. "I'm a Feminist But . . . 'Other' Women and Postnational Feminism." Pp. 57–73 in *Transitions: New Australian Feminisms*, edited by Barbara Caine and Rosemary Pringle. New York: St. Martin's Press.

Appadurai, Arjun. 1990. "Disjuncture and Difference in the Global Cultural Economy." *Theory, Culture and Society* 7: 295–310.

———. 1996. *Modernity at Large: Cultural Dimensions of Globalization*. Minneapolis: University of Minnesota Press.

Armstrong, Elizabeth. 2001. "UN Conference Stumbles on Zionism, Slavery Reparations." *Christian Science Monitor*, 31 July, p. 8.

Armstrong, John. 1982. *Nations before Nationalism*. Chapel Hill: University of North Carolina Press.

Associated Press. 2001a. "Citizens from Many Other Countries Counted in Casualties." 14 September. www.miami.com/herald/content/news/national/digdocs/033629.htm [accessed 15 Sept. 2001].

———. 2001b. "Mexicans Sending More Money Home." 5 June. web.lexis-nexis.com/universe/doc . . . V&—md5=149b228b333b5ab1b1a9a68dcbbae0b3 [accessed 1 March 2003].

Australian Bureau of Statistics. 1999. Australia in Profile. www.abs.gov.au/ [accessed 7 March 2003].

Axtman, Kris. 2002. "A Boom in Citizenship Requests." *Christian Science Monitor,* 11 February, p. 1.

Back, Les, and John Solomos, eds. 2000. *Theories and Race and Racism: A Reader.* London: Routledge.

Bales, Kevin. 1999. *Disposable People: New Slavery in the Global Economy.* Berkeley: University of California Press.

Barber, Benjamin. 1992. "Jihad vs. McWorld." *Atlantic Monthly* (March): 53–63.

———.1994. "Human Rights Report Sets Global Standard." *Christian Science Monitor,* 26 January, p. 8.

———. 1995. *Jihad vs. McWorld.* New York: Random House.

———. 1996. "Constitutional Faith." Pp. 30–37 in *For Love of Country: Debating the Limits of Patriotism,* edited by M. Nussbaum. Boston: Beacon Press.

Barker, Chris. 1999. *Television, Globalization and Cultural Identities.* Philadelphia: Open University Press.

Barrington, Lowell. 2000. "Understanding Citizenship Policy in the Baltic States." Pp. 253–301 in *From Migrants to Citizens: Membership in a Changing World,* edited by T. A. Aleinikoff and D. Klusmeyer. Washington, D.C.: Carnegie Endowment for International Peace.

Basch, Linda, Nina Glick-Schiller, and Cristina S. Blanc. 1994. *Nations Unbound: Transnational Projects, Postcolonial Predicaments, and Deterritorialized Nation-States.* Basel, Switzerland: Gordon and Breach.

Bayes, Jane H., and Rita Mae Kelly. 2001. "Political Spaces, Gender, and NAFTA." Pp. 147–70 in *Gender, Globalization, and Democratization,* edited by R. M. Kelly, J. H. Bayes, M. E. Hawkesworth, and B. Young. Lanham, Md.: Rowman & Littlefield.

Begley, Sharon. 1995. "Three Is Not Enough: Surprising New Lessons from the Controversial Science of Race." *Newsweek* (13 February): 67–69.

Behnke, Andreas. 1997. "Citizenship, Nationhood and the Production of Political Space." *Citizenship Studies* 1, no. 2: 243–66.

Beiner, Ronald. 1995. "Introduction: Why Citizenship Constitutes a Theoretical Problem in the Last Decade of the Twentieth Century." Pp. 1–28 in *Theorizing Citizenship,* edited by R. Beiner. Albany: State University of New York Press.

Bell, Vikki. 1999. "Performativity and Belonging: An Introduction." *Theory, Culture and Society* 16, no. 2: 1–10.

Benería, Lourdes. 2001. "Shifting the Risk: New Employment Patterns, Informalization, and Women's Work." *International Journal of Politics, Culture and Society* 15, no. 1: 27–53.

Bhabha, Homi, ed. 1990. *Nation and Narration.* London: Routledge.

Bhavnani, Kum-Kum. 2001. *Feminism and "Race."* Oxford: Oxford University Press.

Billeaud, Jacques. 2001. "Immigrants Targeted in Arizona, 1 Killed." Associated Press, 16 September, www.modbee.com/24hour/nation/story/841396c.html [accessed 17 Sept. 2001].

Billig, Michael. 1995. *Banal Nationalism.* London: Sage.

Bissoondath, Neil. 1994. *Selling Illusions: The Cult of Multiculturalism in Canada.* Toronto: Penguin.

Bixler, Mark. 2000. Korean Residents Rally to fight Man's Deportation." Cox News Service. Atlanta: Cox Enterprises, Inc. (16 February) [accessed electronically Nov. 2001].

Bonacich, Edna. 1976. "Advanced Capitalism and Black/White Race Relations in the United States: A Split Labor Market Interpretation." *American Sociological Review* 41: 34–51.

Boserup, Edith. 1970. *Woman's Role in Economic Development*. New York: St. Martin's Press.

Bowen, John R. 1996. "The Myth of Global Ethnic Conflict." *Journal of Democracy* 7, no. 4: 3–14.

Braman, Sandra, and Annabelle S. Mohammadi, eds. 1996. *Globalization, Communication, and Transnational Civil Society*. Craskill, N.J.: Hampton Press.

Briggs, Vernon. 2001. *American Unionism and US immigration Policy*. Washington, D.C.: Center for Immigration Studies, August.

Brimelow, Peter. 1995. *Alien Nation: Common Sense about America's Immigration Disaster*. New York: Random House.

Broad, Robin, ed. 2002. *Global Backlash: Citizens Initiatives for a Just World Economy*. Lanham, Md.: Rowman & Littlefield.

Brown, John. 1999. "How Past Is Shaping Serbs' Views." *Christian Science Monitor*, 6 April, p. 1.

Brownmiller, Susan. 1975. *Against Our Will: Men, Women and Rape*. New York: Bantam Books.

Brubaker, Rogers, ed. 1989. *Immigration and the Politics of Citizenship in Europe and North America*. Lanham, Md.: University Press of America.

———. 1992. *Citizenship and Nationhood in France and Germany*. Cambridge: Harvard University Press.

———. 1996. *Nationalism Reframed*. Cambridge: Cambridge University Press.

Bullock, Susan. 1994. *Women and Work*. London: Zed Books.

Burbach, Roger. 1994. "Roots of the Postmodern Rebellion in Chiapas." *New Left Review* (May/June): 113–24.

Buss, David M. 1994. *The Evolution of Desire: Strategies of Human Mating*. New York: Basic Books.

Butler, Judith. 1990. *Gender Trouble*. London: Routledge.

Camarota, Steven. 2001a. "The Slowing Progress of Immigrants: An Examination of Income, Home Ownership, and Citizenship, 1970–2000." Washington, D.C.: Center for Immigration Studies, March.

———. 2001b. "Zogby Poll on Immigration and Terrorism." Washington, D.C.: Center for Immigration Studies, 27 September. www.cis.org/articles/2001/back1201.html [accessed 5 May 2003].

Casimir, Lynn. 2001. "Deportations Soar Up 164% Since Tough New Law." *Daily News* (New York), 7 February, p. 4.

Center for Imigration Studies. 2001. "Competing Blueprints for an Ideal Legal Immigration Policy." (March) www.cis.org/articles/2001/blueprints/release.html [accessed 30 Nov. 2001].

Charsley, S. R. 1974. "The Formation of Ethnic Groups." Pp. 337–68 in *Urban Ethnicity*, edited by Abner Cohen. London: Association of Social Anthropologists of the Commonwealth.

Charter of Fundamental Rights. 2000. "Europa: The European Union On-Line." europa.eu.int/scadplus/leg/en/s50000.htm [accessed 3 Dec. 2001].

Chossudovsky, Michael. 1996. "Economic Genocide in Rwanda." *Economic and Political Weekly* 31, no. 15: 938–41.

CIR. United States Commission on Immigration Reform. 1994. "U.S. Immigration Policy: Restoring Credibility—A Report to Congress." Washington, D.C.: U.S. Government Printing Office.

Cohen, Roger. 2000. "Europe's Migrant Fears Rend a Spanish Town. *New York Times*, 8 May, p. A1.

Commission of the European Communities (CEC). 1975. "Towards European Citizenship." *Bulletin of European Communities* 7/75, p. 7.

———. 1985. Adonnino Report. *Bulletin of European Communities*, Supplement 7/85. Luxembourg: Office for Official Publications of the European Communities.

Connell, Robert W. 1987. *Gender and Power: Society, the Person and Sexual Politics.* Stanford, Calif.: Stanford University Press.

Connor, Walker. 1978. "A Nation Is a Nation, Is a State, Is an Ethnic Group, Is a . . ." *Ethnic and Racial Studies* 1, no. 4: 378–400.

———. 1994. *Ethno-Nationalism: The Quest for Understanding.* Princeton, N.J.: Princeton University Press.

Conzen, Kathleen N., David Gerber, Eva Morawska, and George Pozzetta. 1992. "The Invention of Ethnicity: A Perspective from the USA." *Journal of American Ethnic History* 12, 1: 3–41.

Cornell, Stephen, and Douglas Hartmann. 1998. *Ethnicity and Race: Making Identities in a Changing World.* Thousand Oaks, Calif.: Pine Forge Press.

Cowen, Robert. 1995. "In Industrial Age, World's Languages Dwindle in Number." *Christian Science Monitor*, 21 February, p. 1.

Crawford, Beverly, and Ronnie D. Lipschutz. 1998. *The Myth of "Ethnic Conflict": Politics, Economics and "Cultural" Violence.* Berkeley: University of California Press.

Croucher, Sheila. 1996. "The Success of the Cuban Success Story: Ethnicity, Power, and Politics." *Identities* 2, no. 4: 351–84.

———. 1997. *Imagining Miami: Ethnic Politics in a Postmodern World.* Charlottesville: University Press of Virginia.

———. 1998. "South Africa's Illegal Aliens: Constructing National Boundaries in a Post-Apartheid State." *Ethnic and Racial Studies* 21, no. 4: 639–60.

———. 1999. "Constructing the Ethnic Spectacle." Pp. 123–41 in *The Ethnic Entanglement: Conflict and Intervention in World Politics*, edited by John Stack and Lui Hebron. Westport, Conn.: Praeger.

Csergo, Zsuzsa, and James M. Goldgeier. 2001. "Virtual Nationalism." *Foreign Policy* (July/August): 76–77.

Daly, Martin, and Margo Wilson. 1983. *Sex, Evolution and Behavior.* Boston: Willard Grant Press.

Deans, Bob. 2001. "Foot-Dragger or Leader?" *Palm Beach Post*, 29 July, p. 1E.

Deen, Thalif. 2000. "Women: US Falls Short of UN Goals on Gender Parity." *Interpress Service*, 30 March, n.p.

Degenaar, Johan. 1994. "Beware of Nation-Building." Pp. 23–30 in *Democratic Nation-Building in South Africa*, edited by N. Rhoodie and I. Liebenberg. Pretoria: HSRC Publishers.

Destexhe, Alain. 1995. *Rwanda and Genocide in the Twentieth Century.* New York: New York University Press.

Deutsch, Karl. 1966. *Nationalism and Social Communication.* New York: MIT Press.

Dietz, Mary. 1992. "Context Is All: Feminism and Theories of Citizenship." Pp. 1–23 in *Dimensions of Radical Democracy*, edited by C. Mouffe. London: Verso.

Dodson, Belinda. 2000. "Women on the Move: Gender and Cross Border Migration to South Africa." Pp. 119–50 in *On Borders: Perspectives on International Migration in Southern Africa*, edited by D. A. McDonald. New York: St. Martin's Press.

Dolan, Kathleen. 1997. "Gender Differences in Support for Women Candidates: Is There a Glass Ceiling in American Politics?" *Women and Politics* 17, no. 2: 27–38.

Doty, Roxanne. 1996a. "The Double-Writing of Statecraft: Exploring State Responses to Illegal Immigration." *Alternatives* 21: 171–89.

———. 1996b. "Sovereignty and the Nation: Constructing the Boundaries of National Identity." Pp. 121–47 in *State Sovereignty as Social Construct*, edited by T. Biersteker and C. Weber. Cambridge: Cambridge University Press.

Dugger, Celia. 1996. "African Ritual Pain: Genital Cutting." *New York Times*, 5 October, pp. 1, 4.

Dunlop, Joan, Rachel Kyte, and Mia Macdonald. 1996. "Women Redrawing the Map: The World After the Beijing and Cairo Conferences." *SAIS Review* (Winter–Spring): 153–65.

Dunne, Nancy. 2002. "US Muslims See Their American Dreams Die." *Financial Times*, 27 March, p. 4.

Economist. 1995. "The Miseries of Magnetism." 4 March, pp. 40–41.

Eley, Geoffrey, and Ronald G. Suny. 1996. *Becoming National: A Reader*. New York: Oxford University Press.

Elkins, David. 1997. "Globalization, Telecommunication and Virtual Ethnic Communities." *International Political Science Review* 18, no. 2: 139–52.

Elton, Catherine. 2001. "A New Wall Divides Two Nations." *Christian Science Monitor*, 26 July, p. 6.

Enloe, Cynthia. 1973. *Ethnic Conflict and Political Development*. Boston: Little, Brown.

———. 1981. "The Growth of the State and Ethnic Mobilization: The American Experience." *Ethnic and Racial Studies* 4, no. 2 (April): 123–36.

———. 1989. *Bananas, Beaches and Bases: Making Feminist Sense of International Politics*. Berkeley: University of California Press.

———. 2000. "Daughters and Generals in the Politics of the Globalized Sneaker." Pp. 238–46 in *Rethinking Globalizations*, edited by P. S. Aulakh and M. G. Schecter. New York: St. Martin's Press.

Enriquez, Ana. 1999. "Women Workers and Export Processing Zones." *Asian Labour Update* 28 (May–August): 28–31.

Epstein, Arnold L. 1978. *Ethos and Identity*. London: Tavistock Publications.

Epstein, Cynthia F. 1988. *Deceptive Distinctions*. New Haven, Conn.: Yale University Press.

Esman, Milton. 1994. *Ethnic Politics*. Ithaca, N.Y.: Cornell University Press.

EUROPA. 2002. The E.U. europa.eu.int/scadplus/leg/en/s50000.htm [accessed 1 Dec. 2001].

Faist, Thomas. 2000. "Transnationalization in International Migration: Implications for the Study of Citizenship and Culture." *Ethnic and Racial Studies* 23, no. 2: 189–222.

Feldner, Yotam. 2000. "'Honor' Murders—Why the Perps Get Off Easy." *Middle East Quarterly* 7, no. 4 (December): 41–51.

Fernández Kelly, Maria Patricia. 1994. "Broadening the Scope: Gender and the Study of International Development." Pp. 143–68 in *Comparative National Devel-*

opment, edited by Douglas Kincaid and Alejandro Portes. Chapel Hill: University of North Carolina Press.

Finn, Peter. 2002. "A Turn from Tolerance: Anti-immigrant Movements in Europe." *Washington Post*, 29 March, p. A1.

Fish, Stanley. 2002. "Don't Blame Relativism." *Responsive Community* 12, no. 3: 27–31.

Flanagan, Stephen, Ellen L. Frost, and Richard L. Kugler. 2001. *Challenges of the Global Century: Report of the Project on Globalization and National Security*. Washington, D.C.: National Defense University Press.

Ford, Peter. 2001. "Xenophobia Follows US Terror." *Christian Science Monitor*, 11 October, p. 1.

Foreign Policy. 2001. "Measuring Globalization" (Jan./Feb.): 56–66.

———. 2002. "Globalization's Last Hurrah?" (Jan./Feb.): 38–51.

Fragomen, Austin. 1997. "The Illegal Immigration Reform and Immigrant Responsibility Act of 1996: An Overview." *International Migration Review* 31, no. 2: 438–60.

France, David. 2000. "Slavery's New Face." *Newsweek*, 18 December, pp. 61–65.

Froehling, Oliver. 1997. "The Cyberspace 'War of Ink and Internet' in Chiapas, Mexico." *Geographical Review* 87, no. 2: 291–307.

Fukuyama, Francis. 1989. "The End of History." *National Interest* (Summer): 3–18.

Fussell, Elizabeth. 2000. "Making Labor Flexible: The Recomposition of Tijuana's Maquiladora Female Labor Force." *Feminist Economics* 6, no. 3: 59–80.

Geddes, Andres, and Adrian Favell. 1999. *The Politics of Belonging: Migrants and Minorities in Contemporary Europe*. Aldershot, England: Ashgate.

Geertz, Clifford. 1963. "The Integrative Revolution: Primordial and Civil Politics in the New States." Pp. 105–57 in *Old Societies and New States*, edited by Clifford Geertz. New York: Free Press.

Gellner, Ernest. 1964. *Thought and Change*. London: Weidenfeld and Nicolson.

———. 1983. *Nations and Nationalism*. Oxford: Blackwell.

Giddens, Anthony. 1985. *The Nation-State and Violence*. Cambridge: Polity Press.

———. 1987. *The Nation-State and Violence*. Berkeley: University of California Press.

———. 1995. "The New Context of Politics." *Democratic Dialogue* 1: 8–23.

Goetz, Edward, and Susan Clarke, eds. 1993. *The New Localism: Corporative Urban Politics in a Global Era*. Newbury Park, Calif.: Sage.

Goldman, Philip, Gail Lapidus, and Victor Zaslavsky. 1992. "Introduction." Pp. 1–21 in *From Union to Commonwealth: Nationalism and Separatism in the Soviet Republics*, edited by G. Lapidus, V. Zaslavsky, and P. Goldman. Cambridge: Cambridge University Press.

Gorjanicyn, Katrina. 2000. "Citizenship and Culture in Contemporary France: Extreme Right Interventions." Pp. 138–55 in *Citizenship and Democracy in a Global Era*, edited by A. Vandenberg. New York: St. Martin's Press.

Gould, Stephen J. 1996. *The Mismeasure of Man*. New York: Norton.

Gourevitch, Philip. 1998. *We Wish to Inform You That Tomorrow We Will be Killed with Our Families. Stories from Rwanda*. New York: Picador.

Greenfeld, Liah. 1992. *Nationalism: Five Roads to Modernity*. Boston: Harvard University Press.

Greenhouse, Linda. 1993. "Animal Sacrifice: Court, Citing Religious Freedom, Voids a Ban on Animal Sacrifices." *New York Times*, 12 June, p. 1.

Gribbin, Anthony. 1999. "Dual Citizenship Explodes in U.S." *Washington Times*, 14 November, p. 3.

Grier, Peter. 2001a. "A Changed World." *Christian Science Monitor*, 17 September, p. 1.

———. 2001b. "A Terrorist Version of NATO?" *Christian Science Monitor*, 2 February, p. 1.

Guarnizo, Luis E., Arturo I. Sanchez, and Elizabeth M. Roach. 1999. "Mistrust, Fragmented Solidarity and Transnational Migration: Colombians in New York and Los Angeles." *Ethnic and Racial Studies* 22, no. 2: 367–96.

Guarnizo, Luis E., and Michael P. Smith. 1998. "The Locations of Transnationalism." Pp. 3–34 in *Transnationalism from Below*, edited by M. P. Smith and L. E. Guarnizo. New Brunswick, N.J.: Transaction Publishers.

Guibernau, Montserrat. 1996. *Nationalisms: The Nation-State and Nationalism in the Twentieth Century*. Cambridge: Polity Press.

Gullo, Karen. 2001. "Ashcroft Dangles Prospect of Citizenship for Snitches." *Cincinnati Enquirer*, 30 November, p. A3.

Habermas, Jürgen. 1995. "Citizenship and National Identity." Pp. 255–81 in *Theorizing Citizenship*, edited by R. Beiner. Albany, N.Y.: SUNY Press.

Hall, John. 1993. "Nationalisms: Classified and Explained." *Daedalus* 122, no. 3: 1–28.

———. 1998. *The State of the Nation: Ernest Gellner and the Theory of Nationalism*. Cambridge: Cambridge University Press.

Hall, Stuart. 1996. "Who Needs Identity?" Pp. 1–17 in *Questions of Cultural Identity*, edited by Stuart Hall and Paul Du Gay. London: Sage.

Hannerz, Ulf. 1990. "Cosmopolitans and Locals in World Culture." *Theory, Culture and Society* 7, nos. 2–3: 237–51.

Hargreaves, Alec. 1995. *Immigration, Race and Ethnicity in Contemporary France*. London: Routledge.

Harvey, David. 1990. *The Condition of Postmodernity*. Oxford: Blackwell.

Harvey, Neil. 2001. "The Political Nature of Identities, Borders and Orders: Discourse and Strategy in the Zapatista Rebellion." Pp. 249–74 in *Identities, Borders, Orders: Rethinking International Relations Theory*, edited by M. Albert, D. Jacobson, and Y. Lapid. Minneapolis: University of Minnesota Press.

Hechter, Michael. 1975. *Internal Colonialism: The Celtic Fringe in British National Development*. London: Routledge.

———. 1988. "Rational Choice Theory and the Study of Ethnic Relations." Pp. 265–79 in *Theories of Ethnic and Race Relations*, edited by J. Rex and D. Mason. Cambridge: Cambridge University Press.

Held, David. 1998. "Democracy and Globalization." Pp. 11–27 in *Re-imagining Political Community*, edited by D. Archibugi, D. Held, and M. Köhler. Stanford, Calif.: Stanford University Press.

———, ed. 2000. *A Globalizing World? Culture, Economics, Politics*. London: Routledge.

Hobsbawm, Eric. 1990. *Nations and Nationalism since 1780*. Cambridge: Cambridge University Press.

Holston, John, and Arjun Appadurai. 1996. "Cities and Citizenship." *Public Culture* 8: 187–204.

Holton, Robert. 1998. *Globalization and the Nation-State*. New York: St. Martin's Press.

Holtzman, Michael. 1998. "Information Gap Breeds Techno-Underclass." *Christian Science Monitor*, 6 July, p. 11.

Honig, Bonnie. 1999. "My Culture Made Me Do It." Pp. 35–40 in *Is Multicultur-alism Bad for Women?* edited by S. M. Okin. Princeton, N.J.: Princeton University Press.

Hooper, Charlotte. 2000. "Masculinities in Transition: The Case of Globalization." Pp. 59–73 in *Gender and Global Restructuring: Sightings, Sites and Resistances,* edited by Marianne Marchand and Anne Sisson Runyan. London: Routledge.

Horowitz, Donald. 1985. *Ethnic Groups in Conflict.* Berkeley: University of California Press.

———. 1991. *A Democratic South Africa: Constitutional Engineering in a Divided Society.* Berkeley: University of California Press.

Hossfeld, Karen. 1990. "Their Logic against Them: Contradictions in Sex, Race and Class in Silicon Valley." Pp. 149–79 in *Women Workers and Global Restructuring,* edited by K. Ward. New York: Cornell University Press.

Hroch, Miroslav. 1985. *Social Preconditions of National Revival in Europe.* Cambridge: Cambridge University Press.

Hughes, Donna M. 2000. "The 'Natasha' Trade: The Transnational Shadow Market of Trafficking in Women." *Journal of International Affairs* 53, no. 2: 625–42.

Hunt, Swanee, and Cristina Posa. 2001. "Women Waging Peace." *Foreign Policy* (May/June): 38–47.

Huntington, Samuel. 1993. "The Clash of Civilizations." *Foreign Affairs* (Summer): 22–49.

Hurrell, Andrew, and Ngaire Woods, eds. 1999. *Inequality, Globalization, and World Politics.* Oxford: Oxford University Press.

Hutchinson, John. 2000. "Ethnicity and Modern Nations." *Ethnic and Racial Studies* 23, no. 4: 651–69.

Hutchinson, John, and Anthony D. Smith. 1994. *Nationalism.* Oxford: Oxford University Press.

ICAO. 1998. Annual Civil Aviation Report 1997. Montreal: International Civil Aviation Organisation. www.icao.org [accessed 10 Sept. 2001].

Ifekwunigwe, Jayne. 1999. *Scattered Belongings: Cultural Paradoxes of "Race," Nation and Gender.* London: Routledge.

Ignatieff, Michael. 1993. *Blood and Belonging: Journeys into the New Nationalism.* New York: Farrar, Straus and Giroux.

ILO. 1998. *Labour and Social Issues Relating to Export Processing Zones.* Geneva: International Labour Organization.

Isaacs, Harold. 1974. "Basic Group Identity: The Idols of the Tribe." *Ethnicity* 1: 15–41.

———. 1975. *Idols of the Tribe: Group Identity and Political Change.* Cambridge, Mass.: Harvard University Press.

Jackson, Derrick. 2001. "Who's to Blame on Global Issues." *Boston Globe,* 6 April, p. A25.

Jackson, J. H. 1998. *The World Trade Organisation.* London: Cassell.

Jacobs, Joanne. 2000. "INS Rethinks What It Takes to Become an American." *San Jose Mercury News,* 8 May, p. 9B.

Jacobs, Steven. 2001. "Remittances Up by 40 Percent." *News* (Mexico City), 2 November. www.thenewsmexico.com/noticia.asp?id=11970 [accessed 3 Nov. 2001].

Jacobson, David. 1996. *Rights across Borders: Immigration and the Decline of Citizenship.* Baltimore: Johns Hopkins University Press.

Jameson, Frederic. 1984. "Postmodernism, or the Cultural Logic of Late Capitalism." *New Left Review* 146: 53–92.

Jenson, Jane. 1997. "Fated to Live in Interesting Times: Canada's Changing Citizenship Regimes." *Canadian Journal of Political Science* 30, no. 4 (Dec.): 627–44.

Jervis, Robert. 2002. "An Interim Assessment of September 11: What Has Changed and What Has Not?" *Political Science Quarterly* 117, no. 1: 37–55.

Joekes, Susan, and Ann Weston. 1994. *Women and the New Trade Agenda*. New York: UNIFEM.

Jones, Barry, and Michael Keating, eds. 1995. *The EU and the Regions*. Oxford: Clarendon Press.

Jones, Jeffrey M. 2000. "Americans Remain Split on Immigration." Gallup Press Release, Gallup News Service, 22 September. www.gallup.com/poll/release/pr000922.asp [accessed 30 Sept. 2000].

Jones-Correa, Michael. 2000. "Under Two Flags: Dual Nationality in Latin America and Its Consequences for the United States." Working Papers on Latin America 99/00–3. New York: David Rockefeller Center for Latin American Studies.

Joppke, Christian. 1997. "Asylum and State Sovereignty: A Comparison of the US, Germany and Britain." *Comparative Political Studies* 30, no. 3: 259–98.

———. 1999. "How Immigration Is Changing Citizenship: A Comparative View." *Ethnic and Racial Studies* 22, no. 4: 629–52.

Kacowicz, Arie M. 1999. "Regionalization, Globalization and Nationalism: Convergent, Divergent, or Overlapping?" *Alternatives* 24: 527–56.

Kasfir, Nelson. 1986. "Explaining Ethnic Political Participation." Pp. 88–111 in *The State and Development in the Third World*, edited by A. Kohli. Princeton, N.J.: Princeton University Press.

Kellas, James. 1991. *The Politics of Nationalism and Ethnicity*. London: Macmillan.

Kelly, Rita Mae, Jane Bayes, Mary E. Hawkesworth, and B. Young. 2001. *Gender, Globalization and Democratization*. Lanham, Md.: Rowman & Littlefield.

Kempadoo, Kamala, and Jo Doezema, eds. 1998. *Global Sex Workers: Rights, Resistance, and Redefinition*. New York: Routledge.

Keohane, Robert, and Jospeh Nye. 1977. *Power and Interdependence: World Politics in Transition*. Boston: Little, Brown.

Khor, Martin. 1995. Address to the International Forum on Globalization, New York City, November.

Klein, Naomi. 2000. *No Space, No Choice, No Jobs, No Logo: Taking Aim at the Brand Bullies*. New York: Picador.

Kohn, Hans. 1944. *The Idea of Nationalism*. New York: Macmillan.

Korac, Maja. 1996. "Understanding Ethnic-National Identity and Its Meaning: Questions from Women's Experience." *Women's Studies International Forum* 19, nos. 1/2: 133–43.

Krasner, Stephen. 1993. "Economic Interdependence and Independent Statehood." Pp. 301–21 in *States in a Changing World*, edited by R. H. Jackson and A. James. Oxford: Clarendon.

———. 1999. *Sovereignty: Organized Hypocrisy*. Princeton, N.J.: Princeton University Press.

———. 2001. "Sovereignty." *Foreign Policy* (Jan./Feb.): 20–29.

Kymlicka, Will. 1989. *Liberalism, Community and Culture*. Oxford: Clarendon Press.

———. 1995. *Multicultural Citizenship*. Oxford: Clarendon Press.

Kymlicka, Will, and Wayne Norman. 1995. "Return of the Citizen." Pp. 283–322 in *Theorizing Citizenship*, edited by R. Beiner. Albany: State University of New York Press.

LaFranchi, Howard. 2000a. "Push to Fuel Chiapas Tourism Threatens a Way of Life." *Christian Science Monitor*, 23 August, p. 7.

———. 2000b. "Where Mexico's Voters Are: Here." *Christian Science Monitor*, 19 June, p. 1.

Lamm, Richard. 1985. *Immigration Time Bomb: The Fragmenting of America*. New York: Truman Talley Books.

Lapid, Yosef. 1996. "Culture's Ship: Returns and Departures in International Relations Theory." Pp. 3–20 in *The Return of Culture and Identity in IR Theory*, edited by Yosef Lapid and Friedrich Kratochwil. Boulder, Colo.: Lynne Rienner.

Lapid, Yosef, and Friedrich Kratochwil, eds. 1996. *The Return of Culture and Identity in IR Theory*. Boulder, Colo.: Lynne Rienner.

Lapidoth, Ruth. 1992. "Sovereignty in Transition." *Journal of International Affairs* 45, no. 2: 325–46.

Lee, Jennifer. 2001. "Companies Compete to Provide Internet Veil for the Saudis." *New York Times*, 19 November, p. C1.

Lennon, Tara M. 1998. "Proposition 187: A Case Study of Race, Nationalism, and Democratic Ideals." *Policy Studies Review* 15, nos. 2–3: 80–100.

Lester, Will. 2002. "Dems see Hispanics as Key to House." Associated Press. 5 April. www.washingtonpost.com/wp-dyn/articles/A704–2002Apr5.html [accessed 6 April 2002].

Lichtblau, Eric. 2002. "Bias against US Arabs Taking Subtler Forms." *Los Angeles Times*, 10 February, p. A20.

Lim, Lin Lean., ed. 1998. *The Sex Sector: The Economic and Social Bases of Prostitution in Southeast Asia*. Geneva: International Labour Office.

Lind, Michael. 1995. *The Next American Nation: The New Nationalism and the Fourth American Revolution*. New York: Free Press.

Lipschutz, Ronnie. 1992. "Reconstructing World Politics: The Emergence of Global Civil Society." *Millennium* 21, no. 3: 389–420.

———. 1999. "Members Only?: Citizenship and Civic Virtue in a Time of Globalization." *International Politics* 36, no. 2: 203–33.

Lopez, A. Marin. 1995. "Our Welcomed Guests: Telenovelas in Latin America Soap Opera." Pp. 256–75 in *To Be Continued . . . Soap Opera around the World*, edited by R. Allen. New York: Routledge.

Lyons, Michael. 2001. "EU Candidate Nations Must Control Their Border." Associated Press. 12 October. Web.lexis-nexis.com/universe/doc . . . V&—5= 200ac83061f3017de8be666d67f5a9d [accessed 1 March 2003].

MacKay, Hugh. 2000. "The Globalization of Culture." Pp. 48–84 in *A Globalizing World? Culture, Economics, Politics*, edited by D. Held. London: Routledge.

Malone, Julia. 2002. "Lagging Latino Appeal Looms over Bush Trip." *Atlanta Journal-Constitution*, 29 March, p. 3B.

Mandela, Nelson. 1994. "The Waning Nation State." *New Perspectives Quarterly* 11, no. 3: 58–60.

Marchand, Marianne, and Anne Sisson Runyan. 2000. "Introduction: Feminist Sightings of Global Restructuring." Pp. 1–22 in *Gender and Global Restructuring*, edited by M. H. Marchand and A. S. Runyan. New York: Routledge.

Marshall, Thomas H. 1950. *Citizenship and Social Class and Other Essays.* Cambridge: Cambridge University Press.

Martin-Barbero, Jesus. 1995. "Memory and Form in Latin American Soap Opera." Pp. 276–84 in *To Be Continued . . . Soap Opera around the World,* edited by R. Allen. New York: Routledge.

Martiniello, Marco. 2000. "Citizenship of the European Union." Pp. 342–80 in *From Migrants to Citizens: Membership in a Changing World,* edited by T. A. Aleinikoff and D. Klusmeyer. Washington, D.C.: Carnegie Endowment for International Peace.

Marx, Anthony. 1998. *Making Race and Nation: A Comparison of the United States, South Africa, and Brazil.* Cambridge: Cambridge University Press.

Mathews, Jessica. 1997. "Power Shift." *Foreign Affairs* 76, no. 1: 50.

McLaughlin, Abraham. 1998. "A Move to Extend Vote to Immigrants." *Christian Science Monitor,* 26 October, p. 3.

McNeill, William. 1986. *Polyethnicity and National Unity in World History.* Toronto: University of Toronto Press.

Meade, George. 1998. "Confusion after Euro Vote Law Ruling." Press Association Limited. 19 February.

Meehan, Elizabeth. 1996. "The Debate on Citizenship and European Union." Pp. 201–24 in *Visions of European Unity,* edited by P. Murray and P. Rich. Boulder, Colo.: Westview Press.

Menchu, Rigoberta. 1994."The Mayan Way." *New Perspectives Quarterly* 11 (3): 58–60.

Migdal, Joel, ed. Forthcoming. *Boundaries and Belonging: States and Societies in the Struggle to Shape Identities and Local Practices.* Cambridge: Cambridge University Press.

Miller, John J. 1998. *The Unmaking of Americans: How Multiculturalism Has Undermined the Assimilationist Ethic.* New York: Free Press.

Miller, Mark. 1989. "Political Participation and Representation of Noncitizens." Pp. 129–44 in *Immigration and the Politics of Citizenship in Europe and North America,* edited by R. Brubaker. Lanham, Md.: University Press of America.

Minaar, Anthony, and Mike Hough. 1996. *Who Goes There?* Pretoria: HSRC Publishers.

Mittelman, James H. 2000. *The Globalization Syndrome: Transformation and Resistance.* Princeton, N.J.: Princeton University Press.

———, ed. 1996. *Globalization: Critical Reflections.* Boulder, Colo.: Lynne Rienner.

Mohanty, Chandra. 1991. "Under Western Eyes: Feminist Scholarship and Colonial Discourses." Pp. 51–80 in *Third World Women and the Politics of Feminism,* edited by C. T. Mohanty, A. Russo, and L. Torres. Bloomington: Indiana University Press.

Montagu, Ashley. 1974. *Man's Most Dangerous Myth: The Fallacy of Race.* Oxford: Oxford University Press.

Morgan, Robin. 1984. *Sisterhood Is Global: The International Women's Movement Anthology.* New York: Anchor Press.

Morley, David, and Kenneth Robins. 1995. *Spaces of Identity: Global Media, Electronic Landscapes and Cultural Boundaries.* London: Routledge.

Motyl, Alexander. 1999. *Revolutions, Nations, Empires: Conceptual Limits and Theoretical Possibilities.* New York: Columbia University Press.

———. 2002. "Imagined Communities, Rational Choosers, Invented Ethnies." *Comparative Politics* 34, no. 2: 233–50.

Moynihan, Daniel P. 1993. *Pandaemonium: Ethnicity in International Politics*. Oxford: Oxford University Press.

Nagel, Joane. 1986. "The Political Construction of Ethnicity." Pp. 93–113 in *Competitive Ethnic Relations*, edited by S. Olzak and J. Nagel. New York: Academic Press.

———. 1993. "Ethnic Nationalism: Politics, Ideology, and the World Order." *International Journal of Comparative Sociology* 34, nos. 1–2: 103–12.

———. 1996. *American Indian Ethnic Renewal*. New York: Oxford University Press.

Nairn, Tom. 1977. *The Breakup of Britain: Crisis and Neo-Nationalism*. London: New Left Books.

Nanda, Serena. 2000. *Gender Diversity: Crosscultural Variations*. Prospect Heights, Ill.: Waveland Press.

NATIONALISM: A Report by a Study Group of Members of the Royal Institute of International Affairs. 1939. London: Royal Institute of International Affairs, p. xvi.

NBC News Transcripts. 2000. "Mary Anne Gehris Speaks Out about Her Possible Deportation for Pulling Another Person's Hair." "Sunday Today Show." Anchor Maurice DuBois. 9 January [accessed via Lexis-Nexis, Nov. 2001].

Nederveen Pieterse, Jan. 1994. "Globalisation as Hybridisation." *International Sociology* 9, no. 2: 161–84.

Newman, Saul. 1991. "Does Modernization Breed Ethnic Conflict." *World Politics* 43 (April): 451–78.

Nijeholt, Geertje L. 1995. "Women in International Migration." Pp. 59–60 in *Commitment to the World's Women*, edited by N. Heyzer. New York: UNIFEM.

Nussbaum, Martha. 1996. *For Love of Country: Debating the Limits of Patriotism*. Boston: Beacon Press.

OECD. 2000. *Trends in International Migration: Annual Report*. Paris: Organisation for Economic Co-operation and Development.

Ohmae, Kenichi. 1995. *The End of the Nation State: The Rise of Regional Economies*. New York: Free Press.

Okin, Susan M. 1994. "Gender Inequality and Cultural Differences." *Political Theory* 22, no. 1 (February): 5–24.

———. 1999. *Is Multiculturalism Bad for Women?* Princeton, N.J.: Princeton University Press.

O'Leary, Brendan. 2001. "Nationalism and Ethnicity: Research Agendas on Theories of Their Sources and Regulation." Pp. 37–48 in *Ethnopolitical Warfare*, edited by D. Chirot and M. Seligman. Washington, D.C.: American Psychological Association.

Omi, Michael, and Howard Winant. 1986. *Racial Formation in the United States*. New York: Routledge.

Pan, Phillip. 2000. "Turnabout in Attitudes and Actions." *Washington Post*, 4 July, p. A10.

Pateman, Carole. 1988. *The Sexual Contract*. New York: Polity Press.

Patterson, Orlando. 1994. "Ecumenical America: Global Culture and the American Cosmos." *World Policy Journal* 11 (Summer): 103–17.

Patterson, Wendy. 2001. "Zapatour: A Ride into History?" *Christian Science Monitor*, 7 March, pp. 6–7.

Patton, Charlotte. 1995. "Women and Power: The Nairobi Conference." Pp. 61–76 in *Women, Politics and the United Nations*, edited by A. Winslow. Westport, Conn.: Greenwood Press.

Pear, Robert. 2002. "White House Shifts on Welfare Law." *New York Times*, 10 January, p. A1. www.nytimes.com/2002/01/10/national/10BUDG.html.

Peled, Yoav. 1992. "Ethnic Democracy and the Legal Construction of Citizenship: Arab Citizens of the Jewish State." *American Political Science Review* 86, no. 2: 432–43.

Perez, Lisandro. 1986. "Immigrant Economic Adjustment and Family Organization: The Cuban Success Story Reexamined." *International Migration Review* 20: 4–20.

Peterson, V. Spike, and Anne Sisson Runyan. 1999. *Global Gender Issues*. Boulder, Colo.: Westview.

Pettman, Jan. 1996. *Worlding Women: A Feminist International Politics*. London: Routledge.

Pickus, Noah., ed. 1998. *Immigration and Citizenship in the Twenty-First Century*. Lanham, Md.: Rowman & Littlefield.

Pocock, John G. A. 1995. "The Ideal of Citizenship Since Classical Times." Pp. 29–52 in *Theorizing Citizenship*, edited by R. Beiner. Albany: State University of New York Press.

Portes, Alejandro. 1986. "Global Villagers: The Rise of Transnational Communities." *American Prospect* 25: 74–77.

———. 1998. "Divergent Destinies: Immigration and the Rise of Transnational Communities." Pp. 33–57 in *Paths to Inclusion*, edited by P. Schuck and R. Munz. New York: Berghahn Books.

———. 1999a. "The Study of Transnationalism: Pitfalls and Promise of an Emergent Research Field." *Ethnic and Racial Studies* 22, no. 2: 217–37.

———. 1999b. "Conclusion: Towards a New World—The Origins and Effects of Transnational Activities." *Ethnic and Racial Studies* 22, no. 2: 463–77.

Poster, Winifred R. 2001. "Dangerous Places and Nimble Fingers: Discourses of Gender Discrimination and Rights in Global Corporations." *International Journal of Politics, Culture and Society* 15, no. 1: 77–105.

"Programme for Action." 1980. Copenhagen. 14–30 July. Report of the World Conference of the United Nations Decade for Women. UNDOC. A/Conf. 94/35, UN Publications.

Prusher, Illene. 2000. "Symbol of Both Oppression and Freedom." *Christian Science Monitor*, 11 August, pp. 8–9.

Purnell, Susan. 1999. "Gay Rights Revolution: European Court Will Order Changes in Laws." *Daily Mail* (London) 25 September, p. 39.

Pye, Lucian. 1990. "Political Science and the Crisis of Authoritarianism." *American Political Science Review* 84, no. 1: 3–19.

Pyle, Jean L. 2001. "Sex, Maids, and Export Processing: Risks and Reasons for Gendered Global Production." *International Journal of Politics, Culture and Society* 15, no. 1: 55–75.

Rasmussen, Brigit B., ed. 2001. *The Making and Unmaking of Whiteness*. Durham, N.C.: Duke University Press.

Renshon, Stuart A. 2001. *Dual Citizenship and American National Identity*. Washington, D.C.: Center for Immigration Studies, October.

"Rep. King: Halt Arab Immigration, Saudi Arabia 'Almost an Enemy." 2002. NewMax, 21 April. www.newsmax.com/showinsidecover.shtml?a02/4/21/92650 [accessed 15 May 2002].

Richmond, Anthony. 1994. *Global Apartheid: Refugees, Racism, and the New World Order*. Toronto: Oxford University Press.

Riding, Alan. 2002. "Domino Effect? New Gain for Far Right in Europe." *New York Times*, 23 April, p. A10. www.nytimes.com/2002/04/23/international/europe/23RIGH.html.

Robberson, Tod. 1995. "Mexican Rebels Using a High-Tech Weapon," *Washington Post*, 20 February, p. A1.

Robertson, Roland. 1987. "Globalization and Societal Modernization." *Sociological Analysis* 47 (March): 35–43.

———. 1990. "Mapping the Global Condition: Globalization as the Central Concept." Pp. 15–30 in *Global Culture: Nation, Globalization and Modernity*, edited by M. Featherstone. Thousand Oaks, Calif.: Sage.

———. 1995. "Glocalization: Time-Space and Homogeneity-Heterogeneity." Pp. 25–44 in *Global Modernities* edited by M. Featherstone, S. Lash, and R. Robertson. London: Sage.

Rodrik, Dani. 1997. *Has Globalization Gone Too Far?* Washington, D.C.: Institute for International Economics.

Rohter, Larry. 2000. "Bitter Indians Let Ecuador Know Fight Isn't Over." *New York Times*, 27 January, p. A14.

Rosenau, James. 1990. *Turbulence in World Politics: A Theory of Change and Continuity*. Princeton, N.J.: Princeton University Press.

———. 1992. "Citizenship in a Changing Global Order." Pp. 272–94 in *Governance without Government: Order and Change in World Politics*, edited by J. Rosenau and E. O. Czempiel. Cambridge: Cambridge University Press.

Rosenau, Pauline R. 1992. *Postmodernism and the Social Sciences: Insights, Inroads and Intrusions*. Princeton, N.J.: Princeton University Press.

Ruggie, James G. 1993. "Territoriality and Beyond: Problematizing Modernity in International Relations." *International Organization* 47, no. 1 (Winter): 139–74.

Said, Abdul, and Luiz R. Simmons, eds. 1976. *Ethnicity in an International Context*. New Brunswick, N.J.: Transaction Books.

Sainsbury, Diane. 1994. "Gender and Comparative Analysis: Welfare States, State Theories and Social Policies." Pp. 126–35 in *Different Roles, Different Voices*, edited by M. Githens, P. Norris, and J. Lovenduski. New York: HarperCollins.

Sambo, Dalee. 1994. "A Wave of Change: The United Nations." *Cultural Survival Quarterly* (Spring): 35–44.

Santoro, Lara. 1998. "Echo of 1994 Genocide: Rwanda Slayings Persist." *Christian Science Monitor*, 3 March, p. 7.

Sassen, Saskia. 1996. "Toward a Feminist Analytics of the Global Economy." *Indiana Journal of Global Legal Studies* 4, no. 1 (Fall): 7–41.

Schiller, Herbert I. 1991. "Not Yet the Post-Imperialist Era." *Critical Studies in Mass Communication* 8, no. 1 (March): 13–28.

Schlesinger, Arthur M., Jr. 1992. *The Disuniting of America: Reflections on a Multicultural Society*. New York: W. W. Norton.

Schlesinger, Philip. 1994. "Europe's Contradictory Communicative Space." *Daedalus* 123, no. 2: 25–44.

Schmemann, Serge. 2001. "After the War, Rebuild a Nation. If It's a Nation." *New York Times*, 21 October, sec. 4, p. 1.

Scholte, Jan A. 2000. *Globalization: A Critical Introduction*. New York: St. Martin's Press.

Schuck, Peter. 1989. "Membership in the Liberal Polity: The Devaluation of American Citizenship." Pp. 51–65 in *Immigration and the Politics of Citizenship in Europe and North America*, edited by R. Brubaker. Lanham, Md.: University Press of America.

———. 1998. "Plural Citizenships." Pp. 149–91 in *Immigration and Citizenship in the Twenty-First Century*, edited by N. Pickus. Lanham, Md.: Rowman & Littlefield.

Scott, George M. 1990. "A Resynthesis of the Primordial and Circumstantial Approaches to Ethnic Group Solidarity." *Ethnic and Racial Studies* 13, no. 2: 147–71.

Scott, Joan. 1986. "Gender: A Useful Category." *American Historical Review* 91 (December):1053–75.

Seager, Joni. 1997. *The State of Women in the World Atlas*. New York: Penguin Books.

Seifert, Ruth. 1996. "The Second Front: The Logic of Sexual Violence in Wars." *Women's Studies International Forum* 19, no. 1/2: 35–43.

Selverston, Melina. 1997. "The Politics of Identity Reconstruction: Indians and Democracy in Ecuador." Pp. 170–91 in *The New Politics of Inequality in Latin America*, edited by D. Chalmers. Oxford: Oxford University Press.

Seton-Watson, Hugh. 1977. *Nations and States: An Enquiry into the Origins of Nations and Politics of Nationalism*. Boulder, Colo.: Westview Press.

Shain, Yossi. 1999. *Marketing the American Creed Abroad: Diasporas in the US and Their Homelands*. Cambridge: Cambridge University Press.

Shaw, Paul, and Yuwa Wong. 1989. *Genetic Seeds of Warfare: Evolution, Nationalism, and Patriotism*. Boston: Unwin Hyman.

Shils, Edward. 1957. "Primordial, Personal, Sacred and Civil Ties." *British Journal of Sociology* 8: 130–45.

Simon, Leslie D. 2001. "The Net: Power and Policy in the 21st Century." Pp. 613–33 in *The Global Century: Globalization and National Security*, edited by R. L. Kugler and E. L. Frost. Washington, D.C.: National Defense University Press.

Simpson, Pamela. 1996. "International Trends: Beijing in Perspective." *Journal of Women's History* 8, no. 1 (Spring): 137–46.

Smith, Anthony D. 1986. *The Ethnic Origins of Nations*. Oxford: Blackwell.

———. 1992. "National Identity and the Idea of European Unity." *International Affairs* 68, no. 1: 55–76.

———. 1995. *Nations and Nationalism in a Global Era*. Cambridge: Polity Press.

———. 1998. *Nationalism and Modernism*. London: Routledge.

Smith, Jeffrey. 2000. "Sex Trade Enslaves East Europeans." *Washington Post*, 25 July, n.p.

Smith, Michael P., and Luis E. Guarnizo, eds. 1998. *Transnationalism from Below*. New Brunswick, N.J.: Transaction Publishers.

Smith, Robert. 1998. "Transnational Localities: Community, Technology and the Politics of Membership within the Context of Mexico and US Immigration." Pp. 196–240 in *Transnationalism from Below*, edited by M. P. Smith and L. E. Guarnizo. New Brunswick, N.J.: Transaction Publishers.

Sollors, Werner. 1989. *The Invention of Ethnicity*. Oxford: Oxford University Press.

South African Press Agency. 2001. "Bogus Citizenship Could be Treason," 4 October. Listserv message CISNEWS. 5 Oct.

Sowetan Comment. 1994. "Buthelezi Proposes Punishment for Illegals." 13 August, p. 8.

Soysal, Yasemin. 1994. *Limits to Citizenship.* Chicago: University of Chicago Press.
———. 2000. "Citizenship and Identity: Living in Diasporas in Post-War Europe." *Ethnic and Racial Studies* 23, no. 1: 1–15.
Spelman, Elizabeth. 1988. *Inessential Woman: Problems of Exclusion in Feminist Thought.* Boston: Beacon Press.
Spiro, Peter J. 1997. "Dual Nationality and the Meaning of Citizenship." *Emory Law Journal* 46: 1411–83.
Stack, John, ed. 1981. *Ethnic Identities in a Transnational World.* Westport, Conn.: Greenwood Press.
Staeheli, Lynne A., and Susan E. Clarke. 1995. "Gender, Place, and Citizenship." Pp. 3–23 in *Gender in Urban Research,* edited by J. A. Garber and R. S. Turner. Thousand Oaks, Calif.: Sage.
Steinberg, Stephen. 1989. *The Ethnic Myth: Race, Ethnicity and Class in America.* Boston: Beacon Press.
Stewart, Elizabeth. 1998. "Push on for Cultural Diversity." *Toronto Star,* 28 June, p. A10.
Stienstra, Deborah. 1994. *Women's Movements and International Organizations.* New York: St. Martin's Press.
———. 2000. "Dancing Resistance from Rio to Beijing: Transnational Women's Organizing and UN Conferences, 1992–1996." Pp. 209–24 in *Gender and Global Restructuring,* edited by M. H. Marchand and A. S. Runyan. New York: Routledge.
Strange, Susan. 1996. *The Retreat of the State.* Cambridge: Cambridge University Press.
Sun, Lena H. 1998. "Here Comes the Russian Bride." *Washington Post National Weekly Edition,* 16 March, p. 10.
Suny, Ronald. 1992. "State, Civil Society and Ethnic Cultural Consolidation in the USSR—Roots of the National Question." Pp. 22–44 in *From Union to Commonwealth: Nationalism and Separatism in the Soviet Republics,* edited by G. Lapidus, V. Zaslavsky, and P. Goldman. Cambridge: Cambridge University Press.
Tarrow, Sidney. 1994. *Power in Movement: Social Movements, Collective Action and Politics.* Cambridge: Cambridge University Press.
Thachuk, Kimberly L. 2001. "The Sinister Underbelly: Organized Crime and Terrorism." Pp. 743–60 in *The Global Century: Globalization and National Security,* edited by R. L. Kugler and E. L. Frost. Washington, D.C.: National Defense University Press.
Tilly, Charles. 1975. The *Formation of National States in Western Europe.* Princeton, N.J.: Princeton University Press.
———. 1995. "Citizenship, Identity and Social History." Pp. 1–17 in *Citizenship, Identity and Social History,* edited by C. Tilly. Cambridge: International Review of Social History Supplement 3.
Tishkov, Valery A. 2000. "Forget the 'Nation': Post-Nationalist Understanding of Nationalism." *Ethnic and Racial Studies* 23, no. 4: 625–50.
Tölölyan, Kachig. 1991. "The Nation-State and Its Others: In Lieu of a Preface." *Diaspora* 1: 3–7.
Tomaselli, Sylvana, and Roy Porter, eds. 1986. *Rape.* London: Basil Blackwell.
Tomlinson, John. 1999. "Globalised Culture: The Triumph of the West?" Pp. 22–29 in *Culture and Global Change,* edited by T. Skelton and T. Allen. London: Routledge.

Turner, Bryan. 1990. "Outline of a Theory of Citizenship." *Sociology* 24, no. 2: 189–217.

———. 1997. "Citizenship Studies: A General Theory." *Citizenship Studies* 1, no. 1: 5.

UNCTAD. 2001. *World Investment Report 2001*. Geneva: United Nations Conference on Trade and Development.

UNDP. 1999. *Human Development Report*. United Nations Development Program. New York: Oxford University Press

———. 2002. *Human Development Report*. United Nations Development Program. New York: Oxford University Press.

UNESCO. 1999. "International Flows of Selected Cultural Goods." *Statistical Reports and Studies*. Paris: United Nations Educational, Scientific and Cultural Organization.

UNIFEM [United Nations Development Fund For Women]. 2000. *Progress of the World's Women 2000*. New York: UN Publications.

United Nations. 1992. Declaration on the Rights of Persons Belonging to National or Ethnic, Religious and Linguistic Minorities. [G.A. res. 47/135, annex 47].

U.S. Bureau of the Census. 2000a. *Profile of the Foreign Born in the U.S.* Washington, D.C. www.census.gov [accessed 15 Jan. 2002].

———. 2000b. *Estimates of the Illegal Population*. Appendix A, Report 1. www.census.gov/dmd [accessed 21 June 2002].

Uvin, Peter. 1998. *Aiding Violence: The Development Enterprise in Rwanda*. West Hartford, Conn.: Kumarian Press.

———. 2001. "Reading the Rwandan Genocide." *International Studies Review* 3, no. 3: 75–99.

Vail, Leroy, ed. 1989. *The Creation of Tribalism in Southern Africa*. Berkeley: University of California Press.

Van Den Berghe, Guido. 1982. *Political Rights for European Citizens*. Aldershot: Gower.

Van Den Berghe, P. 1978. "Race and Ethnicity: A Sociobiological Perspective." *Ethnic and Racial Studies* 1: 401–11.

Vargas Llosa, Mario. 2001. "The Culture of Liberty." *Foreign Policy* (Jan./Feb.): 66–71.

Varis, Tapio. 1999. "Sami Radio in Northern Scandinavia." Pp. 439–50 in *Civic Discourse: Intercultural, International and Global Media*, edited by M. H. Prosser and K. S. Sitaram. Stamford, Conn.: Ablex Publishing.

Vertovec, Steve. 1999. "Conceiving and Researching Transnationalism." *Ethnic and Racial Studies* 22, no. 2: 447–62.

Vo, Minh Trina. 1998. "A Look at the World by Numbers: UN Data." *Christian Science Monitor*, 6 November, pp. 8–9.

Vranken, Martin. 1999. "Citizenship and the Law of the European Union." Pp. 25–37 in *Citizenship and Identity in Europe*, edited by L. Holmes and P. Murray. Brookfield, Vt.: Ashgate Publishing.

Wade, Robert. 2001. "Global Inequality: Winners and Losers." *Economist* (28 April): 72–74.

Walker, Alice, and Partha Parmar. 1993. *Warrior Marks: Female Genital Mutilation and the Sexual Blinding of Women*. New York: Harcourt Brace.

Wallerstein, Immanuel. 1974. *The Modern World System: Capitalist Agriculture and the Origins of the European World-Economy in the Sixteenth Century*. New York: Academic Press.

———. 1991. "The Construction of Peoplehood." Pp. 71–85 in *Race, Nation, Class: Ambiguous Identities*, edited by E. Balibar and I. Wallerstein. London: Verso.

"War on Terror: Perspectives." 2001a. *Newsweek*, 8 October, p. 17.

"War on Terror: Perspectives." 2001b. *Newsweek*, 5 November, p. 25.

Waterman, Peter. 1998. *Globalization, Social Movements and the New Internationalisms*. London: Mansell.

Weber, Max. 1948. *Essays in Sociology*. Translated by H. H. Gerth and C. Wright-Mills. London: Routledge.

———. 1968. *Economy and Society*, edited by G. Roth and C. Wittich. Berkeley: University of California Press.

Weil, Patrick. 2001. "Access to Citizenship: A Comparison of Twenty-Five Nationality Laws." Pp. 17–35 in *Citizenship Today: Global Perspectives and Practices*, edited by T. A. Aleinikoff and D. Klusmeyer. Washington, D.C.: Carnegie Endowment for International Peace.

West, Lois A. 1999. "The United Nations Women's Conferences and Feminist Politics." Pp. 177–93 in *Gender Politics in Global Governance*, edited by M. Meyer and E. Prügl. Lanham, Md.: Rowman & Littlefield.

Whitney, Craig. 1996. "Europeans Redefine What Makes a Citizen." *New York Times*, 7 January, p. 6.

Wiener, Antje. 1998. *European Citizenship Practice: Building Institutions of a Non-State*. Boulder, Colo.: Westview Press.

Winant, Howard. 2001. *The World Is a Ghetto: Race and Democracy since World War II*. New York: Basic Books.

Winestock, Gregory. 2001. "Terrorist Attacks Could Undercut Liberal Refugee, Migration Policies." *Wall Street Journal*, 8 October, p. A19.

Wolf, Martin. 2000. "Why This Hatred of the Market." Pp. 9–11 in *The Globalization Reader*, edited by F. J. Lechner and J. Boli. Oxford: Blackwell.

Wood, Daniel B. 1998. "Indians Hear a High-Tech Drumbeat." *Christian Science Monitor*, 19 February, pp. 1, 9.

Woodward, Susan. 1995. *Balkan Tragedy: Chaos and Dissolution after the Cold War*. Washington, D.C.: Brookings Institution.

Woolf, Virginia. 1938. *The Three Guineas*. London: Penguin.

Working Group on Indigenous Peoples. 1993. Draft Declaration on the Rights of Indigenous Peoples. United Nations Economic and Social Council, 23 August [E/CN.4/sub.2/1993/29/Annex I].

Wright, Lawrence. 1996. "One Drop of Blood." *New Yorker* 72 (25 July): 46–55.

Wright, Robert. 1994. "Feminists, Meet Mr. Darwin." *New Republic* (28 Nov.): 34–46.

Wu, Wei. 1999. "Cyberspace and Cultural Community: A Case Study of Cyber-community of Chinese Students in the US." Pp. 75–89 in *Civic Discourse: Intercultural, International and Global Media*, edited by M. H. Prosser and K. S. Sitaram. Stamford, Conn.: Ablex Publishing.

Yack, Bernard. 1999. "The Myth of the Civic Nation." Pp. 103–19 in *Theorizing Nationalism*, edited by R. Beiner. Albany: State University of New York Press.

Yashar, Deborah. 2002. "Globalization and Collective Action," *Comparative Politics* 34, no. 3: 355–75.

Yates, Jon. 2002. "Reared in US, Wisconsin Man Faces Deportation to Afghanistan." *Chicago Tribune*, 17 April, p. 5.

Yelvington, Kevin, ed. 1992. *Trinidad Ethnicity*. Knoxville: University of Tennessee Press.

Young, Crawford. 1993. "The Dialectics of Cultural Pluralism." Pp. 3–35 in *The Rising Tide of Cultural Pluralism*, edited by C. Young. Madison: University of Wisconsin Press.

Yuval-Davis, Nira. 1991. "The Citizenship Debate: Women, Ethnic Processes and the State." *Feminist Review* 39 (Winter): 58–68.

———. 1993. "Gender and Nation." *Ethnic and Racial Studies* 16, no. 4: 621–32.

Yuval-Davis, Nira, and Floya Anthias, eds. 1989. *Woman-Nation-State*. New York: St. Martin's Press.

Zakaria, Fareed. 2001. "Next: Nation-building Lite." *Newsweek* (22 Oct.): 53.

Zedillo, Ernesto. 2001. "More, Not Less, Globalization Is the Answer." *Vital Speeches of the Day* 67, no. 17 (15 June): 514–18.

Zinsser, Judith P. 2002. "From Mexico to Copenhagen to Nairobi: The United Nations Decade for Women." *Journal of World History* 13, no. 1: 139–68.

Zubrzycki, John. 1996. "To Curry Favor in India Debut, McDonald's Sells Maharaja Macs." *Christian Science Monitor*, 17 October, p. 6.

Index

About the Author

Sheila L. Croucher is associate professor of political science and an affiliate in women's studies at Miami University in Oxford, Ohio. Her research and teaching interests focus on issues of comparative identity politics. She is the author of *Imagining Miami: Ethnic Politics in a Postmodern World* (1997) and has published articles on ethnicity and national belonging in journals including *Ethnic and Racial Studies, Identities, International Studies Review,* and *Urban Affairs Review.*